INDIAN BOND MARKET

STRUCTURE, CONDUCT AND MACROECONOMIC IMPACT

GEETIMA DAS KRISHNA
BISWAJIT NAG

ATLANTIC
PUBLISHERS & DISTRIBUTORS (P) LTD

ATLANTIC
PUBLISHERS & DISTRIBUTORS (P) LTD
7/22, Ansari Road, Darya Ganj, New Delhi
Tel.: +91-11-4077 5252, 2327 3880
E-mail: orders@atlanticbooks.com
Web: www.atlanticbooks.com

This edition published in 2026 by Atlantic Publishers & Distributors (P) Ltd.

Registered Office and Editorial Office
Atlantic Publishers & Distributors (P) Ltd.,
7/22, Ansari Road, Darya Ganj, New Delhi-110002, India

Library of Congress Cataloging-in-Publication applied for

ISBN 978-81-269-4502-3

For details of our editorial offices, customer service, and more information about Atlantic Publishers and Distributors (P) Ltd. Products, visit us at www.atlanticbooks.com

Printed and bound in United States of America

Advance Praise

This book fills a much-needed space in the domain of fixed-income instruments and the analysis of bond markets. The analysis of real-world issues enables the readers to develop a better understanding of the market segment that has so far been largely ignored by retail investors. The authors have lucidly tackled conceptual issues using the available analytical or statistical tools. It is a valuable resource for students, researchers, as well as retail investors looking to diversify their portfolio. A timely and relevant publication.

—Dr Rajiv Kumar

Chairman, Pahlé India Foundation, New Delhi

Former Vice Chairman, NITI Aayog

Having engaged closely with India's financial system as Finance Secretary, I recognise how vital a deep and efficient bond market is to the country's growth and fiscal stability. This book by Geetima Das Krishna and Biswajit Nag offers an exceptional analysis of India's government and corporate bond markets, their evolution and policy linkages. It bridges empirical rigour with policy relevance, providing valuable insights for those shaping—and studying—the future of India's financial architecture.

—Dr Arvind Mayaram

Former Finance Secretary, Government of India

This long-awaited volume fills a major gap in understanding India's fixed-income securities markets. Moving beyond scattered studies, it offers a comprehensive and analytical treatment that combines theory, institutional insight, and robust econometric evidence.

Accessible yet rigorous, the book serves both learners and practitioners—students, teachers, bankers and policymakers alike. It makes three key contributions: identifying the determinants of long-term government bond yields in India; introducing the innovative Composite Indicators of Leading Indicators (CILI) to better predict economic activity; and explaining the factors shaping corporate bond markets across Asia.

A landmark reference for scholars and professionals, this work sets a new benchmark in the study of India's financial markets.

—Prof Triptendu Prakash Ghosh

Associate Professor, Indian Institute of Foreign Trade (IIFT), Kolkata

A sharp, market-savvy, data-rich and insight-driven analysis of India's fast-evolving debt market, this book unpacks the structure, behaviour, and macroeconomic drivers shaping bond yields, liquidity, and investment flows. Written for finance professionals, portfolio managers, policy analysts, and serious market watchers, it blends rigorous analysis with real-world relevance—translating complex data into clear, actionable intelligence. With its focus on market structure, yield curve dynamics, and policy impact, the book empowers readers to read the signals, time the shifts, and seize opportunities in one of the world's most dynamic emerging debt markets.

—Indranil Sen Gupta

Professor of Practice (Economics), Shiv Nadar University
Former Head of India Research, CLSA
Former Co-Head of Research & Economist, Merrill Lynch, Bank of America

India's bond markets are an integral component of its financial architecture, facilitating the capital requirements critical to the growth trajectory. This book offers a lucid and comprehensive account of their evolution from administered finance to a market-driven system. It blends historical insight with rigorous empirical analysis, linking monetary policy, fiscal management, and market structure in a coherent narrative. Sovereign, corporate, state, and municipal debt are examined within a single analytical frame, advancing understanding and policy discourse for students, market practitioners and policy makers alike. Balanced in tone and rich in empirical evidence, it stands as a credible and timely contribution to the study of India's fixed-income landscape.

—Tirthankar Patnaik, PhD

Chief Economist, National Stock Exchange of India Limited (NSE)

Contents

PART II

A. SOVEREIGN BOND MARKET

Preface

In this captivating world of financial markets, the term "equity" dominates the conversations. Stock markets are easy to understand and widely discussed, shaping a plethora of articles, blogs, and analyses. Daily market movements are typically seen as reflections of the equity market by most people. However, an equally significant segment often overlooked by retail investors and the public is the bond market.

The bond market, also known as the fixed income market, serves as the primary avenue through which investors loan money to governments or corporates for various projects, typically over a fixed period at a variable or fixed interest rate. However, bonds are not as popular as equities for two main reasons. First, the concept of bond prices is more complex than share prices. Bond prices are based on the Time Value of Money (TVM), where the present value (PV) of a bond is determined by discounting its future cash flows. As a result, bond valuation often remains shrouded in mystery. Second, bonds are seen as the quieter sibling of equities—less flashy, not as exciting, and lacking the volatility and high returns that attract attention. Consequently, the bond market is often overlooked by most investors, particularly retail investors.

David Wessel, a financial journalist and expert on economics, aptly said, "The bond market is the biggest financial market that you've never heard of." This sentiment holds true for India as well. Discussions about financial markets typically focus on stocks and shares, while bonds are often seen as the realm of institutional investors and large corporations. As a result, many people have a limited understanding of what bonds are, the structure and role of the debt market in India, its institutional background, and why bonds are important.

This book aims to bridge the gap between complexity and accessibility, shedding light on the often-misunderstood aspects of the financial system. It is essential to move beyond the fast-paced world of the stock market and explore the quieter waters of the debt market, which offer appealing, attractive opportunities for diversification, stability, and income.

The Indian bond market has undergone significant transformation over the past few decades. Since 1991, a series of reforms have been implemented to develop the necessary market infrastructure, expand and deepen the market, improve risk management practices, and enhance transparency. Once limited to a small group of institutional players, the market is now gradually opening up to retail investors. Today, a wide range of fixed-income products is available, including government bonds, corporate bonds, municipal bonds, and other structured products. To navigate this market, it is crucial to understand concepts like interest rates, yield curves, credit ratings, and the present value of cash flow—fundamental elements that define the bond market.

The Indian economy is on the verge of sustained, high growth, with a significant need for infrastructure financing. However, banks are limited in their ability to provide long-term funding due to their reliance on short-term assets. Both institutional players and individual investors need to recognise the true potential of the debt or bond market. This book aims to demonstrate that understanding the bond market is not only essential for large financial institutions but also for anyone looking to build a more balanced and robust financial future.

Another key aspect explored in this book is the influence of macroeconomic factors on bond market dynamics. From monetary and fiscal policy to inflation, growth, and external factors, everything influences the bond market.

- Interest rates are the primary drivers of the bond market. The monetary policy of the Central Bank (the Reserve Bank of India, RBI) decides benchmark interest rates based on the macroeconomic environment. These rates significantly affect bond returns, as all financial instruments are aligned with RBI's benchmark rate. In turn, this influences borrowing costs throughout the economy.

- Inflation is a crucial macroeconomic factor that bonds are highly sensitive to. Higher inflation erodes the purchasing power of money and reduces real returns on investments. Investors demand higher returns over the life of the bonds to compensate for inflation. This makes inflation a crucial factor not only in determining bond yields but also in shaping investor sentiment regarding future economic growth and central bank policies.
- Economic growth plays a vital role in bond market dynamics. Stronger growth often leads to increased bond issuance, as companies seek loans (capital) for expansion and governments issue sovereign bonds to finance new projects. This can drive interest rates higher, as central banks may tighten monetary policy to manage growth and inflation. Conversely, during a recession, central banks might lower interest rates to stimulate borrowing and spending, which in turn affects bond yields.
- Fiscal policy directly impacts the bond market. When a government increases spending to stimulate the economy, it may need to borrow more to cover budget deficits, leading to a rise in government bond issuance. A government's fiscal health—its debt levels, budget deficits, and overall economic policy—directly impacts bond market behaviour.
- The Indian bond market, like other emerging markets, is affected not only by domestic macroeconomic factors but also by global economic conditions. Factors such as global interest rates, commodity prices, trade imbalances, and geopolitical events can influence investor sentiment and bond prices in India.
- Credit ratings are another important factor influencing the bond market. The credit ratings of a country or company reflect its economic health and potential risk of default. Governments or companies with higher credit ratings are

viewed as less likely to default, often resulting in lower yields for their bonds.

The intricate interconnections between macroeconomic factors and the bond market shape the pricing, demand, and supply of bonds. Bonds are influenced by these macroeconomic elements far more than equities, as they determine the cost of capital, default risk, and real returns for investors. As it is often said, "*The bond market is a reflection of the economy's health, a barometer of interest rates, inflation expectations, and the fiscal policies that shape a nation's financial future.*"

The book explores the bond market not as an isolated entity, but as a mirror reflecting broader economic conditions, highlighting its role as a key indicator of macroeconomic health.

The authors would like to express their sincere gratitude to the publishers and reviewers for their guidance, insightful comments, professionalism and unwavering support throughout the journey of bringing this book to completion. Their belief in the relevance of this work and their meticulous attention to quality have been instrumental in shaping the final manuscript.

Finally, our heartfelt thanks to our family for their constant encouragement, patience and understanding during the long hours of research and writing. This book is as much a reflection of their faith in us as it is of our own efforts.

Geetima Das Krishna

Biswajit Nag

Foreword

In the architecture of modern finance, few institutions command as much quiet influence as the bond market.

James Carville, former political consultant to President Bill Clinton, once quipped with sardonic insight, "I used to think that if there was reincarnation, I wanted to come back as the President or the Pope or as a 400-baseball hitter. But now I would like to come back as the bond market. You can intimidate everybody." His observation captures a timeless truth: the bond market, often operating under the radar, disciplines fiscal conduct, monetary decisions, corporate behaviour and macroeconomic stability in ways that few other forces can.

For an economy like India, which is large, dynamic, and increasingly integrated with global capital flows, the bond market is not merely another funding channel; it is a vital component of financial intermediation and macroeconomic management. It mobilises long-term savings and channels them toward productive investment in infrastructure, industry and innovation. In doing so, it connects households, corporations and governments in a network of trust and discipline that underpins the real economy. A well-functioning bond market not only supplements the banking system but also enhances financial stability by spreading risk and providing reliable benchmarks for pricing capital.

As India aspires to become a developed economy by 2047, the centenary of its independence, the importance of a deep and efficient bond market cannot be overstated. Financing a multi-trillion-dollar infrastructure pipeline, sustaining the green transition and supporting the growth of state and municipal finance will all depend on the country's capacity to raise long-term resources in a transparent and cost-effective manner. A robust bond market also strengthens monetary transmission, improves fiscal responsibility and facilitates the integration of domestic capital with global markets—objectives that lie at the heart of India's growth strategy.

India's fixed-income market has evolved significantly over the past two decades. The government securities market has deepened, the yield curve has lengthened, and regulatory reforms have encouraged broader investor participation. Yet the task is far from complete. The corporate bond market remains shallow relative to the size of the economy, secondary-market liquidity is uneven, and participation by retail investors and smaller institutions remains limited. Overcoming these constraints will require coherent policies across fiscal management, regulation and market infrastructure. It will also demand a sustained effort to enhance transparency, standardise documentation and nurture investor confidence.

Against this backdrop, *Indian Bond Market: Structure, Conduct and Macroeconomic Impact* is both timely and significant. The book offers a comprehensive and empirically grounded analysis of India's bond market, including its institutional design, macroeconomic linkages, and policy relevance. It provides a framework for understanding how fiscal dynamics, inflation expectations, monetary policy, and external capital flows influence yields and, thereby, market behaviour. The authors' treatment of these interactions is meticulous, demonstrating both analytical rigour and a clear sense of practical application.

Particularly valuable is the book's exploration of the Reserve Bank of India's dual role as the government's debt manager and the guardian of monetary stability. The analysis of the yield curve as a communication channel between policy and markets is insightful, as is the discussion of how market expectations both shape and respond to policy decisions. The authors also underscore the interplay between the government and corporate bond segments, showing how a well-functioning sovereign bond market is the foundation upon which corporate debt markets can grow.

"There is no free lunch" is one of the enduring aphorisms of economics. The bond market is a living testament to that time-tested fact. Every fiscal decision, every borrowing programme and every policy commitment carries an implication that the market swiftly and impartially prices in. When governments borrow beyond their means or delay structural reforms, the bond market demands a reckoning through higher yields or diminished confidence. In this sense, it enforces a discipline that is neither punitive nor political—it is simply the discipline of economic truth.

Carville's quip about the intimidating power of the bond market is thus more than light-hearted banter; it is a recognition of accountability in its purest form. Markets, when transparent and efficient, are not adversaries to policy but partners in sound governance. They reward prudence, penalise excess and ensure that capital flows toward the most credible and productive uses. A responsive and transparent engagement between policymakers and market participants strengthens confidence on both sides and ensures that the cost of capital reflects the economy's underlying fundamentals.

The authors, Dr Geetima Das Krishna and Dr Biswajit Nag, have marshalled extensive research, professional insight and analytical depth to produce a book that bridges academic inquiry and policy relevance. Their effort reflects years of careful study of macro-financial linkages and institutional development in India. The book's combination of empirical evidence, conceptual clarity and accessible exposition will make it a valuable reference not only for students and researchers but also for policymakers, regulators and practitioners engaged in India's financial markets.

India's progress towards a developed economy by 2047 will depend as much on the strength of its financial sector as on the dynamism of its real economy. The bond market—often described as the backbone of financial intermediation—will be central to achieving this vision. It will determine the cost and availability of capital, the efficiency of fiscal operations and the credibility of macroeconomic management. Strengthening this market is therefore not just a peripheral objective; it is a national priority.

I commend this book for its comprehensive scope, intellectual balance and the effort that has gone into its writing. It deepens our understanding of a complex yet crucial segment of the financial system and offers a foundation for further policy debate and research. The authors deserve full credit for their thoughtful and rigorous contribution.

Duvvuri Subbarao

Governor (2008–13), Reserve Bank of India

List of Abbreviations

ABS: Asset-Backed Securities

ADF: Augmented Dickey-Fuller

BIS: Bureau of International Settlements

BP: Band-Pass

BSE: Bombay Stock Exchange

CBLO: Collateralized Borrowing and Lending Obligations

CCIL: Clearing Corporation of India Limited

CDS: Credit Default Swap

CILI: Composite Index of Leading Indicators

CMBs: Cash Management Bills

CMIE: Centre for Monitoring Indian Economy

CP: Commercial Paper

CPI: Consumer Price Index

CRR: Cash Reserve Ratio

CSO: Central Statistical Organisation

FE: Fixed Effects

FIIs: Foreign Institutional Investors

FIs: Financial Institutions

FPIs: Foreign Portfolio Investors

FRBM: Fiscal Responsibility and Budget Management

G-Secs: Government Securities

HNI: High Net-Worth Individual

HP: Hodrick–Prescott

IBC: Insolvency and Bankruptcy Code

IIP: Index of Industrial Production

IL&FS: Infrastructure Leasing & Financial Services Limited

IMF: International Monetary Fund

IRDAI: Insurance Regulatory and Development Authority of India

IRF: Interest Rate Futures

IV: Instrumental Variable

LAF: Liquidity Adjustment Facility

MSF: Marginal Standing Facility

NAGDP: Non-Agricultural GDP

NBER: National Bureau of Economic Research

NBFC: Non-Banking Financial Company

NDS: Negotiated Dealing System

NDS-OM: NDS-Order Matching Segment

NEER: Nominal Effective Exchange Rate

NPAs: Non-Performing Assets

NPS: National Pension System

NSDL: National Securities Depository Limited

NSE: National Stock Exchange

NSSF: National Small Savings Fund

OECD: Organisation for Economic Co-operation and Development

OMO: Open Market Operation

OTC: Over-the-Counter

Panel EGLS: Panel Estimated Generalized Least Squares

PCA: Principal Component Analysis

PDs: Primary Dealers

PFC: Power Finance Corporation

PP: Phillips-Perron

PSBR: Public Sector Borrowing Requirement

PSUs: Public Sector Undertakings

RBI: Reserve Bank of India

RE: Random Effects

SDLs: State Development Loans

SEBI: Securities and Exchange Board of India

SLR: Statutory Liquidity Ratio

SPVs: Special Purpose Vehicles

STRIPS: Separate Trading of Registered Interest and Principal Securities

SUR: Seemingly Unrelated Regression

SVAR: Structural Vector Autoregression

T-bills: Treasury Bills

VAR: Vector Autoregression

WPI: Wholesale Price Index

CHAPTER 1

The Fixed Income Market of India

The development of financial markets is not a one-time event but an ongoing process. In India, financial markets have evolved gradually and in calibrated manner in response to a series of reforms since the 1990s. This evolution is evident in the price discovery process, the slackening of restrictions, and the reduction of transaction costs. Over time, financial market integration—reflected in the correlation between different market segments—has increased, enhancing overall efficacy. This progress has bolstered the confidence of both investors and corporations in the market ecosystem.

A well-developed capital market consists of both equity and bond markets, which complement other components of the financial sector, such as banking, insurance and the money market. Within the bond market, the government and corporate segments are the two major categories, and their dynamics are closely linked.

A bond is a fixed-income investment through which an investor loans money to a government or corporation for a specified period at either a fixed or variable interest rate. In return, the investor receives regular interest payments—typically every six months or annually—and the principal amount is returned at the end of the agreed-upon term. Thus, the bond market serves as a crucial link connecting issuers—such as governments, local bodies and corporations—with financing needs to investors who have surplus funds to invest.

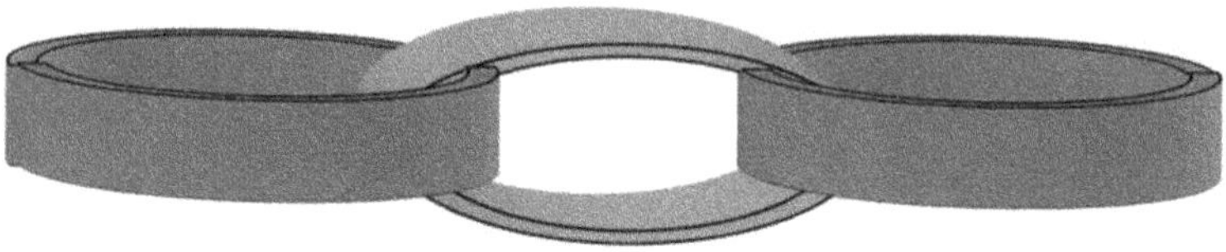

Figure 1.1: Bond Market

An efficient bond market ensures that the needs of both investors and issuers are met effectively at market-determined prices, seamlessly incorporating new information into pricing. The basic pre-requisites for a vibrant bond market include:

- A stable macroeconomic environment.
- Absence of government-controlled interest rates.
- A large base of both investors and issuers.
- Efficient intermediaries and infrastructure for smooth trading and settlement.
- A supportive regulatory and legal framework.

Bond prices are determined by the present value of future cash flows, which are influenced by interest rates, leading to an inverse relationship between the two. It means, when interest rates rise, bond prices fall. This creates interest rate risk in the bond market, as the value of a bond or fixed-income investment suffers whenever interest rates change. This property also makes retail investors a bit wary of investing in this instrument, as they find it difficult to understand this inverse relationship.

While investors find it easy to understand share prices in the equity market, they often struggle with the concept of yield in the bond market. The bond price, or its market value, reflects the amount at which it is currently trading in the open market, similar to a share price. However, bonds are typically quoted in terms of yield, which can be confusing. When an investor buys a bond, they are essentially lending money to the issuer in exchange for periodic interest payments and the return of the principal (the bond's face value) at maturity. Several factors influence a bond's price. Please refer to Box 1.1 to understand the nuances of these factors and how bond prices and yields are related.

Box 1.1: Bond Price and Yield

Let's examine some commonly used terms in the bond market that influence its price:

1. **Face Value (Par Value):** This is the nominal value or principal amount of the bond. It represents the amount the issuer promises to repay to the bondholder at maturity.
2. **Time to Maturity:** This refers to the duration for which money is lent to the issuer of the bond. The length of time until a bond matures also affects its price; generally, longer-term bonds are more sensitive to changes in interest rates than shorter-term bonds.
3. **Coupon Rate:** The coupon rate is the fixed annual or semi-annual interest rate that the bond pays, expressed as a percentage of the bond's face value. For example, a bond with a face value of ₹1,000 and a 5% coupon rate will pay ₹50 in interest annually.
4. **Yield to Maturity (YTM):** YTM is a key concept in bond investing, representing the total return an investor can expect if they hold a bond until maturity. It is the interest rate that equates the present value of the cash flows—interest payments and the final principal amount—to the current market price of the bond. Thus, the bond price and YTM are inversely related.

A robust bond market with a substantial corporate bond segment is vital for the economy, as it ensures the flow of funds into productive sectors. While India boasts a world-class equity market, its corporate bond market remains relatively underdeveloped, with Government Securities (G-Secs) dominating both the primary and secondary markets.

The G-Secs market plays a crucial role in India for several reasons:

- Primary Source of Funding: It serves as the main avenue for the government to raise funds to finance its fiscal deficit.
- Risk-Free Yields: The government or sovereign bond market offers risk-free yields, as governments usually do not default. This allows investors to calibrate the prices of other financial instruments in the economy by adding appropriate risk premiums.
- Monetary Policy Management: The RBI uses the government bond market to manage domestic money supply and inflation through open market operations (OMOs).

Similarly, a robust corporate bond market is equally essential in India for several reasons:

- Alternative Financing: It provides an alternative source of finance for the corporate sector, supplementing bank credit to meet long-term investment needs.
- Stability: It is considered a more stable source of finance compared to the volatile equity market, helping to diversify risks within the financial system.
- Support for Economic Development: A well-developed corporate bond market is vital for economic growth, especially in India, where significant investment is required for the infrastructure sector funding that cannot be met by the banking sector alone.

The maturity of the financial sector is essential for the stability of an economy. In a fast-growing economy like India, an active financial sector is necessary to alleviate the pressures associated with financing economic activities. Without it, even minor crises—whether domestic or international—can undermine macroeconomic foundations. The bond market can play an important role in promoting growth and macroeconomic stability by providing a stable source of financing.

The Indian economy grew by a modest three percent in the fourth quarter of FY 2019–20, marking the slowest growth in approximately eleven years. Investments remained subdued for a prolonged period, while private demand nearly collapsed. One of the primary reasons for the slowdown was the legacy of non-performing assets (NPAs) in the banking sector, which led to banks becoming increasingly risk-averse. Although the banking sector's issues began to improve, the domestic financial markets witnessed further disruption, primarily stemming from Non-banking Financial Companies (NBFCs) in 2018. With outstanding debts of over ₹26 lakh crore, the NBFCs struggled with a severe liquidity crunch following a series of defaults by Infrastructure Leasing & Financial Services Limited (IL&FS). These companies had been borrowing short-term to finance long-term projects and rolling over their debts, which exacerbated the problem as liquidity dried up. According to a report by the RBI, overall financial flows to the commercial sector declined sharply, by around 88 percent in the first six months of FY 2019–20.

Given the challenges in the banking sector, it is important to have a look at the alternative financing sources for the private sector, such as the Corporate Bond Market, and the issues facing this vital segment. Additionally, it's important to understand the factors influencing the government debt market and the impact of various macroeconomic shocks on the entire yield curve. This is because the government yield curve serves as a benchmark for determining the pricing of other financial instruments in the economy.

A well-developed corporate bond market is essential for India's plans to undertake large-scale infrastructure projects. Given that India now needs to look beyond traditional banks for long-term financing needs, it's critical to address the limitations of the banking system. An oversized banking system is often associated with inferior risk assessment, and combined with the system's other weaknesses, this can lead to over-capacity, non-performing loans, and ultimately, an economic crisis (Hakansson, 1999).

The corporate debt defaults following the NBFC crisis in 2019, underscored the urgent need for reforms in the regulatory and operational aspects of the corporate bond market. A robust corporate bond market can play an important role in the economic growth of the country by reducing funding costs and providing infrastructure project developers with more debt-raising options for longer tenors. However, the lack of a solid regulatory framework and investor protection mechanisms exacerbates market imperfections. A weak corporate bond market can have a significant impact on the broader financial system and the country's economic outlook. Therefore, it is crucial to examine the evolution and dynamics of India's bond market and its potential to address the pressing need for funding to finance the government, public sector enterprises, and the private sector.

1.1. The Role of Sovereign Bond Market

According to a 2006 report by the RBI, the government or sovereign securities market plays three key roles—supporting the financial markets, the government, and the central bank.

The government securities market is crucial to the financial system as it provides risk-free credit through highly liquid financial instruments. It is considered the backbone of fixed-income markets because it defines the benchmark yield, with other financial instruments being priced in relation to it. Beyond integrating various segments of domestic financial markets, this market also connects the domestic market with international markets. As a result, government securities are widely used by dealers to hedge against interest rate risk and serve as collateral in other markets, such as repo, futures, and options [Bureau of International Settlements (BIS), 1999].

For the government, as the issuer of securities, a vibrant government securities market allows for borrowing at a reasonable cost. It removes the need for monetising the deficit through central bank funding or relying on captive investors. Instead, investors participate voluntarily, driven by their perception of risk and return.

For the central bank, a developed and deeper government securities market enables the effective use of indirect monetary policy tools, such as OMOs. Market borrowings by the government increase the quantum of eligible collaterals, enhancing the flexibility of the central bank in conducting monetary policy through these tools, particularly in sterilising capital flows. Although the central bank can no longer participate in the primary market for government securities, it can adjust its portfolio by participating in the secondary market. This government securities market helps in monetary policy transmission to the real economy, as changes in policy rates directly impact the short-term yields on government bonds.

The demand and supply dynamics of government securities can influence the investment climate in the economy in two keyways. The risk-free interest rate in the economy is determined by the upward-sloping supply curve and the downward-sloping demand curve for government securities. An increase in the supply of government securities, driven by a higher fiscal deficit, would lead to a drop in prices (and a rise in yields) of these securities, resulting in higher yields on risk-free assets. Higher supply means higher yields. This increase in yields raises corporate borrowing costs, as corporate bond interest rates are typically linked to the risk-free rates of government bonds, plus a risk premium. This creates competition for the economy's limited resources, diverting funds away from the productive commercial sector—a phenomenon known as "crowding out". At the same time, the higher yields on government securities translate into higher borrowing costs for the government, which can further exacerbate the fiscal deficit.

On the other hand, the government securities market can positively influence private investment by supporting the development of the corporate bond market in two key ways—(i) by setting up the basic infrastructure, regulatory and legal framework, institutions, investors, and markets needed by the corporate bond market, and (ii) by developing a complete yield curve that serves as an informational benchmark for all other financial debt instruments.

For investors, sovereign bond yields serve as the benchmark risk-free rates that can influence economic activities. The interest rates of all other debt instruments are determined by using sovereign bond yields as the base, with the addition of the appropriate risk premium (Figure 1.2).

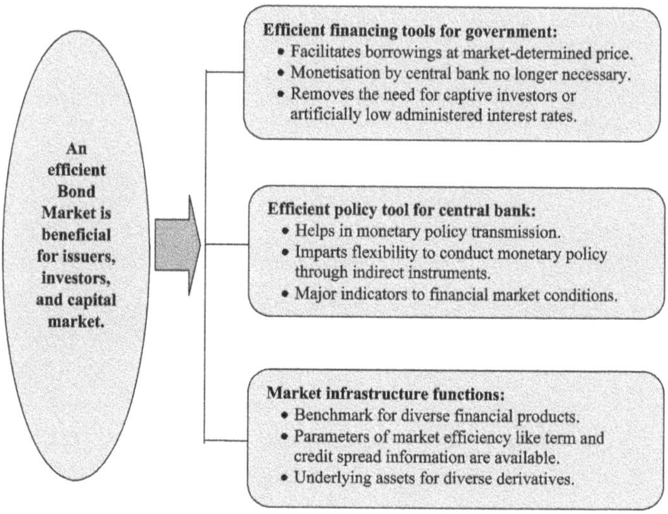

Figure 1.2: Sovereign Bond Market and its Importance

Source: Reddy (2002), RBI

1.2. Structure of the Fixed Income (Bond) Market in India

The Indian bond market evolved rapidly following the economic reforms of the 1990s. During the pre-reform era, the RBI directly monetized or financed the government's fiscal deficit. Banks were mandated to invest in government securities at lower interest rates, forcing them to raise interest rates on commercial loans to compensate for the loss, which negatively impacted economic growth. A series of reforms were introduced after the 1990s to develop the necessary market infrastructure, enhance liquidity, and improve the maturity profile, among other objectives. These reforms are discussed in detail later.

As mentioned earlier, the fixed income market in India is primarily composed of two segments. The first segment is the government or sovereign securities market, which includes both central and state government securities. These fixed-income securities (G-Secs) are issued by the government to borrow funds and finance its fiscal deficit, with the RBI acting as the issuer on behalf of the government. The second segment is the non-government securities market, which includes corporate securities such as bonds issued by financial institutions (FIs) Public Sector Undertakings (PSUs), and private corporations.

In India, banks are mandated by the RBI to maintain a certain percentage of their total liabilities or deposits in government securities and other specified liquid assets. This, in turn, creates a captive demand for government securities. Similar statutory requirements, though in varying proportions, are mandated for FIs, such as insurance companies, provident funds, and non-banking financial institutions. Since most PSU bonds carry an explicit guarantee of the government, they are generally treated as proxies for sovereign securities. Some PSU bonds, such as infrastructure bonds, are tax-free, an advantage not enjoyed even by government bonds. Corporate bonds and debentures typically have maturities of over one year. Additionally, the corporate sector issues bonds with shorter tenures, known as commercial paper, with maturities ranging from 15 days to one year.

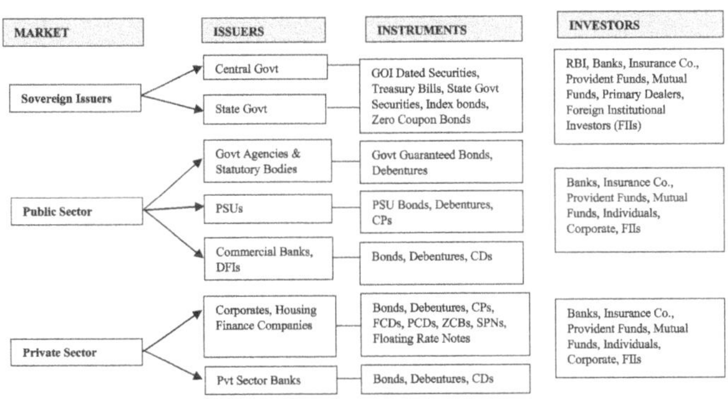

Figure 1.3: Overview of Fixed Income Market of India (Regulator: RBI, SEBI, IRDAI)

Note: CD: Certificate of Deposit, CP: Commercial Paper, FCD: Fully Convertible Debentures, PCD: Partly Convertible Debentures, SPN: Secured Premium Notes, ZCB: Zero-Coupon Bonds, SEBI: Securities and Exchange Board of India, IRDAI: Insurance Regulatory and Development Authority of India.

Box 1.2: Regulators of Bond Market

RBI: The RBI is the Central Bank that plays a major role in the Indian bond market. Some of its key functions include: (i) acting as the regulator of the market, (ii) serving as the debt manager for the government, as government bonds are issued in the market by the RBI, (iii) formulating monetary policy, which influences the interest rates of the bonds issued, and (iv) creating captive demand for these bonds by mandating banks to maintain a certain percentage of their total liabilities or deposits in government securities.

SEBI: The Securities and Exchange Board of India (SEBI) regulates the second segment of the market—non-government securities, which include bonds issued by FIs, PSUs and corporations. Thought the SEBI (Issue and Listing of Debt Securities) Regulations, 2008, the board aims to reduce costs and improve transparency in the corporate debt market. To boost the corporate bond market in India, SEBI made it mandatory for large companies to raise 25% of their incremental borrowings through the issuance of debt securities. However, in September 2023, after consultations with companies, SEBI removed the penalties for companies that were unable to meet this mandatory quota. In addition, SEBI also regulates mutual funds that invest in the bond markets.

IRDAI: Insurance Regulatory and Development Authority of India (IRDAI) is one of the largest components on the demand side of the bond market. It mandates that a certain percentage of pension funds be invested in specified bonds, ensuring the participation of insurance companies in the debt market. Notably, IRDAI has kept pace with the supply-side reforms initiated by the RBI and SEBI.

1.3. Institutional Background

The RBI is the principal operator of the government bond market. It serves as the debt manager for the government and regulates the government bond market, including key participants such as primary dealers (PDs) and banks. The RBI has the authority to issue currency, adjust policy rates and utilise diverse monetary policy tools to achieve its objectives. In addition to regulating the country's financial system, the RBI plays multiple roles, including setting monetary policy, maintaining financial stability, managing government debt, and coordinating with the government on policy matters. The responsibilities provide the RBI with the operational flexibility to influence the nominal yields (interest rates) of government bonds by setting and adjusting short-term interest rates.

Some of the monetary tools used by the RBI include policy rates such as Repo, Reverse Repo, and Marginal Standing Facility (MSF), as well as reserve ratios like CRR (Cash Reserve Ratio) and SLR (Statutory Liquidity Ratio) and OMO (Open Market Operations). These tools are typically categorised into direct and indirect instruments.

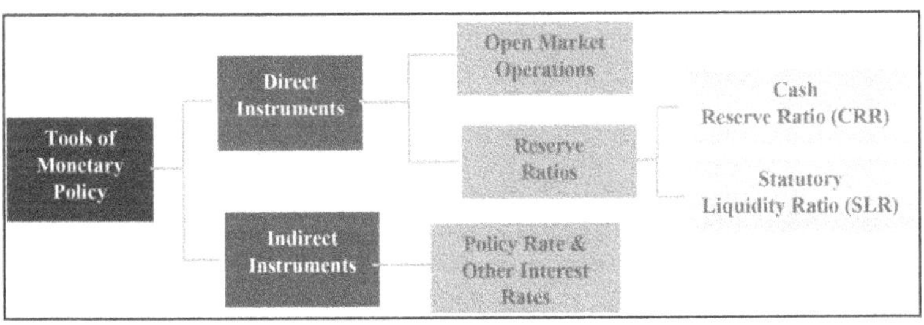

Figure 1.4: Policy Tools of the RBI

The direct and indirect policy tools of the RBI are discussed in detail separately. Standing Deposit Facility (SDF) is the latest policy instrument added to RBI's arsenal in April 2022 for absorbing liquidity to control inflation. The SDF is fixed at 3.75 percent, 25 basis points (bps) below the Repo Rate, and will replace the Fixed

Rate Reverse Repo (FRRR) as the floor of the Liquidity Adjustment Facility (LAF) corridor. (Further details are explained later).

Box 1.3: Direct Monetary Policy Instruments

Direct monetary tools are policy instruments that directly impact market liquidity and interest rates.

1. **Statutory Liquidity Ratio (SLR):** Banks need to maintain a certain ratio of their total deposits as SLR, as decided by RBI from time to time, in the form of approved securities, gold, or cash. As of June 2022, the SLR stands at 18.0%.
2. **Cash Reserve Ratio (CRR):** Banks are also mandated to maintain a certain portion of their total deposits in cash with the RBI, known as the CRR (4.5% as of June 2022), as decided by the RBI periodically. CRR is a cost for banks as they do not earn any interest on it.
3. **Open Market Operations (OMO):** Through OMOs, the RBI can buy or sell government securities in the market to influence liquidity conditions and interest rates.

The RBI directly controls the money supply in the banking system through policy tools such as CRR, SLR, and OMO. When the CRR or SLR is raised, banks have less money available to lend, which tightens liquidity in the system and raises borrowing costs. For example, if the CRR is set at 3%, then for every ₹100 of deposits in banks, ₹3 must be held with the RBI, leaving only ₹97 for the bank to lend. An increase in the CRR reduces the amount of lendable funds available to banks, which in turn raises the cost of borrowing.

Additionally, OMO is a direct tool used by the RBI to inject or drain liquidity in the banking system by buying or selling government bonds. When the RBI buys government bonds, it releases liquidity into the system, and when it sells bonds, it withdraws liquidity from the banking system. By managing liquidity, the RBI can influence bond yields and interest rates in the economy.

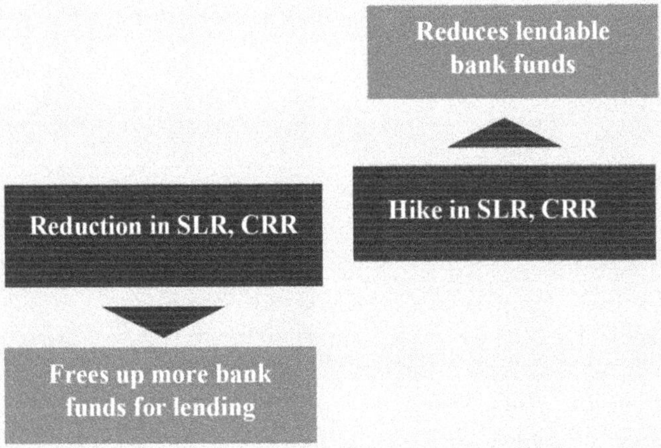

Figure 1.5: Impact of Reserve Ratios

Box 1.4: Indirect Monetary Policy Instruments

Indirect monetary tools are policy instruments that impact market liquidity and interest rates indirectly.

1. **Repo Rate:** The Repo (Repurchase Agreement) Rate is the interest rate at which the RBI lends to banks for short-term funding, with government securities offered as collateral. Banks often borrow from the RBI at the Repo rate to meet their daily operational needs.
2. **Reverse Repo Rate:** The Reverse Repo Rate is the interest rate the RBI pays to banks for accepting short-term deposits. As of June 2022, the Reverse Repo Rate is 65 basis points below the Repo Rate. When banks have excess funds, they can park them with the RBI and earn interest at the Reverse Repo Rate. In return, the RBI offers government securities to banks for the money deposited.
3. **Marginal Standing Facility (MSF):** The MSF rate is the interest rate at which banks can borrow from the

RBI during a liquidity crunch when they lack sufficient collateral. Banks are allowed to lower their SLR requirement to borrow from the RBI at a penalty rate, which is 25 basis points higher than the Repo Rate (as of June 2022).

The Repo, Reverse Repo, and MSF rates are indirect policy tools that help in maintaining adequate liquidity in the system, with the Reverse Repo Rate serving as the floor. These rates keep short-term interest rates within the LAF corridor (Figure 1.6). When the RBI raises the policy rate, short-term rates typically follow the Repo Rate, with the effect gradually extending to longer-term yields. This is why these instruments are referred to as indirect rate tools.

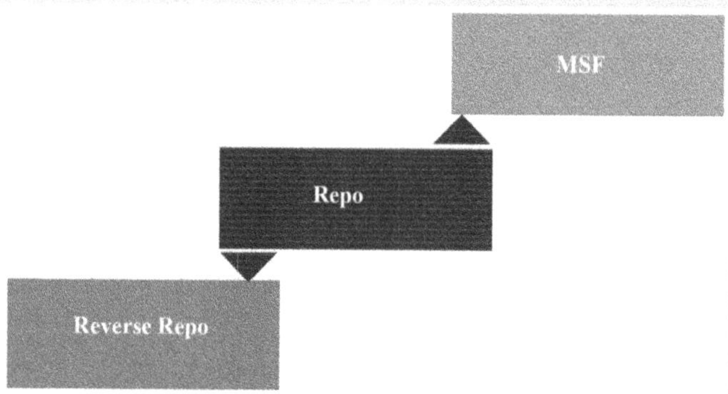

Figure 1.6: The Policy Corridor of RBI

Box 1.5: Standing Deposit Facility (SDF)

On 8th April 2022, the RBI introduced a new monetary tool to its toolkit for absorbing liquidity and controlling inflation: the Standing Deposit Facility (SDF).

The SDF is set at 3.75%, 25 basis points (bps) below the Repo Rate, and will replace the fixed rate reverse repo (FRRR) as the floor of the LAF corridor.

The Reverse Repo rate, now referred to as the Fixed Rate Reverse Repo (FRRR) rate, remains in the toolkit and is set at 3.35%. With this change, the pre-pandemic policy corridor of 50 bps is restored, with the MSF set 25 bps above and the SDF set 25 bps below the Repo Rate.

The idea of an SDF was first proposed in the Urjit Patel Monetary Policy Committee report in 2014. Section 17 of the RBI Act was amended in 2018 to introduce the SDF as an additional tool for absorbing liquidity without the need for collateral. The SDF allows the RBI to absorb excess cash from the economy by sucking liquidity from commercial banks without providing government securities in return. The key difference between the SDF and the Reverse Repo is that while the RBI needs to provide collateral (in the form of government securities) when conducting reverse repo operations, the SDF does not require any collateral. This becomes particularly useful when the RBI does not have adequate bonds to offer as collateral, as was the case during demonetisation. The introduction of the SDF provides the RBI with greater flexibility by removing the collateral constraint, thereby strengthening the operational framework of monetary policy.

During the pandemic, the RBI kept the Repo Rate at an all-time low of 4% since May 2020, while the Reverse Repo rate was set at 3.35% to support economic growth. The central bank also injected liquidity into the system to cushion economic activities during the crisis. As a result, the amount of cash in the system surged significantly. This led to the operative rate in the market falling well below the Repo Rate, as banks parked their large surplus funds with the RBI at the 3.35% Reverse Repo rate.

With inflation surging well above the RBI's comfort zone of 2–6% in the first quarter of FY 2023, there was a need to increase interest rates and absorb liquidity from the system. The introduction of the SDF effectively translates to a 40-bps hike in the Reverse Repo Rate, which will lead to a rise in the cost of money.

Thus, Figure 1.7 visually represents the policy corridor followed by the central bank. The objective is to maintain the overnight or short-term rates within this policy range.

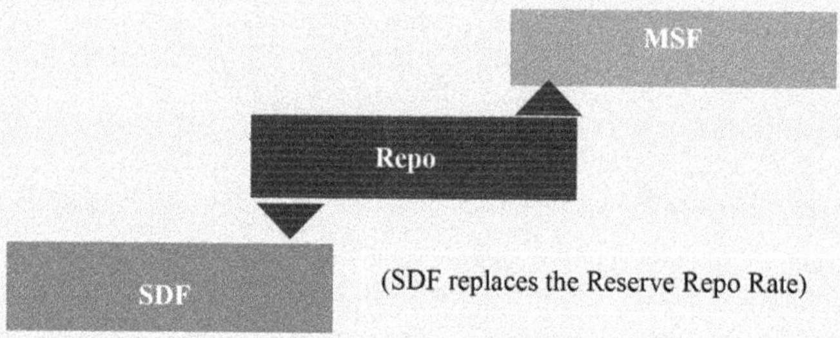

Figure 1.7: The New Policy Corridor of RBI

The trends of the RBI's indirect and direct policy tools can be observed in the charts below.

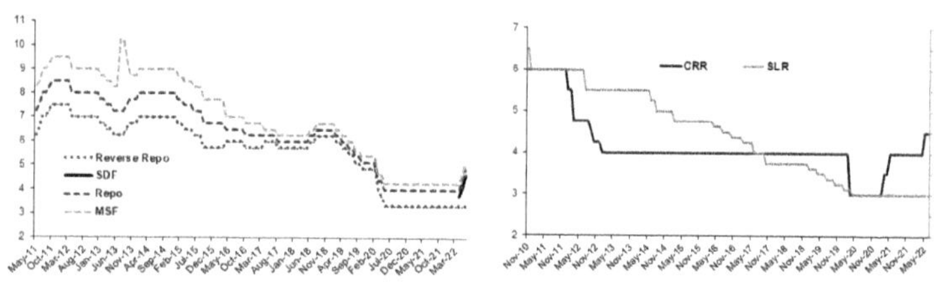

Figure 1.8: Trend of Direct and Indirect Policy Tools of RBI

Source: RBI Database

It is important to understand these policy tools of the central bank, as we will discuss the impact of changes in policy rates on bond yields in later chapters.

In the first chapter, we cover the basics of the fixed income or bond market, including its institutional background and the role of regulators. The following chapters are divided into two parts. In the first part, we will delve more into the evolution of bond markets (both government and corporate), stylised facts, types of bond markets, state government bonds, municipal bonds and select Asian bond markets. In the second part, we try to get more insights through econometric modelling and analysis, such as the long-run determinants of sovereign bond yields, the information contained in the slope of the yield curve, and the factors influencing the development of the corporate bond market.

PART I

Evolution And Structure of The Indian Bond Market

CHAPTER 2

Evolution and Reforms in the Indian Bond Market

India's bond market has witnessed significant transformation since 1990, primarily driven by the need to finance the fiscal deficit of the central government. From its early stages as a basic debt market, the journey to the present vibrant, real-time trading in a variety of debt instruments has been long but rapid.

2.1. Government Bond Market (G-Secs)

The origins of the bond market in India can be traced back to the British period. According to an RBI paper, the concept of borrowing from the public in India was pioneered by the East India Company to finance its campaigns in South India (during the Anglo-French wars) in the eighteenth century. Until 1867, public debt or government borrowing was primarily driven by the need to finance military campaigns. Between 1867 and 1916, public debt was raised to finance infrastructure projects such as railway construction, irrigation canals, and other public works.

In December 1920, the provinces of British India were allowed to float loans for the first time, following the introduction of local government borrowing rules under Section 30(a) of the Government of India Act, 1919. Only three provinces—Bombay, United Provinces, and Punjab—took advantage of this provision. During the World Wars, India's public debt increased significantly, as India was required to contribute to the British exchequer to cover the costs of the war.

After independence, between 1951 and 1985, government borrowing was primarily influenced by the five-year plans. The development of the government bond market in India was slow during the 1970s and 1980s. In the pre-reform era of the 1990s, several factors contributed to the slow growth of the government bond market:

- The government's borrowing (fiscal deficit) was primarily met through a system of ad hoc Treasury bills (T-bills) issued by the government to the RBI. In other words, the RBI directly financed the fiscal deficit.
- Banks were mandated to invest in government securities at pre-determined interest rates by progressively increasing the Statutory Liquidity Ratio (SLR). This disrupted the price discovery process, which is essential for efficient functioning of financial markets.
- Interest rates were kept artificially low to minimise government borrowing costs. This affected the entire interest rate structure, leading to negative real interest rates for several years.
- As banks were forced to lend to the government at lower interest rates, they had no option but to raise interest rates on commercial loans to offset the losses. This adversely affected private sector investment and, in turn, economic growth. Low growth further hurt the financial health of the banking system, as bad loans mounted over time.
- Tepid growth also meant lower tax revenue collections for the government, resulting in a higher fiscal deficit. This created a vicious cycle. This adversely impacted the overall economy and prevented the effective transmission of monetary policy.

The outright monetisation of the central government's budget deficit, along with administered low interest rates, hampered the development of the secondary market for government securities, which was almost absent at the time.

In the early 1990s, the RBI, in consultation with the government, initiated reforms in the government securities market as a part of broader financial sector reforms. Since 1991, India has undertaken wide-ranging reforms in the debt market aimed at developing appropriate market infrastructure, increasing liquidity and maturity profile, widening and deepening the market, improving risk management practices, and enhancing transparency. These reforms were driven by the changing economic environment and the need to address the government's large borrowing requirements.

The reforms in the government securities market can be conceptually divided into three chronological phases (Mohan & Ray, 2009).

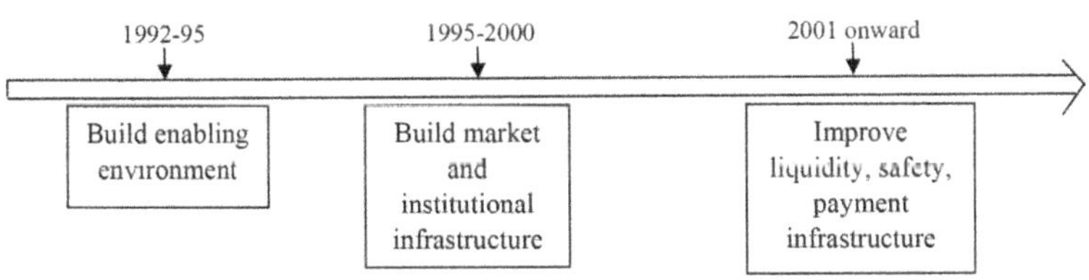

Figure 2.1: Reforms Initiated in Sovereign Bond Market

The first phase, from 1992 to 1995, focused on creating an enabling environment by eliminating automatic monetisation, promoting fiscal discipline, and moving away from administered interest rates to reflect market-driven prices. By 1997, the RBI had completely phased out funding through ad hoc bills.

The second phase, from 1995 to 2000, focused on building the market and institutional infrastructure. The system of PDs was established to support primary issuances and provide liquidity in the secondary market.

The third phase, from 2001 onwards, was focused on improving liquidity, safety, and building payment infrastructure. In 2002, the Negotiated Dealing System (NDS) and Clearing Corporation of India Limited (CCIL) were started, followed by the introduction of trading of G-Secs on stock exchanges. One of the major developments during this phase was the enactment of the Government Securities Act, 2006, which replaced both the Public Debt Act, 1944, and the Indian

Securities Act, 1920, thus modernising the legal framework of the government securities market (Table 2.1).

Table 2.1: Evolution of Government Bond Market in India

Year	Reform	Details
1992–1993	Auction based Pricing Policy	Bond pricing policy was revised and linked to market interest rates. Prior to this, yields on government securities were fixed at artificially low levels. The auction-based sale of government securities coincided with the emergence of primary and secondary dealers in the gilts market.
1993	SLR Reduction	Substantial reduction in the statutory liquidity ratio (SLR) of the banks was seen. The SLR stood at 38.5% in 1992 and is 18.0% at present.
1994	Limit ad hoc T-bills	Agreement between RBI and Government on limiting issue of ad hoc Treasury Bills to remove automatic monetization of government debt. By 1997, ad hoc treasury bills were completely phased out.
1996	Primary Dealer System Introduced	PDs were introduced to support the auction system, strengthen the market intermediation, and support primary issue. PDs have privileged access to preferential finance at the RBI.
1997	FII Investment	Foreign Institutional Investors (FIIs) were allowed to invest in G-Secs within specified limits.
1998	Stamp Duty	Trading in bonds received more encouragement when the government eliminated stamp duty on trades involving debt securities.

Year	Reform	Details
2001	Clearing Corporation of India Ltd. (CCIL)	CCIL established in 2001, is the clearing agency to provide guaranteed clearing and settlement functions for transactions in Money, G-Secs, Foreign Exchange and Derivative markets.
2002	Trading and Settlement Infrastructure	Until 2002, the secondary government bond market was a purely OTC telephone market. In February 2002, NDS and in August 2005, NDS-Order Matching Segment (NDS-OM) were introduced by RBI. NDS-OM, a screen-based anonymous trading and reporting platform, enables electronic bidding in primary auctions with the capability of disseminating trading information with minimum lag.
2003	Collateralized Borrowing and Lending Obligations (CBLOs)	CCIL operates a market for CBLOs—a form of a tripartite repo that allows market participants to place collateral securities (government bonds/treasury bills) at the CCIL. Borrowers can bid for funds through the CBLO system—a transparent, electronic order book. CBLOs are an innovative technique unique to India (Wells & Schou-Zibell, 2008).
2003	Retail Investors allowed	Retail trading of government securities permitted on stock exchanges to widen investor base.
2003	Interest Rate Futures (IRF) introduced	IRF was introduced to facilitate hedging of interest rate risk. Although it did not take off at that time.
2006	When-Issued Market	Introduced in May 2006. It was realised that transparency of issuance allows investors to plan their cash flows and investments more accurately. Now RBI issues auction calendar of forthcoming issues.

Year	Reform	Details
2006	Government Securities Act, 2006	This Act facilitated wider participation in the Government bond market and created the enabling provisions for the issue of Separate Trading of Registered Interest and Principal Securities (STRIPS).
2007	Short Selling	Short selling was prohibited until March 2006. It was then relaxed, allowing PDs and scheduled commercial banks to run intraday short positions.
2010	Cash Management Bills (CMBs)	The government, in consultation with RBI, introduced a new short-term instrument, known as Cash Management Bills (CMBs), to meet the temporary mismatches in the cash flow of the Government of India. The CMBs have the generic character of T-bills but are issued for maturities less than 91 days.
2014	Variable Repo	RBI introduced special variable-rate, short-term repo/reverse repo auctions to manage liquidity and bring stability to the overnight call rates.
2015	IRF on 5y and 15y introduced	IRF was introduced on the 5-year and 15-year on-the-run bonds in addition to the future on 10-year bonds. It was a major push by RBI to make the market more liquid after a weak start of the IRF market in 2003.
2015	Sovereign Gold Bond Scheme	The sovereign gold bond scheme was launched in November 2015 with an objective to reduce the demand for physical gold and shift a part of the domestic savings, used for the purchase of gold, into financial savings.
2016	Market Making	Accepting the recommendations made by H.R. Khan Committee, the RBI allowed market-making in G-Secs to improve market liquidity.

Year	Reform	Details
2017	Municipal Bonds Reintroduced	Pune raised ₹200 crores in first municipal bond issue in 14 years—nearly two years after Sebi issued new norms for municipal bonds. It was first introduced in 1997, and Bangalore Municipal Corporation was the first to issue, followed by Ahmedabad. Later lost momentum.
2021	RBI Retail Direct Scheme	Launch of the RBI Retail Direct Scheme—a one-stop solution to facilitate investment in G-Secs by individual investors.
2023	Sovereign Green Bonds for non-Residents	Through the circular (RBI/2023-24/81) dated Nov 2023, RBI designated all Sovereign Green Bonds issued by the Government in the fiscal year 2023–24 as "specified securities" under the Fully Accessible Route (FAR).

In September 2023, JPMorgan Chase & Co. announced that Indian government bonds would be included in the GBI-EM Global Index suite and all relevant derivative benchmarks starting on 28 June 2024. The inclusion of Indian bonds will be staggered over a 10-month period, from 28 June 2024 to 31 March 2025. As per the index inclusion criteria, eligible instruments must have a notional outstanding value of over $1 billion (or equivalent) and at least 2.5 years of remaining maturity. It is estimated that the inclusion of Indian bonds in the global indices will increase index yields by 33 basis points and 8 basis points, respectively, once the inclusion process is complete.

2.2. Corporate Bond Market

For an emerging economy like India, a well-developed bond market is a critical source of funds for the corporate sector. Indian corporate bond market is yet to mature and is small relative to other large economies. According to Asian Development Bank (2016), the total Indian domestic bond market stands at 58 percent of GDP (primarily due to low outstanding corporate bonds) which is low compared to other developed and developing Asian countries. For example, Japan has the highest outstanding domestic debt at 213 percent of GDP, followed by S. Korea (111 percent), Malaysia (94.3 percent), China (75 percent) and Singapore (57.6 percent).

According to an RBI report, the solid growth of the government securities market, favourable tax treatment, and reduced cost of capital in the equities market have made the corporate bond market less attractive to many firms and investors. While the corporate bond market has grown over the years, this growth has largely been in private placements. The presence of development financial institutions, public sector banks, and commercial banks has made it easier for most corporates to access capital at low interest rates, making the public placement of bonds more expensive and less appealing. Private placements of bonds (with a specific bank or a few banks) were more cost-effective, and less cumbersome than public placements. This has led to information asymmetry in the corporate bond market, increasing its risk and making it less attractive to most investors.

Even today, most of the large issuers in the corporate debt market segment are "quasi-government" entities, such as public sector oil companies, PSU banks, and government-sponsored FIs. The challenges in this segment are manifold, including weak market infrastructure, low liquidity in the secondary market, a narrow investor base, inadequate credit assessment skills, high cost of issuance, lack of transparency, and underdeveloped securitisation of products.

Several committees, including the RH Patil Committee (2005), the Percy Mistry Committee (2007), the Committee on Financial Sector Reforms (2008), and most recently the HR Khan Committee (2016), have recommended measures to augment bond market liquidity. Key agencies such as the RBI, SEBI, and the government have undertaken significant reforms in the Indian corporate bond market. These reforms aim to widen the investor base with retail participation, create a liquid and transparent secondary market, improve clearing and trading mechanisms, and reduce the cost and duration of the issuance process. Despite all these reform measures, considerable work still needs to be done before India's corporate bond market can fully take off. A list of the reforms undertaken since 2006 in the Indian corporate bond market is provided below (Table 2.2).

Table 2.2: Evolution of Corporate Bond Market in India

Year	Reforms	Objectives
December 2006	SEBI allows the Bombay Stock Exchange (BSE) to set up a reporting platform.	The platform would capture all trade information about corporate bonds to help efficient price discovery and consistent clearing and settlement processes.
January 2007	SEBI to be responsible for the primary and secondary market. RBI, for the repo/reverse repo transactions in corporate debt. Existing exchanges at the National Stock Exchange (NSE) and BSE would be used for trading of Corporate Bonds. There would be no separate trading platforms for different kinds of (retail vs Institutional) investors.	Improves clarity on the responsibilities of different agencies for different segments of the corporate debt market. Efficient use of existing infrastructure.
April 2007	SEBI allows both BSE and NSE to have in place corporate bond trading platforms, clearing, and settlement mechanisms. Moreover, SEBI reduces tradable lots in corporate bonds.	Develop a transparent and efficient secondary market for corporate bonds that capture all trading information to enable efficient price discovery and reliable clearing and settlement process. Encourage participation of retail investors.
August 2007	SEBI makes it mandatory for companies issuing debentures to disseminate all information (default to pay interest, revision of ratings, etc) about the debentures to the investors and the people in general.	Provide access to better information about companies issuing debentures.

Year	Reforms	Objectives
May 2009	SEBI puts in place a simplified listing agreement.	Reduction in time and cost of the issuance process.
August 2009	Mutual funds are mandated to report inter-scheme transfers of corporate bonds (on NSE, BSE, and FIMMDA).	More detailed information dissemination of trading.
October 2009	SEBI makes it compulsory that the clearing and settlement of all trades should be through National Securities Clearing Corporation (NSCCL) or the Indian Clearing Corporation Limited (ICCL).	Clearing and settlement of trades to follow the International Organisation of Security Commissions (IOSCO) standards and the global best practices by way of well-established clearing and settlement procedures through recognised clearing and settlement agencies.
2014	Issuance of long-term bonds by banks allowed for the infrastructure sector.	Banks were allowed to issue long term bonds for funding their long-term commitments. This will help in reducing asset-liability mismatches in the longer-term maturities.
2014	Masala Bond—bonds issued outside India but denominated in Indian rupees.	Masala bond makes the investors bear the currency risk. The first Masala bond was issued by the World Bank-backed IFC in November 2014 when it raised 1,000 crore bonds to fund infrastructure projects in India.
2015	Green Bond	Yes Bank and Exim Bank of India issued a five-year $500 million green bond, which is India's first dollar-denominated green bond. The Indian Green Bonds Council, formed in late 2017.

Year	Reforms	Objectives
2017	RBI increased the corporate bond investment limit for foreign investors (FPIs) by taking out Masala bonds, from the ambit of the total investment limit.	The limit for investment by FPIs in corporate bonds was ₹2,44,323 crores including ₹44,001 crores of Masala bonds. Now, Masala bonds will form part of the ECBs.
2021	Permanent institutional framework announced in budget.	To instill confidence during times of stress and to enhance secondary market liquidity, a permanent institutional framework is proposed. The proposed body would purchase investment grade debt securities both in stressed and normal times and help in the development of the market.
2024	Inclusion of Corporate Bonds and Removal of Cap in held-to-maturity (HTM) basket of banks.	Removal of the 23% limit on bond holdings within the held-to-maturity (HTM) basket. Previously confined to G-Secs, banks can now include corporate bonds in their HTM portfolio, signalling a paradigm shift in investment dynamics.
2024	Recognition of mark-to-market (MTM) gains and losses in banks' Profit & Loss accounts.	The RBI's reforms allow banks to recognise both mark-to-market (MTM) gainsand losses, enhancing transparency and potentially encouraging greater investment in the corporate bond market.

The government's Committee on Financial Sector Reforms has made the following recommendations to help revive the corporate bond market: (i) Allow domestic financial institutions greater flexibility to invest in corporate bonds, (ii) Steadily raise the limit on foreign investment in corporate bonds, (iii) Amend the bankruptcy code to protect the rights of unsecured creditors, (iv) Reduce transaction costs in the corporate bond market, and (v) Eliminate the artificial preference for bank loans by subjecting both loans and bonds to similar mark-to-market requirements. In the Union Budget 2018 speech on 1 February, the then Finance Minister, Mr. Arun Jaitley, proposed that SEBI, the stock market regulator, might consider mandating that a quarter (25%) of corporate financing requirements be raised through the bond market. The regulators may also permit investments in bonds with an "A" grade rating, whereas, at present, investments are restricted to bonds with a rating of "AA" or higher. These measures are expected to help deepen the market.

Despite two and a half decades of economic reforms, the corporate bond market remains small and underdeveloped, although it has shown some growth. An analysis of funding sources reveals that Indian companies have usually relied on bank loans rather than corporate bonds to finance their investment needs. This may be due to existing regulations that favour bank loan financing over corporate bond financing.

CHAPTER 3

Varieties of Bonds: Colours and Flavours

A bond is a form of debt for the issuer, who receives funds from investors for a defined time frame. Bonds can be issued by governments or corporations in need of capital. Typically, bonds have a fixed maturity date, and the issuer promises to repay the principal amount to investors after that date. In addition, most bonds pay periodic interest, known as coupons, to bondholders along with the principal at maturity.

Bonds can be categorised based on factors such as coupon rates, maturity, embedded options or convertibility, and so on. Moreover, the issuer of bonds may choose to raise funds from foreign markets, in addition to domestic investors. What may initially seem like staid bonds can become exotic as they take on the characteristics of foreign cuisines, cultures and financial landscapes. We'll explore some of the more interesting types of bonds, classified by their offered interest rates, embedded options, or targeted geographies. These different bonds cater to different needs of the issuers and serve the diverse interests and risk profiles of investors.

3.1. Various Interest Rate Bonds

Bonds can be classified based on the types of interest rates paid on the principal amount. These classifications are illustrated in Figure 3.1.

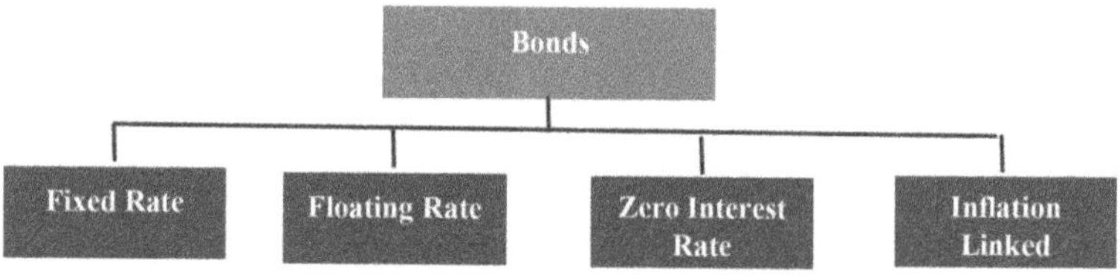

Figure 3.1: Types of Bonds based on Interest Rate

1. **Fixed Rate Bonds:** In fixed rate bonds, the interest paid remains fixed throughout the tenure of the bond. These bonds are less affected by market interest rate fluctuations.
2. **Floating Rate Bonds:** Floating rate bonds have an interest rate (coupon) that fluctuates according to a market reference rate at that point of time.
3. **Zero Interest Rate Bonds:** Zero interest rate bonds or Zero-Coupon Bonds (ZCB) do not pay regular interest to investors. Instead, the issuer repays the principal amount to the bond holders at the end of the holding period.
4. **Inflation-Linked Bonds:** Inflation-linked bonds are tied to inflation, with interest rates typically lower than those of fixed-rate bonds.

3.2. Embedded Bonds

Bonds can also be classified based on embedded options, meaning the issuer or bondholder may have the option or right to buy back or sell the bond prior to the maturity.

These embedded options can include a call option or a put option. Bonds with these features are commonly referred to as callable bonds or puttable bonds.

1. **Callable Bond:** A callable bond is one in which the issuer has the right to redeem (buy back) the bond from the investor before its maturity, at a price determined when the bond is issued. This price is usually higher than the bond's principal amount. For example, a 15-year bond paying 12% interest may include a call option allowing the issuer to redeem the bond after 5 years at a set price. The callable

option is particularly beneficial in a falling interest rate environment. If market interest rate declines from 12% (the original bond rate) to 8%, the issuer can call back the bond and issue a new one at the lower 8% rate, thus reducing their debt servicing costs. In this case, the issuer would exercise the call option after 5 years, redeem the bond, and raise fresh funds at the more favourable interest rate.

2. **Puttable Bond:** A puttable bond, on the other hand, gives the investor the right to sell the bond back to the issuer before maturity, at a price specified when the bond is issued. While the call feature gives an advantage to the issuer, the put option provides protection to the investor by limiting downside risk. For example, if an investor holds a bond with a 7% coupon rate, and the market rate suddenly increases to 11%, the bondholder would be losing out on potential returns, as they could earn 4% (11%–7%) more in the market. In this case, the investor would exercise the put option, get the bond redeemed, and reinvest the funds at the prevailing rate of 11%.

3.3. Foreign Bonds

A foreign bond is issued by a foreign or international entity or government in a domestic market, denominated in the domestic currency, to raise capital. It is a common practice for foreign firms with a significant presence in the domestic market to issue bonds in the domestic currency. These bonds allow domestic investors to diversify their portfolios, as they are traded on local exchanges.

Risks in Foreign Bonds

Foreign bonds carry both implicit and explicit risks associated with them, including the effects of interest rates, inflation, currency exchange rates, and geopolitical factors.

1. **Interest Rate Risk:** Foreign bonds are subject to fluctuations in market interest rates. A rise in interest rate will lower the price of the bond.

2. **Inflation Risk:** Real interest rate is the nominal rate minus the inflation rate. The real value of the bond is determined by inflation, which erodes the yield. For example, if an investor purchases a bond with a 5% interest rate during a time when inflation is 2%, the investor's real payout is 3%. However, if inflation increases to 3%, the real payout decreases accordingly.
3. **Currency Risk:** Currency risk is an implicit issue for all foreign bonds. When income from a bond yielding 8% in a foreign currency is converted into US dollars, the payout will depend on the prevailing exchange rate. As exchange rates fluctuate, the amount received in US dollar will change accordingly.
4. **Political Risk:** Before investing in foreign bonds, investors assess the political risks associated with the issuing country. Key considerations include the stability of the government (or issuing company), the legal framework surrounding the bond issuance, the functioning of the judicial system, and other relevant factors.
5. **Repayment Risk:** Foreign bonds carry repayment risk if the issuer lacks sufficient funds to meet its debt obligations. In such cases, investors may lose some or all of their principal and interest.

Foreign bonds reflect the diversity of different cultures and markets. Few types of foreign bonds are given in Figure 3.2.

Yankee bonds	Yankee bonds are dollar-denominated bonds within the U.S. These bonds are issued by a foreign company or country registered with the Securities and Exchange Commission (SEC).
Bulldog bonds	A bulldog bond is issued in the United Kingdom, in British pound sterling, by a foreign corporation for raising funds in the UK.
Matilda or Kangaroo Bonds	A Matilda or Kangaroo bond is a bond issued in the Australian market by a non-Australian company.
Samurai Bonds	A samurai bond is a corporate bond issued in Japan by a non-Japanese company in Japanese Yen.
Panda Bonds	Panda bonds are onshore Chinese renminbi-denominated debt issued in China by overseas companies.

Figure 3.2: Types of Foreign Bonds

All the bonds mentioned above are onshore bonds, meaning they are issued by foreign companies in the domestic market and denominated in domestic currencies. In addition to these, there are offshore foreign bonds, such as China's Dim Sum Bonds and India's Masala Bonds.

Dim Sum Bonds: These are bonds denominated in Chinese renminbi but issued in Hong Kong, a relatively autonomous region of China. They are attractive to foreign investors seeking direct exposure to renminbi-denominated assets while avoiding China's capital controls on domestic Chinese debt.

The term "Dim Sum" is inspired by a popular Hong Kong cuisine, where a variety of small delicacies are served.

Masala Bonds: A Masala bond is a unique type of bond issued outside India but denominated in Indian rupees, primarily used to fund infrastructure projects.

The first Masala bond was issued by the World Bank-backed International Finance Corporation (IFC) in November 2014, with the aim of boosting foreign investment in India and mobilizing international capital markets to support infrastructure development.

The term "Masala Bond" was coined by the IFC to evoke the culture and cuisine of India. In August 2015, the IFC issued Green Masala Bonds, raising $3.15 billion for private sector investments aimed at addressing climate change in India.

The term "masala" refers to the blend of Indian spices that give Indian cuisine its characteristic flavor, and Masala bonds have helped India secure a place on the global bond trading map.

A unique feature of Masala bonds is that Rupee currency risk associated with the instrument is borne by the bond investors, rather than the issuers. These bonds are typically issued by Indian entities seeking to raise debt in the overseas market without taking on foreign currency risk. This allows corporate to borrow from offshore markets at lower interest rates and reach a broad base of investors.

Masala bonds are typically bought by non-resident Indians and foreign investors seeking exposure to local currency bonds. The interest payments on these bonds are usually higher than other bonds denominated in major foreign currencies like USD, EUR, and JPY, due to India's relatively higher inflation rate. This makes the yield on Masala bonds attractive to foreign investors. For example, the yield on NTPC's Masala bond maturing in 2021 was 8.39% if held to maturity. This was 4.77% higher than the yield on NTPC's USD-denominated bond maturing in the same year.

The RBI allowed Indian corporates to issue Masala bonds on 29 September 2015. In July 2016, HDFC became the first Indian company to issue Masala bonds, raising ₹3,000 crores. The first corporate green Masala bonds, worth ₹2,000 crores, were issued in August 2016 by National Thermal Power Company Limited (NTPC Ltd.). Currently, the top issuers of Masala bonds include HDFC Ltd., NTPC Ltd., and Indiabulls Housing Finance.

In March 2019, Kerala became the first Indian state to issue Masala bonds. The Kerala Infrastructure Investment Fund Board (KIIFB) raised ₹2,150 crores at a 9.72% yield for a 5-year maturity period. Until 2019, Masala bonds were primarily issued by large, AAA-rated Indian corporates and public institutions like NHAI and NTPC. With a BB rating, KIIFB is much below the Central government's BBB rating. The money raised will be used for funding the infrastructure development projects cleared by the KIIFB Board of Directors.

3.4. Social Impact Bonds

3.4.1. Green Bond

Green bonds are fixed-income instruments issued by an entity to raise funds from investors, with the proceeds earmarked for financing "green" projects—those that offer environmental benefits.

The green bond market started in 2007 when the European Investment Bank (EIB) issued its first climate awareness bonds, raising USD 800 million. This was followed by a USD 400 million green bond issuance by the World Bank in 2008. Corporates entered the green bond market only in 2013, with the first sizable "green" bond issuance (classified by the "use of proceeds") by Électricité de France.

There is no universally accepted definition of "green bonds". However, the Climate Bonds Initiative, in 2009, came up with the "Green Bond Principles" (GBP), which have since been adopted by a consortium of banks and FIs as the standard for defining "green". The Green Bond Principles focus on addressing key concerns such as climate change, natural resource depletion, loss of biodiversity and pollution.

The GBP consists of four components:

- Use of Proceeds
- Process for Project Evaluation and Selection
- Management of Proceeds
- Reporting

The categories of investments eligible for green bonds include (but not restricted to) the following:

1. **Renewable energy** (including production, transmission, appliances, and products).
2. **Energy efficiency** (such as in new and refurbished buildings, energy storage, district heating, smart grids, appliances and products).

3. **Pollution prevention and control** (including reduction of air emissions, greenhouse gas control, soil remediation, waste prevention, waste reduction, waste recycling, and energy/emission-efficient waste-to-energy).
4. **Environmentally sustainable management of living natural resources and land use** (including climate-smart farm inputs such as biological crop protection or drip-irrigation; environmentally sustainable agriculture, fishery, and aquaculture; forestry, including afforestation, etc.)
5. **Terrestrial and aquatic biodiversity conservation** (including the protection of coastal, marine, and watershed environments).
6. **Clean transportation** (such as electric, hybrid, public, rail, non-motorised, multi-modal transportation, infrastructure for clean energy vehicles, and reduction of harmful emissions).
7. **Sustainable water and wastewater management** (including sustainable infrastructure for clean and/or drinking water, wastewater treatment, sustainable urban drainage systems, and river training and other forms of flood mitigation).
8. **Climate change adaptation** (including efforts to make infrastructure more resilient to the impacts of climate change, as well as information support systems, such as climate observation and early warning systems).
9. **Circular economy-adapted products, production technologies and processes** (such as the design and introduction of reusable, recyclable, and refurbished materials, components, and products; circular tools and services).
10. **Green buildings** that meet regional, national, or internationally recognised standards or certifications for environmental performance.

The global green bond market has been growing rapidly, with a compounded annual growth rate (CAGR) of 9%. More and more institutional investors and FIs are publicly pledging to increase green bond holdings.

In 2021, Green bond issuers in Emerging Markets and Developing Economies (EMDE) had their strongest year, recording USD 95 billion in issuance—more than double the USD 41 billion issued in 2020 and exceeding the USD 53 billion in 2019.

In India, the SEBI issued guidelines on Green bonds in 2017, including provisions for the listing of Green Bonds on Indian stock exchanges, to promote their adoption. The green indices in India, such as the S&P BSE CARBONEX (2012), MSCI ESG India (2013), and S&P BSE 100 ESG Index (2017), provide opportunities for passive and retail investors to invest in "green" companies. As of December 2020, eight Environmental, Social, and Governance (ESG) mutual funds have been launched in India. Green bonds have proven to be an effective vehicle of raising capital for renewable energy projects while helping India meet its climate targets.

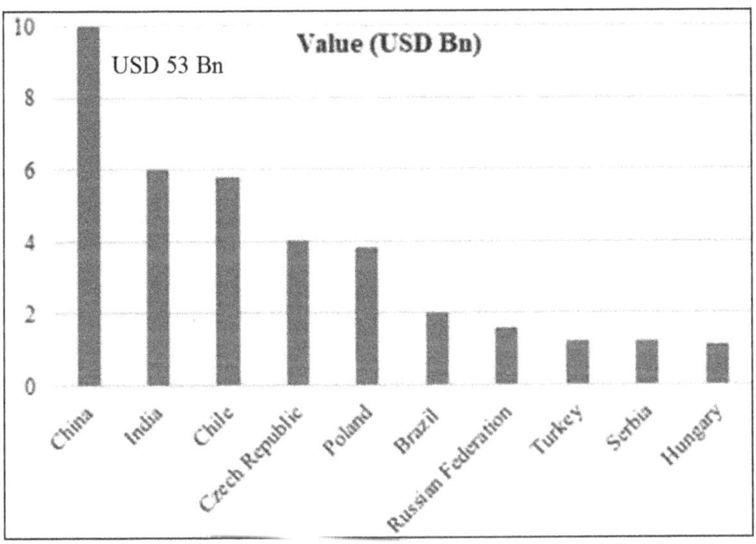

Figure 3.3: Top 10 Emerging Market Green Bond Issuance, 2021

Note: The column for China represents much higher number than the scale.

Source: Emerging Market Green Bonds Report 2021, IFC, World Bank.

China remains the leader as the largest Green Bond issuer among EMDEs, with issuance of USD 59 billion in 2021, accounting for 63% of the total, followed by India, Chile, the Czech Republic, Poland, and Brazil (Figure 3.3). New issuers in the market include Bangladesh and Pakistan. Over the period 2012–2023, 13 countries accounted for 92% of the $466.2 billion in emerging market green bonds issued. China alone accounted for $292 billion, or 63% of the cumulative tally. Other major issuers include India with a cumulative total of $25 billion.

India issued USD 6.3 billion of Green bonds in 2021. It was the strongest issue since the first issue in 2015. Of these, USD 6.2 billion was raised through green bonds targeting renewable energy, USD 85 million towards low carbon buildings, and USD 20 million towards water management. Several 2021 Climate Bonds Certified deals also financed renewable energy projects, particularly solar and wind. These were issued by Azure Power Energy (USD 414 million), Power Finance Corporation (PFC) (EUR 300 million/USD 352 million), Renew Power (USD 1 billion), and Vector Green Energy (INR 12.37 billion/USD 166 million). Between September 2021 and February 2022, Adani Green Energy along with its three subsidiaries had raised a total of more than USD 1.21 billion through domestic (rupee denominated) and overseas (dollar denominated) green bonds.

The Indian government has initiated Renewable Purchase Obligations (RPOs) to promote renewable energy. RPOs mandate that electricity distribution companies purchase a minimum percentage of their total power from renewable energy (RE) sources. RPOs help create a market for renewable energy in the absence of pricing externalities associated with conventional power generation. In July 2018, the Government of India notified a long-term growth trajectory for RPOs, applicable uniformly across all States and Union Territories. This target is set to increase each year, aiming for 43.3% of total power demand from renewables by 2030.

While presenting the Union Budget for 2022–23, India's Finance Minister, Nirmala Sitharaman, announced a proposal to issue sovereign green bonds worth INR 24,000 crores (~USD 3.3 billion) to push green financing initiatives in India. The proceeds from these bonds are expected to support India's commitment to achieving net-zero emissions by 2070. This will be a big step for India, especially amongst the BRICS nations, as it will be the first country to issue such a bond.

India issued its first-ever sovereign green bond in January 2023, a $1 billion deal that was followed again for a similar amount the following month. This came in the wake of the release of India's Green Bond Framework in November 2022. On 8 November 2023, the RBI, through its circular (RBI/2023-24/81), included Sovereign Green Bonds in the Fully Accessible Route (FAR). This is a significant milestone in India's financial landscape, as it allows non-resident investors to participate in these securities. This proactive move by the RBI aims to promote sustainable finance and reinforce India's position as a responsible player in the global financial market. It also reflects the growing importance of Environmental, Social, and Governance (ESG) factors in investment decisions, catering to the evolving preferences of investors worldwide.

3.4.2. Rhino Bond

In March 2022, the World Bank issued the world's first Wildlife Conservation Bond (WCB), also known as the "Rhino Bond", to support South Africa's efforts to conserve the endangered species of Black Rhino. This five-year, $150 million Sustainable Development Bond aims to help reverse the decline in the Black Rhino population, which had fallen from over 65,000 in 1970 to around 2,600 today. The amount raised through this bond will be used for the conservation of the animals, including expenses for medicine, food, protection and other related efforts.

The bond includes a potential performance payment from the Global Environment Facility (GEF), meaning investors will receive a payment based on the growth rate of Black Rhino populations in two South African reserves—Addo Elephant National Park and Great Fish River Nature Reserve. If the population declines, no payment will be made. For a population growth rate of 0–2%, a partial payment will be paid; for growth between 2–4%, a higher payment will be paid; and the highest payment will be made for a growth rate exceeding 4%.

If this works, this model could lead to similar bonds being issued to protect rhinos in Kenya's reserves as well as other endangered species. Such impact investing has immense potential in India to address various issues, including girls' education, malnutrition, and more. On one hand, it will help improve social well-being by harnessing the power of finance; on the other hand, it opens up avenues for private players to contribute to social goods, such as environmental conservation and biodiversity.

CHAPTER 4

Stylised Facts about Indian Sovereign and Corporate Bond Markets

To understand the bond markets in India and the policy impact on these markets, we first need to examine the size, maturity profile, liquidity and investor base of these markets, as well as how they have evolved over the years.

The Indian bond market is largely dominated by government bonds, with the corporate bond market accounting for only about 33% of the total outstanding bonds. Let us review some stylised facts about these markets to better understand the various policy impacts.

4.1. Government or Sovereign Market

4.1.1. Size and Liquidity

The reforms initiated in the bond market post-1990 helped develop a strong institutional structure, fast clearing and settlement infrastructure, improved regulatory and legal systems, and the introduction of new technologies. These advancements, in turn, led to the expansion of trading volumes and a diversification of both participants and instruments.

The Indian government securities market has undergone significant transformation since the early 1990s. As shown in Table 4.1, the outstanding stock of government securities (both central and state) increased almost fivefold in nominal terms, reaching ₹107 lakh crores during the period 2010 to 2021. As a proportion of GDP, it grew substantially from 14.7% in 1992 to 54% in 2021.

Table 4.1: Government Securities Outstanding

Year	In ₹ Crores			Share in total (%)	
	Centre	States	Total	Centre	States
2002–03	6,19,105	1,33,066	7,52,171	82.3	17.7
2003–04	7,07,965	2,08,901	9,16,866	77.2	22.8
2004–05	7,58,995	2,43,362	10,02,357	75.7	24.3
2005–06	8,62,370	2,60,506	11,22,876	76.8	23.2
2006–07	9,72,801	2,68,828	12,41,629	78.3	21.7
2007–08	11,04,564	3,21,651	14,26,215	77.4	22.6
2008–09	13,38,194	4,23,615	17,61,809	76.0	24.0
2009–10	17,46,619	5,34,569	22,81,188	76.6	23.4
2010–11	20,72,033	6,18,518	26,90,551	77.0	23.0
2011–12	25,16,953	7,52,683	32,69,635	77.0	23.0
2012–13	29,84,309	8,83,268	38,67,576	77.2	22.8
2013–14	34,41,641	10,57,599	44,99,241	76.5	23.5
2014–15	38,91,734	12,72,103	51,63,838	75.4	24.6
2015–16	42,98,784	15,16,071	58,14,855	73.9	26.1
2016–17	46,49,487	18,57,110	65,06,597	71.5	28.5
2017–18	50,68,408	22,06107	72,74,515	69.7	30.3
2018–19	55,00,141	25,61,387	80,61,528	68.2	31.8
2019–20	59,86,127	30,58,827	90,44,954	66.2	33.8
2020–21	71,35,144	37,22,110	1,08,57,254	65.7	34.3
2021–22	80,26,725	42,35,944	1,22,62,669	65.5	34.5
2022–23	91,41,233	47,78,760	1,39,19,993	65.7	34.3
2023–24	1,02,51,585	55,00,712	1,57,52,297	65.1	34.9

Note: Central government securities include only the dated securities and not the special securities or treasury bills. The state government securities include the UDAY bonds issued amounting to ₹98,960 crores in FY 2016 and ₹2.1 lakh crores in FY 2017.

Source: RBI database.

One important point to note is that central government securities form a large part of the overall debt. As of 31 March 2021, Central Government dated securities amounted to ₹71.5 lakh crores (36% of GDP), while State government securities amounted to ₹36.2 lakh crores (18% of GDP). However, the outstanding state government securities have been steadily increasing since 2016–2017.

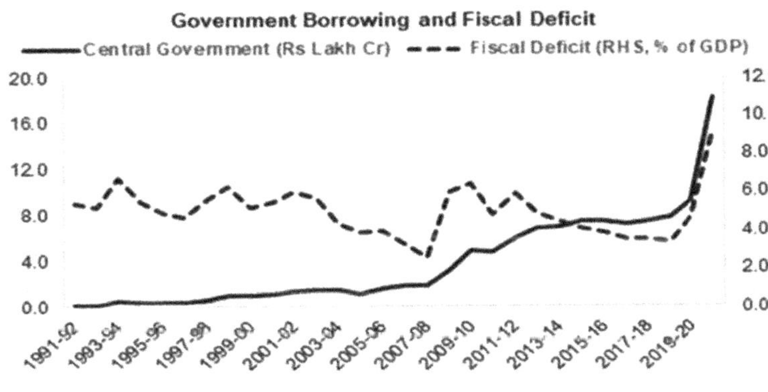

Figure 4.1: Central Govt Borrowing vs Fiscal Deficit

Source: Centre for Monitoring Indian Economy (CMIE), RBI database.

Government market borrowings rose significantly in the 1980s and 1990s, as shown in Figure 4.1. In response, the Central Government enacted the Fiscal Responsibility and Budget Management Act (FRBM) in 2003 to rein in public debt following a prolonged attempt to control public finances. The act required the government to reduce the fiscal deficit to less than 3% of GDP by 2009 and prohibited the RBI from participating in the primary market to avoid conflicts of interest in its dual role as both the monetary authority and debt manager for central and state governments. Although the fiscal deficit initially declined after 2003, it surged again during the global financial crisis of 2009, as the government had to increase spending to cushion the economy against the downturn. The government, once again, embarked on prudent fiscal policy in 2012. However, despite some progress, government borrowing remained high in absolute terms. The situation changed dramatically after the COVID-19 pandemic in 2020, when the government had to significantly increase borrowing to support the economy during the crisis. As a result, the fiscal deficit once again ballooned, derailing the FRBM roadmap.

As a result of market development, the volume of transactions in the secondary market for government securities has increased substantially over the past decade. The turnover of central government securities has increased more than eightfold, while that of state government securities has increased 48 times between 2007–08 and 2019–20. Table 4.2 shows that central government securities are primarily traded actively. Before 2004–05, the share of state government securities in the annual turnover of the total government securities market was minuscule, accounting for less than 1%, while their share in outstanding government securities was around 22–23%. However, the share of state government securities in total turnover has improved to about 7% in 2022–23 (Table 4.2).

Table 4.2: Liquidity (Turnover) of Government Securities

Year	In ₹ Crores			Share in total (%)	
	Centre	States	Total	Centre	States
2002–03	10,32,185	6,519	10,38,704	99.4	0.63
2003–04	14,58,665	14,169	14,72,834	99.0	0.96
2004–05	8,62,820	24,700	8,87,520	97.2	2.78
2005–06	6,57,213	17,700	6,74,913	97.4	2.62
2006–07	8,83,248	11,332	8,94,580	98.7	1.27
2007–08	14,67,704	14,234	14,81,938	99.0	0.96
2008–09	19,55,412	34,385	19,89,797	98.3	1.73
2009–10	24,80,850	69,757	25,50,607	97.3	2.73
2010–11	25,52,181	43,677	25,95,858	98.3	1.68
2011–12	30,99,108	43,859	31,42,967	98.6	1.40
2012–13	59,20,929	1,18,159	60,39,088	98.0	1.96
2013–14	79,68,661	1,54,847	81,23,508	98.1	1.91
2014–15	91,49,608	1,83,083	93,32,691	98.0	1.96
2015–16	85,57,672	3,16,479	88,74,151	96.4	3.57
2016–17	1,51,98,472	6,02,213	1,58,00,685	96.2	3.81
2017–18	98,30,117	5,63,709	1,03,93,826	94.6	5.42

Year	In ₹ Crores			Share in total (%)	
	Centre	States	Total	Centre	States
2018–19	79,07,618	5,09,050	84,16,668	94.0	6.05
2019–20	1,12,65,755	6,86,469	1,19,52,224	94.3	5.74
2020–21	75,96,059	5,86,295	81,82,354	92.8	7.17
2021–22	66,30,083	6,78,923	73,09,006	90.7	9.29
2022–23	80,49,756	6,42,605	86,92,361	92.6	7.39
2023–24	1,09,01,607	7,12,661	1,16,14,268	93.9	6.14

Note: Central Government Dated Securities and State Development Loans considered.

Source: RBI Annual Report, CCIL.

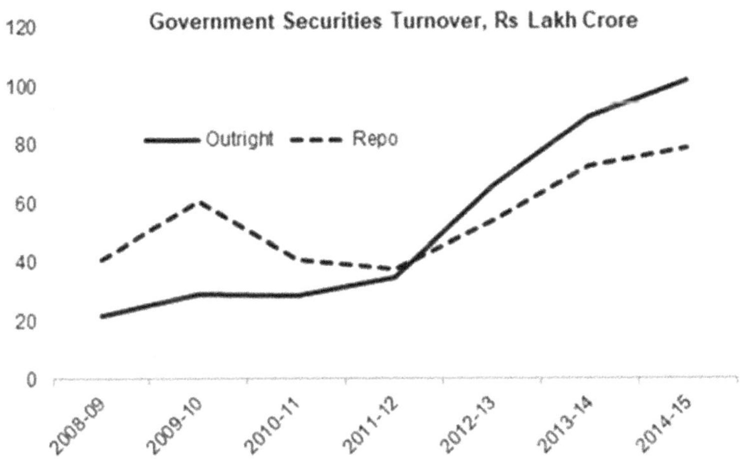

Figure 4.2: Outright vs Repo Turnover

Source: RBI Annual Report, CMIE

An interesting aspect of secondary market transactions in government securities is the distinction between two types of transactions: Outright and Repo. Outright transactions refer to the actual trading of government bonds in the secondary market, while Repo stands for repurchase agreements. In a repo transaction, holders of government securities typically use them as a form of overnight borrowing. A dealer or other holder of government securities sells the securities to a lender and agrees to repurchase them at an agreed future date at an agreed price. The bonds are used as collateral for the overnight loan. Figure 4.2 shows that until 2011–12, the turnover of repurchase agreements (repo) was higher than outright transactions, indicating that more borrowers were using government bonds as a financing tool, rather than investors trading them.

However, this trend shifted after 2012, indicating that the Indian bond market has structurally matured, as non-repo transactions in the secondary market have increased, adding depth to the market.

The above discussion shows that, in India, the central government securities market dominates the overall debt market, both in terms of outstanding securities and trading volumes. The dominance of central government securities in the secondary market is even more pronounced, as they account for more than 90% of the transactions.

4.1.2. Elongation of Maturity Profile

For prudent debt management, the RBI extended the maturity profile of the outstanding stock of government securities by issuing bonds with longer maturities. The maximum maturity of government securities was extended to 25 years in 2001–02 and further extended to 30 years in 2002–03. This extension was also driven by investor demand for such long-tenured securities, particularly from non-bank investors such as insurance companies and pension funds, which have long-term liabilities. A positive outcome of this elongation of the maturity profile was the formation of a yield curve that now extends over a longer horizon.

The share of securities with maturities of more than 10 years increased to 62% of total issuances in 2016–17, while those with maturities of less than 5 years remained insignificant. However, the issuance of securities with less than 5 years maturities increased in the last three years during the pandemic.

In line with the increase in the maturity of primary issuances, the tenure structure of outstanding government securities also evolved, with a sharp increase in the share of securities with maturities longer than 10 years in the total outstanding stock since 1995–96 (Table 4.3).

Table 4.3: Maturity Profile of Market Loans of Central Government

Year	Raised During the Year			Amount Outstanding on March End		
	< 5 years	5-10 years	> 10 years	< 5 years	5-10 years	> 10 years
1995–96	42.0	58.0	0.0	45.2	29.0	25.8
1996–97	50.0	50.0	0.0	41.0	40.8	18.2
1997–98	18.0	82.0	0.0	41.4	42.4	16.1
1998–99	18.0	68.0	14.0	37.5	38.7	23.9
1999–00	0.0	35.0	65.0	35.0	39.3	25.7
2000–01	6.0	41.0	53.0	30.6	35.6	33.8
2001–02	2.0	24.0	74.0	26.4	34.7	39.0
2002–03	0.0	36.0	64.0	22.4	30.9	46.6
2003–04	5.0	18.0	77.0	23.8	30.5	45.7
2004–05	11.0	11.0	78.0	25.0	31.0	44.0
2005–06	0.0	26.0	74.0	25.0	32.0	43.0
2006–07	7.0	47.0	46.0	26.0	35.0	39.0
2007–08	0.0	61.0	39.0	26.0	38.0	36.0
2008–09	6.0	55.0	39.0	26.0	40.0	34.0
2009–10	12.4	45.0	42.6	29.0	38.0	33.0
2010–11	2.5	34.8	62.7	23.7	37.6	38.6
2011–12	3.5	45.9	50.6	21.5	24.8	53.7
2012–13	8.4	34.2	57.4	31.0	35.0	34.1
2013–14	2.0	40.9	57.1	29.9	31.5	38.5
2014–15	0.0	39.7	60.3	28.2	30.4	41.4
2015–16	0.0	34.2	65.8	26.8	29.6	43.5
2016–17	3.1	38.1	61.9	25.0	33.3	41.7
2017–18	1.5	44.9	53.6	26.2	32.1	41.7
2018–19	9.1	27.5	63.4	28.3	31.2	40.5
2019–20	7.9	21.0	71.1	29.0	30.0	41.0
2020–21	9.8	20.6	69.6	29.3	29.0	41.7
2021–22	5.4	18.2	76.4	29.3	28.8	41.9
2022–23	6.2	26.0	67.8	29.1	28.8	42.1

Source: Various RBI Annual Reports.

The prevailing benign interest rates in the early 2000s facilitated the process of maturity elongation as the cost of borrowing came down. As a result, the weighted average maturity of primary issuances of the central government securities increased from 5.8 years in 1995–96 to 14.5 years in 2020–21. Similarly, the weighted average maturity of the outstanding stock of government securities increased from 6.5 years at the end of March 1998 to 11.3 years at end of March 2021. On the other hand, the weighted average yields began moderating from 1996–97 and declined to 5.7 percent for central government securities by 2003–04. Figure 4.3 below shows the movement of the weighted average maturity and the weighted average yield on central government bonds since 1995–96.

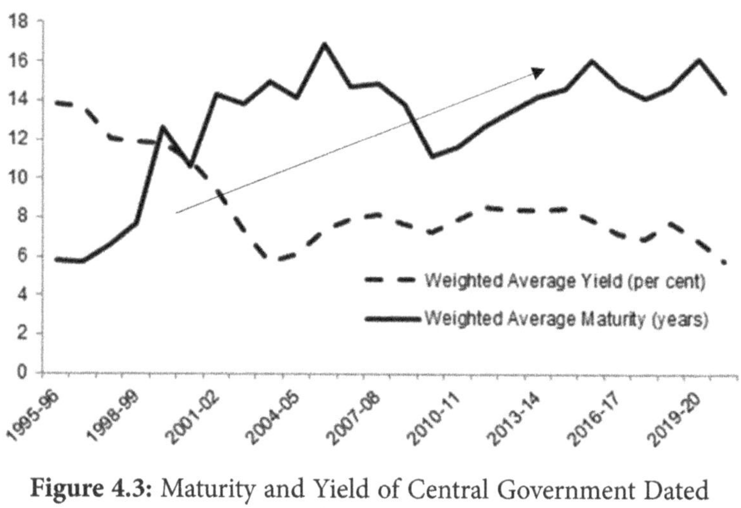

Figure 4.3: Maturity and Yield of Central Government Dated Securities

Source: RBI Annual Reports

4.1.3. Ownership Pattern of the Government Securities

A vibrant bond market requires the existence of a large and diverse investor base with different liquidity requirements for increasing competition and better price discovery in the market. This, in turn, reduces the borrowing cost for the government. Prior to reforms, the investor base for government securities in India was very narrow and primarily consisted of institutions such as banks, insurance companies, and pension funds, which were mandated to invest in these securities.

To generate captive demand for government securities, the SLR for banks was gradually increased, reaching a peak of 38.5% of net demand and time liabilities in February 1992. Since then, the SLR has been progressively reduced to 18.0% as of April 2020. However, banks, of their own volition, continue to hold investments in government securities and other approved securities over the mandated requirement, driven by their need for liquidity and trading purposes. Additionally, banks often increase their investment in government securities in the absence of credit demand or during the period of risk aversion.

Over time, the investor base has diversified with the inclusion of cooperative banks, regional rural banks, mutual funds (especially gilt funds), and NBFCs. The introduction of 100% gilt mutual funds has also helped expand the retail investor base.

The RBI has tried to attract foreign investments in Indian debt by gradually increasing the upper limits for investments by Foreign Portfolio Investors (FPIs) over the years (Table 4.4). In September 2015, the RBI established a medium-term framework for FPI limits in consultation with the government, with plans to increase the limits in phases to 5% of the outstanding stock by March 2018. Starting in January 2018, FPIs were allowed to invest up to ₹2.56 lakh crore in central government securities and ₹45,100 crores in state loans. In April 2022, the RBI announced updated limits for investment in government securities (G-Secs), state development loans (SDLs) and corporate bonds, set at 6%, 2%, and 15%, respectively, of the outstanding stock of securities for FY 2023. The limits remained unchanged at 6%, 2% and 15% respectively of the outstanding stocks of securities for 2025–26.

Table 4.4: Upper Limit of FPI Investment in Government Debt

FPI Limit	Upper Limit (in ₹ Crores) Government Debt
Dec 31, 2014	1,53,569
Dec 31, 2015	1,86,500
Dec 30, 2016	2,27,500
Dec 28, 2017	2,89,300
Mar 14, 2018	3,01,500
June 17, 2022	3,90,188

As of 28 March 2024, FPIs had utilised about 30% of their investment limit in central government securities, but only 4.6% of their limit in state loans, reflecting their risk-averse stance (Table 4.5).

Table 4.5: Debt Utilization Status by FPIs as on 28 March 2024.

Instrument Type	Upper Limit (in ₹ Cr)	Total Investment (in ₹ Cr)	% of Limits Utilised	Limit Available (in ₹ Cr)
Central Government Debt-General	2,67,890	68,396	25.6	1,99,454
Central Government Debt-Long Term	1,36,890	6,299	4.6	1,30,590
State Development Loans-General	92,828	4,233	4.6	88,595
State Development Loans-Long Term	7,100	0.0	0.0	7,100
Total Government Securities	5,04,708	78,928	35.0	4,25,739

Source: NSDL Report.

However, weakness in the rupee and rising yields overseas led FPIs to sell Indian debt in the last few years. As of 15 June 2022, FPI investment in G-Secs (under both general and long-term categories) stood at ₹89,297 crores against an upper limit of ₹3,90,188 crores. FPI utilisation in G-Secs was as high as 60% as of March 2019, but it declined to 53.95% by the end of March 2020, and further shrank to 25.6% by the end of FY 2024.

As a result, FPI holdings in government debt, which had increased to 2.5% in 2016–17 (up from 1.25% in 2011–12), came down to 1.9% in 2020–21. However, commercial banks and insurance companies continue to hold the largest share of government securities. The share of insurance companies holding the central government securities consistently increased to 25% by the end of March 2021, up from 19.7% at the end of March 2008. The share of commercial banks' holdings, on the other hand, declined steadily from 51% to 38% during the same period, reflecting the reduction in the SLR. Overall, the investor base has widened over the years, as shown in the charts (Figure 4.4).

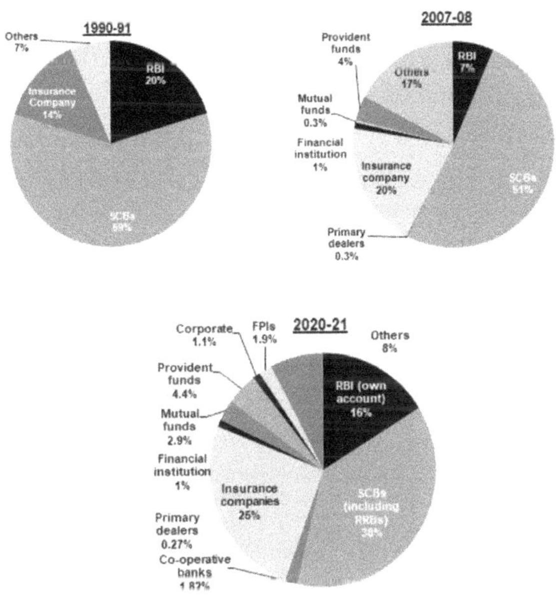

Figure 4.4: Holding Pattern of Central Government Securities (in % share of total).

Source: RBI Annual Report

Box 4.1: Impact of Inclusion of Indian Bonds in Global Index

In September 2023, JPMorgan Chase & Co. announced that Indian bonds would be included in its widely tracked emerging market debt index starting in June 2024, resulting in billions of dollars of inflows into the world's fifth-largest economy.

RBI Governor Shaktikanta Das remarked, "The first thing that has to be recognised in this is that it's a kind of a vote of confidence about the Indian economy and about the Indian financial markets. The bond market had been anticipating the announcement, and the yield of government bonds had softened accordingly."

Some of the expected impacts of this inclusion in the Global Index are:

1. Diversification of the Investor Base:

Most of the investors in the government debt market are captive in nature, as discussed before. Banks, insurance companies, and pension funds are the largest investors, holding about 60% of the total outstanding debt. The share of FPIs is less than 2%. The inclusion in the global index is expected to increase foreign investor holdings of government securities to 3-4% of the outstanding stock.

2. Lower Cost of Borrowing and Crowding in of Private Investment:

Increased demand for government bonds could lead to lower yields of these bonds. This, in turn, would reduce the cost of borrowing for the corporate sector and help crowd in private investment, as government bond yields serve as a benchmark in financial markets.

Additionally, this could expose foreign investors to the capital needs of Indian corporations, which they have largely overlooked so far. Foreign investors would gain access to a significantly larger pool of Indian corporate issuers.

3. Fiscal Prudence and Macroeconomic Stability:

India was one of the most affected countries when the US Federal Reserve decided to taper its bond purchases in 2013. During the taper tantrum episode, India was regarded as one of the "Fragile Five" due to its vulnerable external and fiscal balances, which were sensitive to sudden foreign fund outflows.

As India's bonds are included in global indices and its investor base diversifies, the government will be forced to follow fiscal prudence. Any deviation from this path could trigger large outflows by foreign funds, leading to higher yields. Moreover, the quality of government expenditure, tax buoyancy, and off-balance-sheet accounting will be closely monitored by investors. Even the balance of payments and current account position will also face greater scrutiny from foreign investors. This heightened oversight will compel India to focus on improving its macroeconomic fundamentals.

4. Management of the Impossible Trinity:

There are various estimates regarding the amount of inflows that would result from the inclusion of Indian bonds in the Global Index. Goldman Sachs expects an overall inflow of around $30 billion, while Barclays estimates around $25 billion, and UBS Global Research estimates an inflow of about $15–$20 billion, staggered over at least three quarters in FY 2024. This will place increased focus on the RBI's management of the "impossible trinity". There are two possible scenarios:

i) The foreign capital inflows will put appreciation pressure on the rupee. Higher demand for G-secs will lower bond yields, resulting in reduced cost of borrowing. However, a strong INR may hurt exporters.

ii) On the other hand, if the RBI chooses to keep the exchange rate within a certain band, it will likely intervene in the forex market. The RBI will buy US dollars and supply INR, increasing forex reserves and preventing significant appreciation of the rupee. However, this would also inject more liquidity into the system, raising the risk of inflation. To absorb excess liquidity, the RBI may sell government bonds, reducing its balance sheet and putting a floor under bond yields. Balancing the exchange rate, liquidity, and inflation simultaneously could become a significant challenge.

It has also been pointed out that, as the share of Indian bonds in the Global Index rises to 10%, the share of some other countries may go down. According to Barclays, this could adversely impact other emerging Asian economies.

4.2. Corporate Bond Market in India

4.2.1. Size of the Corporate Bond Market

Resources raised from the corporate bond market have steadily increased from 2000–2001 to 2020–21 (Table 4.6). Resources mobilised rose sharply by 51% to ₹175,827 crores in 2008–09 from the previous year. Since then, funds mobilised from the primary debt markets have continued their uptrend and stood at ₹670,042 crores in 2016–2017 (vs. gross market borrowings by the government ₹6,24,670 crores in FY 17). It is seen that even though funds mobilized from the debt market had increased, private placement accounted for 98% of the total resources mobilised from the debt markets in 2023–2024.

Table 4.6: Resources Raised from Corporate Bond Market (Crores)

	Year	2000-01	2004-05	2008-09	2016-17	2020-21	2023-24
Debt Issues (in ₹ Cr.)	Public Issues	4,139	4,095	1,500	29,327	10,588	19,168
	Private Placement	52,433	55,184	1,74,327	6,40,715	7,71,840	8,37,756
Total Debt Issue		56,572	59,279	1,75,827	6,70,042	7,82,428	8,56,924
Share of Pvt. Placement/ Total Debt		92.7%	93.1%	99.1%	95.6%	98.6%	97.8%

Sources: SEBI reports.

According to market participants, the public issue of corporate bonds is often viewed as difficult, slow, expensive, and inflexible. On the contrary, private placements are relatively easier, quicker and cheaper. The largest investors in public placements in India are banks—sometimes, a single bank buys up the entire issue placed by a company. As a result, these private placements can be seen as little more than syndicated loans (Sarma, 2014).

The issuer base has remained narrow in the corporate bond market, with most issuers coming from the finance or infrastructure sectors (Table 4.7).

Table 4.7: Corporate Bond Issuance by Sectors in FY 2024

Sectors	% Share
Finance	75
Infrastructure	20
Manufacturing	1
Oil	2
Others	3

Source: CCIL

4.2.2. Corporate vs Government Debt Market

In India, the government bond market (encompassing both central and state governments) forms an overwhelming part of the overall debt market, both in terms of outstanding securities and trading volumes. As of 2020, the total outstanding debt, including both government and corporate debt, amounted to ₹121 lakh crores, representing 60% percent of GDP. Out of the total outstanding, more than 70% was accounted for by government securities (Table 4.8). Corporate bonds, on the other hand, accounted for a mere 16% of GDP in 2020. Corporate bond outstanding is only around 22.4% of the total in FY 2023.

The dominance of government securities in the secondary market is even more pronounced, accounting for a whopping 88% of transactions in recent years. Although the share of corporate debt trading in the secondary market gradually decreased from 18.7% in

2010–11 to 6.6% in 2016–17 (Table 4.9), it has since begun to rise again, reaching 11.6% in FY 2023.

Table 4.8: Outstanding Government and Corporate Bonds

Year	In ₹ Crores			Share in Total (%)	
	Government	Corporate	Total	Government	Corporate
2011–12	32,69,635	8,89,510	41,59,145	78.6	21.4
2012–13	38,67,576	10,51,639	49,19,215	78.6	21.4
2013–14	44,99,241	12,90,147	57,89,388	77.7	22.3
2014–15	51,63,838	14,67,397	66,31,235	77.9	22.1
2015–16	58,14,855	17,50,320	75,65,175	76.9	23.1
2016–17	65,06,597	20,19,296	85,25,893	76.3	23.7
2017–18	72,74,515	24,04,911	96,79,426	75.2	24.8
2018–19	80,61,528	27,42,259	1,08,03,787	74.6	25.4
2019–20	90,44,954	30,67,228	1,21,12,182	74.7	25.3
2020–21	1,08,57,254	32,53,921	1,41,11,175	76.9	23.1
2021–22	1,22,62,669	36,12,604	1,58,75,273	77.2	22.8
2022–23	1,39,19,993	40,17,025	1,79,37,018	77.6	22.4

Source: CCIL Reports, SEBI

Table 4.9: Turnover in Secondary Market

Year	In ₹ Crores			Share in Total (%)	
	Government	Corporate	Total	Government	Corporate
2010–11	25,95,858	5,98,604	31,94,462	81.3	18.7
2011–12	31,42,967	5,91,979	37,34,946	84.2	15.8
2012–13	60,39,088	7,36,347	67,75,435	89.1	10.9
2013–14	81,23,508	9,72,156	90,95,664	89.3	10.7
2014–15	93,32,691	10,13,504	1,03,46,195	90.2	9.8
2015–16	88,74,151	9,05,333	97,79,484	90.7	9.3
2016–17	1,58,00,685	11,24,988	1,69,25,673	93.4	6.6
2017–18	1,03,93,826	13,50,033	1,17,43,859	88.5	11.50
2018–19	84,16,668	10,90,407	95,07,075	88.5	11.47
2019–20	1,19,52,224	15,55,518	1,35,07,742	88.5	11.52
2020–21	81,82,354	14,49,926	96,32,280	84.9	15.05

2021–22	73,09,006	11,97,730	85,06,736	85.9	14.08
2022–23	86,92,361	11,44,028	98,36,389	88.4	11.63

Source: CCIL Reports

4.2.3. Narrow Investor Base

As we have already seen, most corporate bonds are privately placed with banks, leading to a limited supply of bonds available for trading in the secondary market. Moreover, government bonds dominate both public and private sources of bond financing in India.

The investors in the Indian corporate debt markets include banks (Indian, foreign and PDs), pension and insurance funds, mutual funds, and other entities such as FPIs and corporates. Banks represent the largest segment of investors in corporate debt markets in India, typically preferring higher-rated bonds. However, Indian banks are highly regulated by the RBI, with mandatory investments in government bonds. As a result, banks rarely participate in secondary trading, which restricts the depth and liquidity of the secondary corporate bond market.

Insurance companies, provident funds, and pension funds invest in corporate bonds that align with their long-term liabilities. However, they are subject to stringent regulatory restrictions and are allowed to invest only a small portion in high investment-grade corporate bonds. Moreover, regulations require that once these entities subscribe to corporate bonds, they must hold them to maturity and cannot trade them in the secondary market.

The FPI investment limit in Indian corporate debt markets has increased over the years, but the utilisation of these limits has remained low (Table 4.10). In 2017, the RBI removed Masala bonds (rupee-denominated debt securities sold abroad) from the corporate bond investment limit in order to encourage more investment in the domestic corporate bond market. This increased the investment limit for corporate bonds to ₹2,44,323 crores, excluding Masala bonds. The actual utilisation of these limits by FPIs reached a record high of 95% in December 2017 (Table 4.11). However, in recent times, the utilisation of these limits by FPIs has been dismal, standing at around 20% in December 2021.

FPIs have never been very excited about investing in the Indian corporate bond market, primarily due to the illiquid secondary market, which limits exit options. Following the pandemic, several factors—such as rising yields on risk-free US government bonds, increasing inflation, a widening current account deficit (CAD), and a weakening rupee—have contributed to a decline in foreign investors' interest in the debt market.

Table 4.10: Upper Limit of FPI Investment in Corporate Debt.

FPI Limit	Upper Limit (in ₹ Crores) Corporate Debt
Dec 31, 2014	2,44,323
Dec 31, 2015	2,44,323
Dec 30, 2016	2,44,323
Dec 28, 2017	2,27,322
Mar 14, 2018	2,44,323
Mar 31, 2019	2,89,100
Mar 31, 2020	3,17,000
Mar 31, 2021	5,41,488
Mar 31, 2022	6,07,039
Mar 31, 2023	6,67,871

Source: NSDL Report

Table 4.11: Debt Utilization Status of Corporate Debt by FPIs.

	Upper Limit (in ₹ Cr.)	Total Investment (in ₹ Cr.)	% of Limits Utilised	Limit Available (in ₹ Cr.)
Dec 31, 2014	2,44,323	1,43,848	58.88	1,00,475
Dec 31, 2015	2,44,323	1,79,344	73.40	64,979
Dec 30, 2016	2,44,323	1,67,909	68.72	76,414
Dec 28, 2017	2,27,322	2,15,522	95.00	11,800
Dec 31, 2018	289,100	203,663	70.45	85,437
Dec 31, 2019	317,000	183,523	57.89	133,477
Dec 31, 2020	541,488	141,110	26.06	4,00,378
Dec 31, 2021	607,039	121,110	19.95	4,85,929

Dec 30, 2022	667,871	109,822	16.44	5,58,049
Dec 29, 2023	667,871	105,348	15.77	5,62,523

Source: NSDL Report.

Retail investors are notably absent from the corporate bond market, largely due to a lack of awareness about the concept of risk and return. Currently, only corporate bonds from companies in the infrastructure sector are eligible under Section 80C of the Income Tax Act. There is a need to expand the scope to attract retail investors. This segment typically participates in the corporate debt market through debt mutual funds.

A broad investor base with diverse requirements is a prerequisite for healthy corporate debt markets. However, there is hardly any diversity among issuers, as the market is dominated by banks, FIs, and quasi-government bodies (PSUs). This limited set of issuers and the lack of diverse instruments fail to attract a wide range of investors. As a result, the narrow investor base leads to shallow trading in the secondary market, leaving it illiquid. Most issuers opt for private placements in this illiquid market, engaging with only a small number of investors. There is an urgent need to break this vicious circle.

From the discussion above, we can conclude that the bond market in India has developed significantly over the years. The reforms initiated since the 1990s have led to the expansion of trading volumes, an elongation of the maturity profile, and greater diversification of both participants and instruments in the government bond market. The outstanding stock of government securities has increased more than five times in nominal terms during the period 2010 to 2021. As a proportion of GDP, it has also increased significantly, rising from 14.7% in 1992 to 54% in 2021.

Moreover, in India, the government bond market forms an overwhelming part of the overall debt market, both in terms of outstanding securities and trading volumes. Out of the total outstanding, more than 70% of debt instruments are government securities. The dominance of government securities in the secondary market is even more pronounced, accounting for a whopping 90% of transactions in recent years.

The corporate bond market in India has remained quite insignificant, with only large companies dominating the market. There is a need to study the various issues and challenges faced by the corporate bond market in India. The problems can be manifolds ranging from weak market infrastructure, low liquidity in the secondary market, a narrow investor base, inadequate credit assessment skills, high cost of issuance, a limited set of issuers, and a lack of diverse instruments. Addressing these challenges is crucial for the growth and development of India's corporate debt market.

The domestic environment appears conducive to the development of a liquid corporate bond market, given the prevailing macroeconomic environment, large investment needs to fund infrastructure in India, constraints in the banking sector to provide funding, and the emerging legal frameworks on bankruptcy. It is important to assess whether a large, efficient sovereign bond market is a prerequisite for the corporate bond market or if it crowds out private credit and negatively impacts its growth.

CHAPTER 5

Indian Corporate Bond Market and its Challenges

5.1. Corporate Bond Market: A Perspective

Despite its relatively long history, numerous committee recommendations, and ongoing reforms, the Indian corporate bond market has remained small in size. It is besieged by several problems both from the supply and demand sides, including an illiquid secondary market, a narrow investor base, a lack of diversity of instruments, crowding out by large public issuance, high costs of borrowing, information asymmetry, regulatory restrictions on demand, unavailability of repo options, and a lack of a well-functioning derivatives market and credit enhancement facilities to mitigate interest and default risks.

The NBFC crisis a few years ago had the potential to spill over into the banking sector, ultimately affecting the corporate bond market. The default of the Infrastructure Leasing and Financial Services (IL&FS) in 2018 took many by surprise. Dewan Housing Finance Limited (DHFL) and other NBFCs focused on housing finance also defaulted on their loan payments, leading to a series of downgrades of their bonds by rating agencies. Several banks and mutual funds had significant exposure to corporate bonds issued by these troubled NBFCs. This chain of events had an adverse impact on the development of the corporate bond market in India.

In 2018, NBFCs, with outstanding debts of over ₹26 lakh crore, faced a sudden drying up of their funding sources following a series of defaults by IL&FS, which triggered a liquidity crisis. The NBFCs had been borrowing short-term to finance long-term projects and rolling over debt, which exacerbated the problem. In the aftermath, corporate debt issuance became even more challenging for smaller firms, as the risk aversion prompted by the liquidity crisis sparked off by the infrastructure financier (IL&FS) significantly heightened. It was not a good sign for a slowing Indian economy.

IL&FS, which had been arranging financing for Indian infrastructure projects for more than 30 years, was considered "systemically important" by the RBI[1]. The government had to step in after it amassed huge debt in failed projects and defaulted on multiple obligations. Credit rating agencies came under lens for missing the warning signs. IL&FS's long-term bond, which had held a AAA rating until July 2018, was downgraded to AA+ on 6 August, to BB on 8 September, and finally to D on 17 September. These sharp and sudden downgrades raised serious questions about the methodology and processes adopted by the rating agencies in evaluating companies and their bonds. Four leading rating agencies—ICRA, CARE, India Ratings, and Brickwork—were involved in rating various papers and schemes of different IL&FS group entities. In the budget of 2019, the finance minister proposed that PSU banks would purchase high-rated pooled assets from financially sound NBFCs, amounting to ₹1 lakh crore during that financial year. Moreover, it was announced that NBFCs and Housing Finance Companies would be brought under RBI oversight to improve regulatory supervision.

Not only credit rating agencies but also auditors came under scrutiny. Between January and May 2019, a staggering 32 auditors resigned prematurely, with 15 resignations occurring in the month of May itself. The primary reasons for these departures included insufficient information about the company's businesses, unresolved tax observations, and a preoccupation with "mutual exits".

1. As of 31 March 2019, there were 9,659 NBFCs registered with the RBI, 88 of which were deposit accepting and 263 systemically important non-deposit accepting NBFCs' Financial Stability Report of RBI, June 2019.

The corporate bond market cannot develop without credible credit rating agencies, reliable auditors, strong regulation, and a robust investor protection mechanism. The NBFC liquidity crisis can be leveraged by the policymakers to deepen the corporate bond market. This approach would serve as an ideal solution in the absence of a long-term lender in the Indian financial system at a time when there has been a vacuum in the segment after the likes of ICICI and IDBI were converted into banks. Given India's capital shortage for infrastructure development, building a vibrant and strong corporate bond market is essential.

5.2. Importance of Corporate Bond Market

A corporate bond is a fixed-income instrument issued by a firm to raise capital for the purposes such as building a new plant, purchasing equipment, funding acquisitions, or expanding its business. Typically, these bonds are longer-term debt instruments with a maturity of more than one year, while shorter-term instruments are referred to as "commercial paper".

Private firms can secure funding from three primary sources: equity, bonds, and bank loans. The corporate sector has both short-term and long-term funding needs. While short-term or working capital requirements are primarily met by the banking sector and money markets, long-term funding requirements are met through investors in the debt or equity markets. By utilising multiple financing sources such as equity, debt, and bank borrowings, companies can also lower the systemic risk within the financial system.

An efficient corporate bond market is known to reduce financial sector fragility and provide an alternative cheap capital for firms (Yoshitomi & Shirai, 2001). A deep and vibrant bond market helps to modify the currency and maturity mismatches, as long-term assets are financed by long-term liabilities and currency exposure is aligned between assets and liabilities. In addition, it improves risk pricing by reducing information asymmetry, facilitates efficient asset management, and enhances the competence of capital markets in the country (Plummer & Click, 2005). Thus, a robust corporate bond market enables firms to raise funds at a lower cost, facilitates infrastructure financing, lowers risk, and reduces over-reliance on bank financing. It also promotes the process of "disintermediation," enabling corporates to directly access the capital markets for funding, bypassing traditional banks.

Since the introduction of Modigliani and Miller's capital structure theory in the 1950s, corporate finance and risk analysis have primarily focused on determining the optimal debt-to-equity ratio, with very little attention paid to understanding the optimal balance between bank financing and bond financing. This is strange as one of the reasons for the Asian financial crisis in 1997–98 was the excessive dependence of those economies on commercial banks for domestic financing (Bhattacharya, 2011), while other major sources, such as bond markets, were small. These banks borrowed short-term from international markets to invest in long-term projects at home.

An underdeveloped corporate bond market often leads to an over-dependence on bank funding. In the presence of imperfect banking regulatory supervision and high levels of government interference in credit allocation, distorted lending preferences can result in poor risk assessments. This, in turn, may lead to NPAs and undesirable systemic risk, as was observed in India.

The capital market structure in India is dominated by a large commercial bank sector, mostly publicly owned. It was believed that the government-owned banking system would serve as a powerful channel for targeted investment and economic development. However, in the absence of a deep corporate bond market, we have witnessed how, in its over-enthusiasm to boost growth, the government incentivised or coerced the public sector banks to channelise bank credit flows to the infrastructure sector during the boom period of 2005–2008. This huge infrastructure funding by banks resulted in an asset-liability mismatch, as long-term projects were financed with short-term liabilities. As economic growth stumbled, many of these projects became unviable, resulting in a significant increase in NPAs on bank books. There were also instances of "crony capitalism" and the evergreening of loans, often with the tacit or explicit approval of the government. The economy is still recovering from these excesses. Unfortunately, the asset creation of the Indian corporate sector now largely depends on borrowing at higher rates or seeking international financing.

In contrast, studies have shown that the risk assessment process in developed corporate bond markets, involving credit analysts and credit rating agencies, is significantly stronger. An independent corporate bond market is better equipped to accurately assess the inherent value of investments, due to the disciplinary role of free-market forces. Competitive commercial banks can improve the efficiency of the capital market by improving lending to private businesses, thereby benefiting the broader economy (Bose & Coondoo, 2003). Without competition, however, banks become more susceptible to moral hazard and adverse selection processes.

5.3. Relatively Small Size of Corporate Bond Market in India

A deep and liquid bond market, with a significant corporate bond segment, is considered important for the economy as it ensures the flow of funds toward productive sectors. The corporate bond market has been in existence in India for a long time; however, despite its long history, the size of the public issue segment of the corporate bond market in India has remained quite insignificant, even though the equity market is quite active. Even today, most of the large issuers in the corporate debt market segment are "quasi-government" entities, such as banks, public sector oil companies, or government-sponsored FIs. The government bond market forms an overwhelming part of the overall debt market, both in terms of outstanding securities (Table 5.1) and trading volumes. By the end of March 2018, the accumulated value of outstanding corporate bonds accounted for only 16.3% of GDP, while the ratio for government securities was around 30 percent (including market loans of central and state governments), and general government debt stood at close to 70% of GDP. The dominance of government securities in the secondary market is even more pronounced, as they account for a whopping 90% of transactions in recent years.

Table 5.1: Outstanding Fixed Income Securities (Bonds) in India

Year	In ₹ Crores			Share in Total (%)	
	Government	Corporate	Total	Government	Corporate
2010–11	26,90,551	8,89,510	35,80,061	75.2	24.8
2011–12	32,69,635	10,51,639	43,21,274	75.7	24.3
2012–13	38,67,576	12,90,147	51,57,723	75.0	25.0
2013–14	44,99,241	14,67,397	59,66,637	75.4	24.6
2014–15	51,63,838	17,50,320	69,14,158	74.7	25.3
2015–16	58,14,855	20,19,296	78,34,151	74.2	25.8
2016–17	65,06,597	24,04,911	89,11,508	73.0	27.0
2017–18	72,74,515	27,42,259	1,00,16,774	72.6	27.4
2018–19	80,61,528	30,67,228	1,11,28,756	72.4	27.6
2019–20	90,44,954	32,53,922	1,22,98,876	73.5	26.5
2020–21	1,08,57,254	32,53,921	1,41,11,175	76.9	23.1
2021–22	1,22,62,669	36,12,604	1,58,75,273	77.2	22.8
2022–23	1,39,19,993	40,17,025	1,79,37,018	77.6	22.4

Source: CCIL Reports.

*Government bonds include central and state govt market loans, no Uday or other PSU bonds are included.

A comparison with its Asian peers indicates that the Indian corporate debt market is relatively small. The corporate debt-to-GDP ratio in India is significantly lower than that of other developing countries like South Korea, Malaysia and China (Table 5.2).

Table 5.2: Corporate Debt Market Penetration (as percent of GDP)

Country	Corporate	Total Bond Market
India	18.0	75.8
China	35.3	98.0
Indonesia	2.8	31.0
Japan	16.8	239.9
South Korea	85.1	145.7
Malaysia	56.5	122.7

Country	Corporate	Total Bond Market
Philippines	8.8	51.0
Singapore	34.9	107.8
Thailand	23.7	89.0
Vietnam	4.2	23.5

Note: Data for the Asian Bond Market as of March 2021.

Source: Asia Bond Monitor; CCIL

5.4. Challenges in Corporate Bond Market in India

The challenges surrounding the development of the Indian corporate bond market must be examined from both the supply and demand sides. Often, the issues on both sides are intertwined, resembling the typical "chicken and egg" dilemma.

5.4.1. Demand-Side Issues

1. Demand Capped by Regulations or Capabilities

The demand for corporate bonds in India is constrained by both regulations and ratings. Historically, mutual funds (MFs), retirement funds (such as the Employees' Provident Fund Organisation, exempted trusts, and National Pension System (NPS)), banks, FPIs, corporates, high net-worth individuals, and Alternative Investment Funds are the key investors in the Indian corporate bond market. The demand from these investors is influenced by their investment objectives, end-investor mandates, and regulatory limits. For long-term investors like insurance funds, pension funds, and provident funds, investment norms are heavily skewed towards government and PSU bonds, which make up around 50% of their corpus. Additionally, these funds are typically restricted from investing in instruments with ratings lower than AA. As a result, in practice, these funds allocate a very minuscule portion of their investments to private corporate bonds. Mutual funds, on the other hand, are mostly active at the shorter end of the yield curve, aligned with their liability profile, and are more willing to invest in bonds with ratings lower than AA. However, banks are not natural investors in corporate bonds, as they primarily provide credit to the private sector. Banks tend to favour loans over corporate bonds, as there are no mark-to-market concerns with bank credit. There is limited appetite among retail investors due to a lack of awareness, liquidity issues, limited product flexibility, and insufficient tax sops. These factors collectively contribute to a narrow investor base.

In addition to restrictions that limit their investments to high-grade papers, insurance, pension, and provident funds generally lack the inclination or resources to invest in structured products. They prefer balance-sheet financing over asset financing. Mostly, their funding is directed to public sector companies in the infrastructure sector, rather than through investments in private infrastructure bonds.

2. Uncompetitive Risk-Return Trade-Off

Rising yields in the bond market in 2018 led to a decline in corporate bond issuance, following a sustained increase over the previous three years. SDLs, considered risk-free, offered higher returns than the debt of top-rated public sector companies for much of the year, which dampened demand for corporate bonds.

Government spending on infrastructure is mostly carried out through various PSUs, and off-balance-sheet borrowings by the government have increased in recent years through these PSUs. These quasi-government securities, with high credit ratings, are often preferred by investors over debt issued by private companies.

3. Volatile Demand from FPIs

Foreign portfolio investment (FPI) in corporate bonds has been allowed and has increased over the years. The government is also trying to attract foreign capital. However, these inflows are highly dependent on global dynamics, such as currency fluctuations and global interest rates. As a result, FPIs cannot be relied upon as a sustainable source of funds, as there have been years when macroeconomic vulnerabilities led to significant foreign fund outflows.

4. Lack of Liquidity

There is a lack of secondary market liquidity in the corporate bond market. By nature, pension and insurance funds typically do not sell their investments in bonds in the secondary market, as these bonds are held to maturity. Even if they are allowed to buy in the secondary market, they generally prefer to do so in the primary market. As a result, there is a difference between actual liquidity and perceived liquidity. Mutual funds do take part in the secondary market, but primarily for shorter-duration bonds. Secondary market activity is dominated by the top 5–10 issuers, with no demand for bonds rated below AA. Thus, this thin secondary market is hurt by issues such as the absence of market makers, limited liquidity, a lack of pricing benchmarks, and a narrow institutional investor base.

Table 5.3 below shows that government bonds dominate the secondary market, significantly overshadowing corporate bonds. However, it needs to be mentioned that trading in the secondary market for corporate bonds increased by 95% between FY 2016 to FY 2020, with higher FPI activity contributing to this trend.

Table 5.3: Turnover in Secondary Market

Fiscal Year	Corporate Bonds	Government Bonds	Share in Total	
	Average daily Trading (in Rs Cr)	Average daily Trading (in Rs Cr)	Corporate (%)	Government (%)
FY09	630	8,254	7	93
FY10	1,613	10,353	13	87
FY11	2,437	10,238	19	81
FY12	2,476	12,973	16	84
FY13	3,047	24,462	11	89
FY14	4,025	32,710	11	89
FY15	4,584	38,645	11	89
FY16	4,171	35,560	10	90
FY17	5,520	62,973	8	92
FY18	6,907	40,739	14	86
FY19	7,147	32,628	18	82
FY20	8,117	46,558	15	85

Source: Crisil Debt Report, 2021.

5. Lack of Diversity of Instruments

A study on the Indian bond market by Mitra (2009) highlights the problem of lack of diversity in available instruments as a major factor hampering the development of corporate debt markets in India. While various types of instruments, such as step-up bonds, step-down bonds, deep discount bonds, reverse floater bonds, indexed bonds, and currency bonds are common internationally, the Indian corporate bond market is primarily dominated by fixed-rate coupon bonds. Furthermore, the average maturity of bonds issued is typically limited to just 5 to 7 years.

Table 5.4: Historical Tenor-wise Issuance

	Number of Instruments											
Maturities	**FY 09**	**FY 10**	**FY 11**	**FY 12**	**FY 13**	**FY 14**	**FY 15**	**FY 16**	**FY 17**	**FY 18**	**FY 19**	**FY 20**
Up to 3 y ₹	317	335	466	1,096	1,203	2,609	3,805	1,180	1,196	937	1,093	1,029
3 - 5 y ₹	190	160	195	228	505	472	744	1,557	1,688	1,494	1,401	1,144
5 - 10 y ₹	151	172	178	386	577	354	454	625	771	721	536	763
>10	59	76	117	220	158	81	106	429	469	473	303	286
N.A	157	136	0	0	0	0	0	0	0	0	0	0
Total	874	879	956	1,930	2,443	3,516	5,109	3,791	4,124	3,625	3,333	3,222

Table 5.5: Tenon-wise Issuance Analysis in May 2019

Tenor Bucket	No	Amount (Rs Cr)	Fixed	Floating	Zero-Coupon	Avg. Fixed Coupon	Max Coupon	Min Coupon	Floating Bench-mark
<=1 year	3	675.0	3	-	-	7.48%	9.30%	5.00%	-
> 1 year –<=2 years	11	1,389.7	11	-	-	11.16%	18.00%	8.40%	-
> 2 years –<=5 years	24	8,650.3	24	-	-	11.37%	18.00%	5.00%	-
>5 years –<=10 years	20	2,624.9	20	-	-	8.12%	16.75%	0.00%	-
>10 years– <=15 years	3	4,048.5	3	-	-	11.44%	12.00%	10.32%	-
>15 years	3	1,017.7	3	-	-	13.50%	15.50%	10.00%	-
Perpetual	-	-	-	-	-	-	-	-	-

Source: Crisil Debt Report, FIMMDA; Rakshitra, CCIL.

Table 5.4 shows that about 70% of historical issuances have been in the under-5-year tenor bucket. However, interestingly, in recent years, there has been an increase in issuances with tenors of more than 10 years. This trend is also evident in the issuance data for May 2019 (Table 5.5). Moreover, most of the corporate bonds are fixed coupon bonds, with a lack of variety in the instruments offered. As MFs are particularly active in the 3 to 5-year tenor bucket, demand in this range remains strong. Moreover, investors prefer shorter tenures, as the yields are attractive and there are lower mark-to-market losses.

6. Information Asymmetry

The corporate bond market is heterogeneous, unlike the government bond market, as each firm raising capital operates in different sectors with unique balance sheets. The problem is that most of the corporate bonds are privately placed (>90%) with limited disclosure. These deals usually happen privately between the issuer and the investor, making credit rating difficult. The market perceives the disclosure and documentation requirements for private placements as comprehensive and easy, whereas the disclosure requirements for public debt issuance are considered expensive, time-consuming, extremely burdensome, and difficult to comply with. As observed in Table 5.6, the share of private placements in total issuances is above 95% on average (with 99% in 2018). Unless investors have their own strong credit teams, they have to rely on external credit rating agencies. This leads to significant information asymmetry, which deters potential investors.

Table 5.6: Resources Raised through Primary Issuance

Fiscal Year	Private Placements						Mobilised Amount through Public Placements (Rs Cr)	Share of Privately Mobilised (%)	Total Amount Mobilised as % of GDP
	No of Issuers	No of Deals	No of Instruments	Mobilised Amt. (Rs Cr)	Growth (%)	Amount Mobilised as % of GDP			
FY09	167	799	874	1,74,327	51	3.1	1,500	99	3.1
FY10	192	803	879	1,89,478	9	2.9	2,500	99	3.0
FY11	182	825	956	1,92,127	1	2.5	9,451	95	2.6
FY12	184	1,327	1,939	2,51,437	31	2.9	35,611	88	3.3
FY13	267	1,828	2,443	3,51,848	40	3.5	16,982	95	3.7
FY14	245	1,473	3,524	2,70,946	-23	2.4	42,383	86	2.8
FY15	344	1,765	5,109	4,32,692	60	3.5	9,713	98	3.5
FY16	589	2,682	3,791	4,92,047	14	3.6	33,812	94	3.8
FY17	663	1,837	4,124	7,05,174	43	4.6	29,547	96	4.8
FY18	694	2,398	3,625	6,55,799	-7	3.8	4,953	99	3.9
FY19	568	2551	3333	6,35,239	-3	3.3	36,679	94	3.5
FY20	587	2250	3222	6,75,236	6	3.3	14,984	98	3.4

Source: Crisil report on Debt 2021, SEBI, RBI.

7. Evolving Bankruptcy Code

Bankruptcy reforms have led to significant growth in the corporate bond market in several countries (Table 5.7). India's Insolvency and Bankruptcy Code (IBC) is expected to play a similar role, but it is still evolving and has yet to be fully tested on financial entities.

Table 5.7: Corporate Bonds to GDP Nearly Doubles Five Years After Bankruptcy Reforms

Country	Year of Bankruptcy Reforms*	Pre-Reforms (%)	Post-Reforms* (%)
UK	2002	68.40	106.80
Brazil	2005	12.70	26.30
China	2007	18.80	33.40
Russia	2009	8.10	13.10
India	2016	13.40	Effect to be seen.

Source: BIS

*Five-year average corporate bonds to GDP ratio.

Table 5.8: Status of Six Large Accounts Initiated by the RBI (in ₹ Billion)

Name of Corporate Debtor	Claims of Financial Creditors under Resolution		
	Amount Admitted	Amount Realised	Realisation as a % of Claims
Electrosteel Steels Ltd.	131.8	53.2	40.38
Bhushan Steel Ltd.	560.2	355.7	63.50
Monnet Ispat & Energy Ltd.	110.2	28.9	26.26
Essar Steel India Ltd.*	494.7	*	*
Alok Industries Ltd.	295.2	50.5	17.11
Jyoti Structures Ltd.	73.7	36.8	50.02

Source: Insolvency and Bankruptcy Board of India (IBBI) quarterly newsletter for FY 2018–19.

* In a major judgment on 15 November 2019, the Supreme Court cleared the hurdles for Arcelor Mittal to the takeover of Essar Steel for ₹42,000 crore—the biggest takeover of bad loans in Indian corporate history.

According to the RBI report on Financial Sector: Regulation and Developments, for the first batch of referrals to IBC, the resolution plan of six out of the 12 large borrowers of Scheduled Commercial Banks (SCBs) has been approved. The outcomes of these six large accounts, which concluded with resolution plans, are presented in Table 5.8.

The IBC code has significantly overhauled regulatory measures regarding the resolution of impaired assets and is expected to boost investors' confidence in the protection of their rights, potentially developing an appetite for bonds below the AA category. In particular, the judgment on Essar Steel was expected to improve the effectiveness of the IBC, speed up the resolution of other cases under the bankruptcy code, and assist Indian banks in attracting foreign capital to address their bad loans. However, it will take some time for the system to become fully effective and efficient. A few exemplary cases can serve as testimony to the solid foundations of the IBC.

8. Non-availability of Products for Credit Risk Management

Credit enhancement is a mechanism that improves the credit rating of an instrument, typically through a guarantee, collateralisation of security, or cash. In 2016, the RBI allowed banks to provide Partial Credit Enhancement to bonds issued by corporates or special purpose vehicles (SPVs), covering up to 50% of the total bond issue size, with a cap of 20% of the bond issue for an individual bank. However, some experts warn that this might expose banks, insurance and pension funds, and their customers to increased risk (Chandrasekhar, 2016). Despite these concerns, credit enhancement can improve tradability, increase risk appetite, and boost market liquidity by attracting more investors. It can be especially helpful for infrastructure companies seeking to raise funds. However, the credit insurance or Credit Default Swap (CDS) market has not yet evolved in India. According to Crisil, the growth of the CDS market is constrained by unattractive pricing, lack of secondary market liquidity, and the absence of specialised players. There is a need to incentivise both domestic and foreign participants to promote the growth of the CDS market.

9. Lack of Inter-Regulatory Coordination

Wells and Schou-Zibell (2008) highlight how fragmented regulation hampers participation in the Indian market. Regulatory responsibility for corporate bond markets is divided among various entities with often conflicting objectives. While SEBI regulates corporate bonds, brokers, and mutual funds, the RBI oversees banks and PDs. Pension funds are regulated by the Pension Fund Regulatory and Development Authority, and insurance companies fall under the IRDAI. Foreign investment limits are imposed by both SEBI and RBI. The study emphasises the need for stronger and more coordinated regulatory frameworks to facilitate market participation.

10. Lack of Repo Options

One of the reasons for the underperformance of the corporate bond market is the non-availability of the Repo option. Usually, a Repo transaction involves two entities, where the borrower raises funds by selling securities with the promise to repurchase them on a specified date at a mutually agreed price. The tri-party repo was part of the recommendations of the H.R. Khan Committee's 2016 report on the development of the corporate bond market.

In 2018, the NSE and BSE launched an electronic platform for Repos. However, the securities allowed on this platform are limited to AAA-rated bonds, A+ rated commercial papers, and certificates of deposit. Although the RBI introduced repos in corporate bonds in 2010, the response was tepid because of the non-availability of guaranteed settlement and an electronic dealing platform.

5.4.2. Supply-Side Issues

1. Crowding Out of Corporate Borrowings

A study by Acharya and his co-researchers covering the period 1997 to 2016 shows that for every 10 percent increase in government debt as a share of GDP, corporate debt issuances fall by 7.3%, indicating a crowding-out effect. In 2015–16, when total government debt rose by 12.6%, corporate debt declined by 9.1%. A bulk of this effect was driven by the bank credit channel, which accounted for 6.7% to the decline in corporate borrowing.

Although the fiscal deficit trend at the center shows credible consolidation since FY 2011–12, the actual level of government debt is significantly understated. The Comptroller and Auditor General's (CAG's) report details how various government expenses—such as subsidies and project financing—have been kept off the books, often funded through public sector companies or simply rolled over to subsequent years. This practice has persisted for years, regardless of the political party in power at the center.

Table 5.9: Adjusted Central Fiscal Deficit and State Fiscal Deficit

	% of GDP			
	Central Fiscal Deficit	**Adjusted Fiscal Deficit**	**State Fiscal Deficit**	**Total**
FY12	5.9	5.9	1.9	7.8
FY13	4.9	4.9	2.0	6.9
FY14	4.5	4.5	2.2	6.7
FY15	4.1	4.1	2.6	6.7
FY16	3.9	3.9	3.0	6.9
FY17	3.5	4.0	3.7	7.7
FY18	3.5	4.3	3.1	7.4

Source: ICICI Securities Primary Dealership, CMIE database.

*Fiscal deficit adjusted for special bond issuance and NSSF loans undertaken by public sector entities. Bank recapitalization bonds are not included in the analysis.

In the last two financial years, part of the food subsidy bill to the Food Corporation of India (FCI) has been converted into loans from the National Small Savings Fund (NSSF). Loans have been extended by NSSF to public sector entities like the National Highways Authority of India and the Indian Railway Finance Corporation (IRFC), which accounts for a large chunk of public sector capital spending. The adjusted fiscal deficit shown in Table 5.9 includes all such borrowings through special bonds, NSSF loans, and government-serviced bonds issued by public sector entities. An actual picture of government debt can be obtained by examining the Public Sector Borrowing Requirement (PSBR), which includes borrowing not only by the central government but also by the state governments. By adding the state government fiscal deficit to the adjusted central deficit, we arrive at a total deficit of around 7.5% of GDP. This figure does not account for bank recapitalisation bonds issued.

As there are no official data available on PSBR, there has been a number of such estimates done by researchers. According to Sajjid Chinoy of JPMorgan & Chase Co., the PSBR for the Centre and states in FY 2018 could be as high as 8.5% of GDP. This estimate does not account for off-budget loans of state governments and their agencies. If these are included, the total PSBR could exceed 9% of GDP. Other such studies also estimate the PSBR to be around 8-9% of GDP.

India's savings rate declined to 30% of GDP by the end of March 2017, down from 31.3% in 2015–16 and 34.6% in FY 2012, primarily due to slow growth in household savings. Household savings, which are channelled through banks and other non-banking financial entities, are a major source of investment funding for the Indian economy. According to the RBI's annual report, net household financial savings fell to 6.7% of GDP in FY 2017, down from 8.1% in FY 2016. As a result, the PSBR, estimated at around 8%, is consuming virtually all household financial savings. This is one of the reasons why real interest rates in India remain high.

Government borrowing for productive capital investment is essential, as it can help crowd in private investment. However, much of this borrowing is still being used to finance loan waivers, non-merit subsidies, and inefficient schemes. This allocation is consuming valuable resources in the economy, thereby crowding out the private corporate sector.

2. High Cost of Borrowings

The high supply of government and PSU bonds has put pressure on risk-free bond yields, forcing private players to offer higher interest rates in the domestic market. As shown in Table 5.10, the risk premium paid by issuers of bonds rated below A is exorbitant. The spread on BBB-rated bonds is nearly 11%, and that of debt papers with ratings below BBB is significant too. This has resulted in the exclusion of small and medium enterprises from accessing the debt market, which typically fall below the investment-grade BBB rating. As a result, these small private players have no option but to tap the bank credit, leveraging their long-standing relationships with banks.

The high cost of borrowing through corporate bonds, compared to other forms of financing, and the inadequate liquidity in the corporate debt market deter firms from issuing bonds in the market.

Table 5.10: Historical Spread Analysis of Corporate Bonds (Average, in Basis Points)

Year	Ratings										
	AAA	AA	A1	A2	A	BBB	BB	B	C	D	P1	NA
2011-12	119	189	248	-	202	185	227	-	-	-	-	205
2012-13	98	161	231	-	220	308	262	182	-	-	193	181
2013-14	85	140	275	-	163	291	254	-	-	-	189	176
2014-15	46	123	179	141	149	351	83	138	566	-	-	148
2015-16	62	164	205	-	237	593	710	281	-	-	-	167
2016-17	73	221	240	-	343	720	1,042	1,699	-	-	-	170
2017-18	74	171	177	825	352	500	957	1,052	-	-	-	135
2018-19	105	183	199	-	232	460	602	885	687	656	-	256
2019-20	114	282	-	-	391	1135	659	1185	781	807	-	220

Source: Rakshitra, CCIL.

The large corporates can source funds from abroad, and even after adjusting for hedging costs, the cost of borrowing internationally tends to be lower than borrowing through domestic sources. For example, in June 2019, Adani Ports and Special Economic Zone Ltd. raised $750 million through an offshore bond sale listed on the Singapore Exchange. The funds were intended for capital expenditure, including on-lending to subsidiaries to meet their capital needs, as well as repaying existing debt. The US dollar-denominated bonds were priced at a mark-up of 265 basis points over the 10-year US benchmark yield, making them cheaper than domestic interest rates.

3. Dominance of Higher-Rated Bonds

Due to risk aversion and regulatory restrictions, market demand for AAA and AA-rated bonds remains high. From FY 2018–20, the total issuance of AAA and AA-rated bonds were at about 88% of total issuance (Table 5.11). Even in secondary market trading, almost 70% of trading happens in papers rated above AA, indicating low liquidity for lower-rated papers (Table 5.12). There was a slight increase in the issuance of below AA-rated bonds in FY 2016 and FY 2017, but the strong market preference for very safe AA and above-rated papers has resulted in a thin market for lower-rated bonds. As a result, there is little demand for low-rated papers, and supply remains limited. The share of A-rated bonds is a mere one-twentieth of the total market.

Table 5.11: Ratings Assigned to Corporate Bonds (Maturity ≥ 1 yr)

Grade/ Period	% Share in Rated Amount				
	Highest Safety (AAA)	**High Safety (AA)**	**Adequate Safety (A)**	**Moderate Safety (BBB)**	**Non-Investment Grade**
FY12	55%	25%	9%	5%	6%
FY13	65%	20%	7%	4%	4%
FY14	70%	23%	5%	2%	0%
FY15	65%	26%	6%	2%	1%
FY16	56%	23%	5%	13%	2%
FY17	56%	28%	5%	8%	2%
FY18	60%	28%	5%	1%	2%
FY19	72%	16%	4%	1%	2%
FY20	76%	13%	3%	1%	2%

Source: Crisil report on Debt

Table 5.12: Rating-wise Trading of Corporate Bonds

Grade/ Period	% Share in Rated Amount				
	Highest Safety (AAA)	High Safety (AA)	Adequate Safety (A)	Moderate Safety (BBB)	Ratings NA
FY13	56%	11%	1%	0.1%	31%
FY14	72%	13%	2%	0.3%	12%
FY15	71%	13%	3%	0.1%	12%
FY16	64%	17%	4%	0.2%	15%
FY17	51%	11%	2%	0.1%	36%
FY18	62%	16%	2%	0.3%	19%
FY19	75%	16%	3%	0.2%	6%
FY20	60%	7%	1%	0%	32%

Source: Rakshitra, CCIL.

4. Supply Limited to Few Sectors

Financials are the largest issuers in India's corporate bond market (Table 5.13). More specifically, PSU financials, such as PFC, Rural Electrification Corporation, and National Bank of Agriculture and Rural Development, are the biggest issuers. The next major segment is the housing finance sector, which has experienced significant growth in the last few years, with companies like HDFC Housing Finance and Dewan Housing Finance leading the way. There is limited issuance from other sectors (Table 5.14).

Table 5.13: Industry-wise Historical Analysis in Secondary Market

Year	% Share				
	Finance	Infrastructure	Manufacturing	Oil	Others
2013-14	60%	19%	4%	2%	15%
2014-15	53%	24%	4%	2%	17%
2015-16	61%	29%	5%	0%	6%
2016-17	64%	23%	3%	1%	9%
2017-18	68%	20%	6%	0%	6%
2018-19	67%	19%	6%	0%	8%
2019-20	59%	25%	4%	3%	10%

Source: Rakshita, CCIL.

Table 5.14: Industry-wise Classification of Bond Issuance in Primary Market

Major Industries	% Share			
	FY16	FY17	FY18	FY19
Non-Financial	24.9	26.8	25.8	27.9
Manufacturing	4.4	4.3	5.1	2.3
Mining	1.2	0.3	-	3.3
Electricity	6.7	7	3.8	1.3
Services (other than financial)	6.3	12.1	13.1	14.6
-Transport Services	0.8	5.1	6.8	5.5
-Communication Services	2.7	3.3	-	7.3
Construction and Real Estate	6.4	3.1	3.6	6.4
Financial Services	75.1	73.2	74.2	72.1
Asset Financing services	33.2	30.8	32.7	29.5
-Auto Financing Services	1.0	2.1	1.3	3.8
-Housing Finance Services	4.9	8.4	3.4	7.5
-Other Asset Financing Services	27.2	20.4	27.9	18
Other Financial Services	35.1	33.5	28.1	37.9

Source: CARE Ratings, CMIE.

Investment demand from the manufacturing sector has gone down in recent years, both in green-field and brown-field projects. Overall investment demand has also been on the decline. Excluding PSUs, there are only a handful of private players with AAA or AA ratings. Over the last three years, power generation and supply witnessed a 30% spurt in bond issuance, driven by focused reforms undertaken by the government. According to Crisil, the top ten issuers contributed 50 percent of total issuance from FY 2019 to the first half of FY 2021. Housing Development Finance Corporation (HDFC) was the top issuer over the past decade. However, in the first half of FY 2021, PFC remained on the top, followed by HDFC and Reliance Industries (a new entrant in the list of top five issuers).

5.5. Conclusion and Recommendations

In summary, the Indian corporate debt market is riddled with several problems. Access to domestic bond issuance has largely been confined to large and highly rated corporates, primarily attributed to the risk aversion of investors, investment restrictions on institutional investors like pension funds and insurance companies, as well as the lack of tools for reliable credit pricing and risk assessment in these markets. According to the Crisil Yearbook on the Indian Debt Market 2018, demand for corporate bonds increased between 2014 to 2017, prior to the NBFC liquidity crisis, due to: (i) increased flow of household savings into financial instruments, which boosted demand from mutual funds, (ii) higher allocation by banks resulting from a lowered statutory liquidity ratio (SLR) and increased deposits after demonetisation, (iii) increased demand from pension schemes as new states adopted the NPS and more employees enrolled, and iv) higher utilisation limits of FPIs, which rose from 40-50% to 70-90% after 2014, driven by political stability. With India's GDP growth currently below potential, authorities are trying to revive growth through coordinated monetary and fiscal policies. To support this, it is imperative to remove any financing constraints by developing alternative financing channels that can supplement bank credit. India must now need to look beyond banks to meet its large infrastructure financing needs. We list out a few recommendations for the development of the corporate debt market in India.

First, it is well understood that large public debt issuance can render monetary policy actions ineffective by interfering with monetary policy transmission and crowding out private investment. The 2019 budget announcement that the government would tap international markets for a portion of sovereign borrowing was generally well-received, though the associated risks with it were perceived to be higher. Many of the problems in the corporate debt market will be solved if the government reduces public borrowings. Part of the fiscal deficit can be met by divesting shares in public sector enterprises, monetising non-core public assets (like golf-courses), and cutting back on wasteful subsidies, freebies, and programs that do not contribute to growth. Increasing the share of capital expenditure will also help crowd in private investment. With more resources available to the corporate sector, the cost of funds will come down, addressing some of the supply-side challenges.

Second, there is a need to deepen the market for A-rated bonds, as this would enable smaller corporates to tap funding at lower interest rates and enable investors to diversify their portfolios without significantly increasing risks, thus addressing both supply and demand issues. The FY 2019 budget recognised some of these problems and took steps to address the skewness in the market. The Finance Minister announced in 2019 that the government would collaborate with the RBI and the SEBI to set up a Credit Guarantee Enhancement Corporation aimed at deepening the corporate debt market, with a special focus on infrastructure. At present, there is a Credit Guarantee Fund Scheme for Micro and Small Enterprises to provide collateral-free credit to these small firms. The credit guarantee would enhance the ratings of such issuance, increasing demand from pension funds, insurance companies, and provident funds, which are constrained by regulatory restrictions on their investment. Hence, the supply of such papers would increase, reducing the dominance of only very high-rated bonds in the market.

Third, the development of a tri-party repo market for corporate debt securities is expected to provide an opportunity for borrowing against securities, offering short-term liquidity to market participants. The government, in collaboration with the RBI and SEBI, will work to enable stock exchanges to accept AA-rated bonds as collateral. This initiative will increase the demand for and liquidity in lower-rated corporate bonds.

Fourth, there should be better coordination amongst the regulatory authorities like RBI, SEBI, IRDAI and PFRDA. These agencies should increase consultation and avoid working at cross-purposes.

Fifth, the corporate bond market tends to be less vibrant in countries with underdeveloped securities laws. A robust corporate bond market cannot be expected if investors have little confidence in corporate management and the agencies responsible for protecting investors' interests. Creditors' confidence depends on corporate governance, accounting and auditing standards, financial reporting systems, disclosure standards, and the legal protection of their rights. The credibility of the rating process can be enhanced by complementing ratings from domestic rating agencies with those from credible international rating agencies. The lack of sophisticated credit risk assessments has been a major limitation to the growth of corporate bond markets in emerging economies. As the Insolvency and Bankruptcy Code (IBC) becomes more effective, it will instil greater confidence in investors regarding recoveries through timely resolution. This, in turn, will give a fillip to the demand for the market for A-rated bonds.

Sixth, regulators should review the disclosure requirements for public debt issuance to reduce the cost, time, and complexity of compliance. On the other hand, disclosure requirements for private placements should be increased to address information asymmetry. Private issues are not traded in secondary markets and, therefore, lack the liquidity of public issues, as they change hands much less frequently. Moreover, private placements are often considered close substitutes for syndicated bank loans.

Seventh, as more resources become available and the cost of funds goes down, we can expect to see debt issuance from a diverse sectors, such as manufacturing, mining, and services, beyond just the financial sector. Over time, as demand for such bonds grows and liquidity improves, a variety of instruments, such as floating-rate bonds or step-up bonds, will become more prevalent in the market.

Lastly, there is a need to expand the investor base. Foreign investors usually impose positive pressure to develop robust market infrastructure and promote transparent market practices. However, this should be supplemented with a developed repo market, hedging instruments, and consistent, supportive taxation policies to attract foreign investment.

Furthermore, retail investors mostly invest in the corporate bond market through mutual funds. Given that financial literacy in our country remains relatively low, the government can incentivise individuals through favourable taxation policies to encourage a shift in household savings from traditional assets like gold and real estate into financial instruments.

A well-functioning corporate bond market can play a critical role in the economy by bridging the funding gap for infrastructure financing in the country. The private sector can access this market to raise long-term capital without depending on the banking sector, which is already stressed with NPAs. However, developing the corporate bond market cannot be achieved through regulations alone. Investors' confidence needs to be nurtured through strong corporate governance, improved market credibility through adequate disclosure and transparency, and better investor protection. Now is the right time to address the issues hindering the development of a liquid and vibrant corporate bond market in India.

CHAPTER 6

Importance of State Government Bonds: State Development Loans (SDLs)

India follows a federal structure of government, where governance powers are shared between the central and state governments. Certain subjects, such as external affairs, are exclusively under the central government, while others, like law and order, fall completely under the jurisdiction of state governments. In addition, the Concurrent List includes subjects of common interest to both the union and state governments, such as education and forests.

India follows a model of "Competitive Cooperative Federalism". After independence, the country adopted the idea of cooperative federalism, where the centre and states shared a horizontal relationship, working together to promote the larger public interest. However, over time, states began competing to attract capital and investment, aiming to stimulate economic growth and improve efficiency. This led to the emergence of Competitive Federalism, which fosters a vertical relationship between the states and the central government. It encourages healthy competition among states, ensuring minimum waste and maximum resource utilisation. As a result, states in India have the autonomy to create their own policies to govern the state, manage revenue sources, set budgets, and define developmental priorities.

The states are the major growth drivers of India. In recent years, the size of state governments' budget has grown significantly, with their combined expenditure surpassing that of the central government. In FY 2019–20, total state government expenditure was around ₹33.3 lakh crore, exceeding the central government's expenditure of ₹26.8 lakh crore. Since 2011–12, the growth in aggregate expenditure of states has outpaced that of the central government every year. However, states' revenue sources are limited, and states often depend on market borrowings and transfers from the central government to meet their revenue shortfalls.

According to Part XII of Article 293(1) and (3) of the Constitution, state governments can independently borrow loans and issue guarantees, similar to the central government, subject to any limits set by the state's legislature through law. State governments' market borrowings or bonds are known as SDLs, which are managed by the RBI, just like the central government's borrowings.

6.1. Stylised Facts about State Government Bonds

6.1.1. Fiscal Health

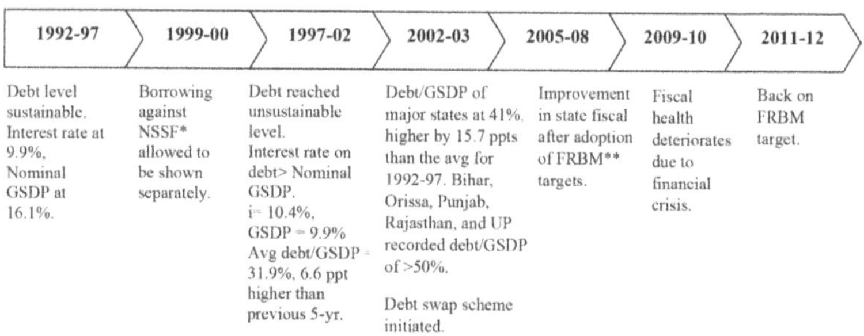

**NSSF*: National Small Savings Fund;

***FRBM*: Fiscal Responsibility and Budget Management.

Figure 6.1: Historical Background of State Finances or Fiscal Health

States have experienced several phases of debt unsustainability and subsequent debt consolidation. Various schemes have been introduced to assist states in restructuring their debts. Figure 6.1 gives a snapshot of the changes in the fiscal health of states.

Various schemes have been introduced over time, based on the recommendations of the Finance Commission (FC), to help states restructure their debts. A few of these are:

1. Debt Swap Scheme (DSS)

DSS was initiated in 2002–03, allowing states to prepay their high-cost loans (with interest rates greater than 13%) to the centre through additional market borrowings and a portion of small savings receipts. In 1999–2000, changes were made to the accounting procedure, allowing proceeds from the National Small Saving Funds (NSSF) to be shown as part of internal borrowings or internal debt. By 2002–03, NSSF had emerged as the most important source of funding, accounting for over 50% of the total. In 2003–04, 61% of the debt was financed through additional market borrowings at interest rates below 6.5%, with the remaining portion funded through special securities issued to NSSF, carrying an interest rate fixed at 9.5%.

2. Conditional Debt Write-off

The 12th Finance Commission (FC) offered conditional write-offs on debt repayments and concessions on interest rates. The central loans to states, outstanding as of March 2005 and amounting to ₹1,28,795 crores, were rescheduled for a fresh term of 20 years at a reduced interest rate of 7.5%. This rescheduling was contingent upon the enactment of the FRBM Act, which included five key features:

(i) Elimination of the Revenue Deficit (RD) by FY 2009.

(ii) Reduction of the Fiscal Deficit (FD) to 3% of GSDP.

(iii) Setting annual reduction targets for deficits.

(iv) Issuance of annual statements outlining the related fiscal strategy.

(v) Provision of special statements along with the budget detailing expenditure on salaries.

Additionally, another debt write-off scheme was introduced for repayments due from FY 2006–10 on central loans contracted up to March 2004, with eligibility linked to an absolute reduction in the revenue deficit.

(vi) If a state achieved a zero-revenue deficit by 2008–09, it would receive a full write-off in 2009–10, regardless of its fiscal deficit.

Figure 6.2 illustrates the trend of Fiscal and Revenue Deficits of states as a percentage of GSDP. It shows that after reaching unsustainable levels between FY 1998 and FY 2002, most states were able to achieve and maintain the Fiscal Deficit (FD) target and eliminate the Revenue Deficit (RD) following the adoption of the FRBM Act. Several external factors contributed to this improvement, including: (i) increased central transfers, (ii) higher tax revenues driven by strong GDP growth and the adoption of VAT, and (iii) lower interest payments owing to debt restructuring.

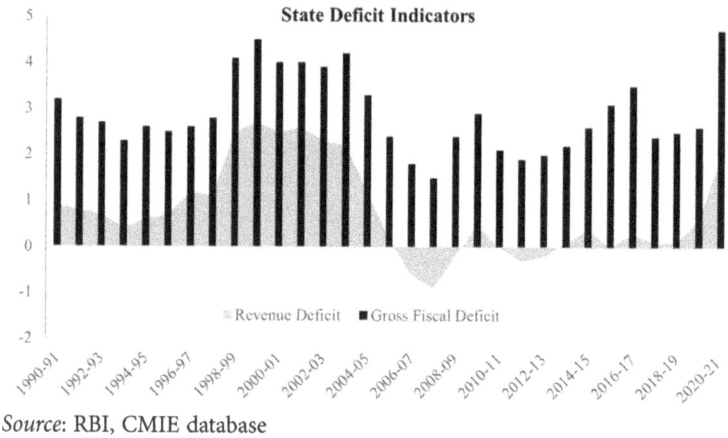

Source: RBI, CMIE database

Figure 6.2: States Fiscal and Revenue Deficit Trend (as a % of GSDP)

In response to the Global Financial Crisis, the FRBM Act was put on hold during 2008–13. During this period, states also took on part of the liabilities of state power utilities under the UDAY Scheme, which led to an increase in the fiscal deficit, pushing it above the FRBM target. However, by FY 2002 and FY 2018, states managed to maintain their Gross Fiscal Deficit (GFD) at 2.4% of GDP, supported by higher revenue receipts from tax devolution, despite an increase in both revenue and capital expenditures.

For the fiscal year 2020–21, states had budgeted a combined Gross Fiscal Deficit (GFD) of 2.8% of GDP, with more than half of them planning for revenue surpluses. However, the huge expenditures related to COVID-19 and lower revenue receipts significantly undermined these targets, with the GFD-GDP ratio climbing to 4.1%, much higher than budgeted. Subsequently, states managed to lower their GFD-GDP ratio to 2.7% in 2022–23, 10 basis points lower than that in 2021–22. This consolidation was achieved through a reduction in the revenue deficit, while maintaining the quality of expenditure.

6.1.2. Sources of Financing State Bonds (SDLs)

The sources of financing the fiscal deficit of states have changed over time (Table 6.1). From FY 1991–1999, loans from central government were the major source of financing the fiscal deficit, accounting for nearly 47% on average.

As mentioned earlier, since FY 2000, states have been encouraged to use proceeds from small savings (NSSF) to finance their deficit, which was recorded as part of internal borrowings. In FY 2006 and FY 2007, almost 77% of the total deficit was financed through NSSF.

As these sources were expensive, states were encouraged to tap the market to bridge the fiscal gap. From FY 2008 onwards, market borrowings became the primary source of financing for the fiscal deficit, with an increase in the issuance of state bonds. In FY 2020, 89% of the fiscal deficit was financed through SDLs.

Table 6.1: Sources of Financing Gross Fiscal Deficit of States (Percentage of Total).

Years	Loans from Central Government	Market Borrowings	Special Securities Issued to NSSF	Others
1991–92	50	17	0	33
1992–93	43	17	0	41
1993–94	46	18	0	36
1994–95	52	15	0	33
1995–96	46	19	0	35
1996–97	46	18	0	37
1997–98	52	17	0	31
1998–99	41	14	0	44
1999–00	14	14	29	43
2000–01	9	14	37	39
2001–02	12	18	38	32
2002–03	0	29	49	23
2003–04	12	39	15	34
2004–05	-9	32	60	17
2005–06	0	17	82	1
2006–07	-11	17	72	22
2007–08	-1	71	8	22
2008–09	-1	77	1	22
2009–10	-1	60	13	28
2010–11	0	55	24	21
2011–12	0	80	-5	24
2012–13	1	75	0	24
2013–14	0	66	1	33
2014–15	0	63	7	29
2015–16	0	61	6	32
2016–17	1	66	-6	39
2017–18	1	84	-8	23
2018–19	2	74	-6	30
2019–20	3	89	-6	14

Source: RBI Report on State Finances

The same can be seen from the chart (Figure 6.3) below.

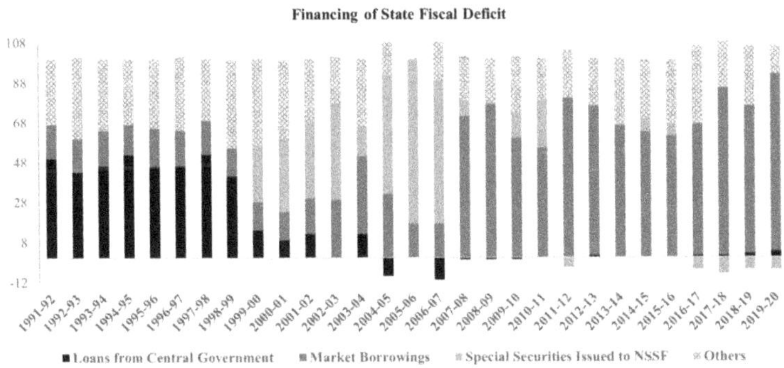

Figure 6.3: Financing of State Fiscal Deficit

The share of market borrowing to finance states' fiscal deficits has increased significantly, from 24% during 2001–07 to 67% in 2008–17, and nearly 90% in 2019–20.

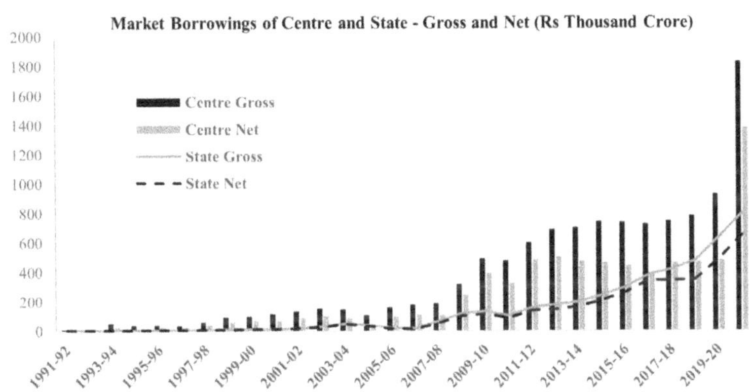

Source: RBI Report on State Finances.

Figure 6.4: Market Borrowings by Both Centre and State (in ₹ Thousand Crore)

Market borrowing by states and UTs—both gross and net—has become almost comparable to that of the centre (Figure 6.4). The share of states' borrowings in total general government borrowing has more than doubled in the last five years, partly due to rising redemptions. In 2019–20, net borrowings by states increased by about 40%, while gross market borrowings, at ₹6.3 lakh crore, rose by 32.7%, marking one of the highest increases in recent years. (Gross borrowing is the sum of net borrowing and redemptions.)

According to the RBI report, states like Odisha and Haryana have been pragmatic in managing their higher fiscal deficits by using their rainy-day funds, rather than resorting to higher permissible market borrowings. In contrast, states like Gujarat and Punjab have over-borrowed, despite efforts at fiscal consolidation. Uttar Pradesh stands out as an extreme case, having borrowed more than 20% above the budgeted amount, even though it registered a fiscal surplus in 2019–20, contrary to the budgeted deficit (Figure 6.5).

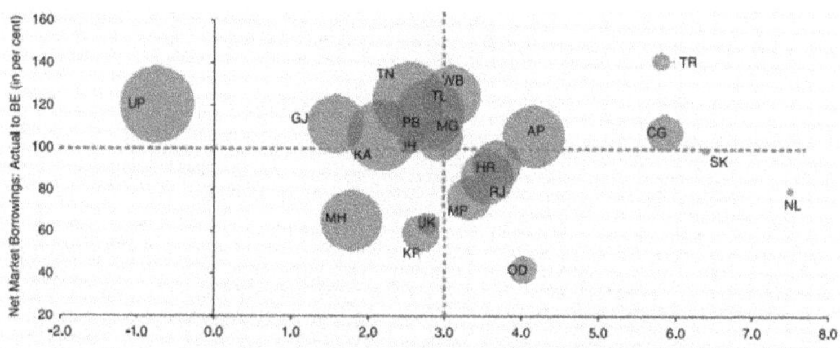

AP: Andhra Pradesh, CG: Chhattisgarh, HR: Haryana, KA: Karnataka, KR: Kerala, MH: Maharashtra, MG: Meghalaya, MP: Madhya Pradesh, NL: Nagaland, OD: Odisha, PB: Punjab, RJ: Rajasthan, SK: Sikkim, TN: Tamil Nadu, TL: Telangana, TR: Tripura, UP: Uttar Pradesh, UK: Uttarakhand, WB: West Bengal.
Note: Size of bubble represents size of net market borrowings.
Sources: CAG and budget documents of state governments.

Figure 6.5: GFD-GSDP Ratio and Market Borrowing Gap (Actual to BE): 2019–20.

6.1.3. Trend of Outstanding SDLs

As of 31 March 2021, the total government securities included central government dated securities amounting to ₹71.5 lakh crore (36% of GDP) and state government securities totalling ₹36.2 lakh crore (18% of GDP). The market share of SDLs in outstanding securities has increased from 17.7% in 2002–03 to 34.3% in 2022–23, while the share of central government bonds (G-Secs only) has decreased from 82.3% to 65.7% during the same period.

Table 6.2: Government Securities Outstanding

Year	In ₹ Crore			Share in Total (%)	
	Centre	States (SDL)	Total	Centre	States (SDL)
2002–03	6,19,105	1,33,066	7,52,171	82.3	17.7
2009–10	17,46,619	5,34,569	22,81,188	76.6	23.4
2014–15	38,91,734	12,72,103	51,63,838	75.4	24.6
2015–16	42,98,784	15,16,071	58,14,855	73.9	26.1
2016–17	46,49,487	18,57,110	65,06,597	71.5	28.5
2017–18	50,68,408	22,06107	72,74,515	69.7	30.3
2018–19	55,00,141	25,61,387	80,61,528	68.2	31.8
2019–20	59,86,127	30,58,827	90,44,954	66.2	33.8
2020–21	71,35,144	37,22,110	1,08,57,254	65.7	34.3
2021–22	80,26,725	42,35,944	1,22,62,669	65.5	34.5
2022–23	91,41,233	47,78,760	1,39,19,993	65.7	34.3

Note. Central government securities include only the dated securities and not the special securities or treasury bills; The state government securities include the UDAY bonds issued, amounting to ₹98,960 crores in FY 2016 and ₹2.1 lakh crores in FY 2017.

Source: CCIL, CMIE

6.1.4. Off-Budget Financing

The FRBM Review Committee report of 2017 observed that some states have been delivering public services, such as drinking water, schools, hospitals, and housing for the poor, through off-budget financing (e.g., Kerala Infrastructure Investment Board and Maha Infra). This means these expenditures and borrowings are not reflected in the state budget. PSUs or SPVs are used to borrow from the market to provide these services. Since the government does not directly borrow, this is not included in the state's debt or fiscal deficit. These expenditures do not require legislative approval but are subject to audits by the Comptroller and Auditor General (CAG) and additional scrutiny due to the government's explicit or implicit guarantee. Such guarantees, whether explicit or implicit, represent contingent liabilities for the states in case of a default. Debt takeover from DISCOMs under the UDAY scheme (₹2.1 lakh crore) is one such example of contingent liability. Such guarantees are not risk-free. According to RBI, while central government-guaranteed claims attract a zero-risk weight, state government-guaranteed claims carry a 20% risk weight.

Table 6.3: RBI Master Circular on Capital Adequacy and Market Discipline for Banks (2015)

Investment Provisioning	
Central Government Securities	Zero Risk weight
Central Government Guaranteed Securities	Zero Risk weight
State Government Securities	Zero Risk weight
State Government Guaranteed Securities	20% Risk weight

6.2. Issues in SDL

6.2.1. Narrow Investor Base

The investor base in SDL has improved since 1990–91, but it has not diversified significantly (Figure 6.6). In FY 1991, nearly 80% of total SDLs were owned by commercial banks. The share of commercial banks steadily declined from 78.5% in FY 1991 to 52.3% in FY 2008, and further to 35.8% in FY 2018, as the Statutory Liquidity Ratio (SLR)—the mandatory investment requirement for banks in sovereign bonds—was gradually reduced. As the share of commercial banks declined, the share of Insurance and Provident funds increased. By FY 2018, Provident and Insurance funds collectively owned about 54% of total SDLs. Consequently, almost 90% of SDLs are owned by just three investor segments: insurance companies, pension funds, and commercial banks.

Although FPIs are allowed to invest in SDLs, they have cited the lack of information on the financial position of states as one of the main reasons for their lacklustre interest in SDLs, despite the higher yields these bonds offer.

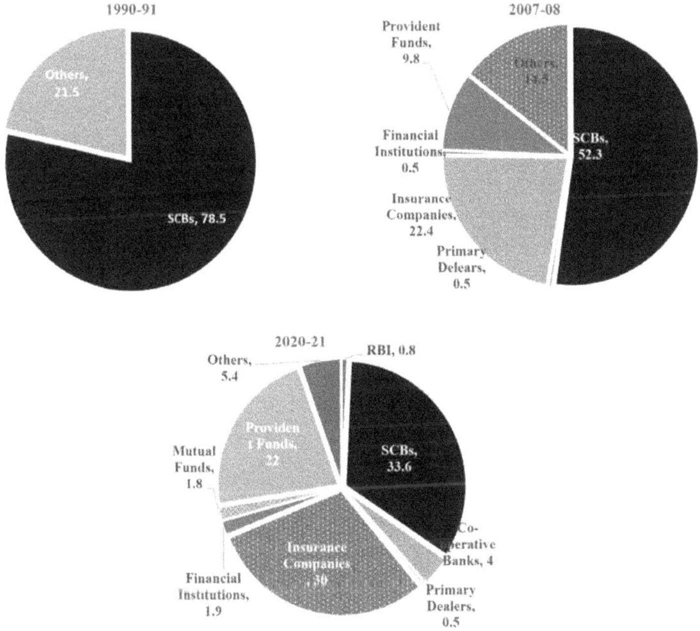

Figure 6.6: Ownership Pattern of SDLs.

6.2.2. Lack of Liquidity

The SDL market is relatively illiquid compared to central government bonds. This illiquidity is evident in Table 6.4, which shows the turnover of both central and state government bonds in the secondary market. A liquid asset is one that can be easily converted into cash in a short period of time, allowing investors to sell it quickly when they need money. In contrast, illiquid assets are difficult to sell due to low trading activity.

Before 2004–05, the share of state governments' securities in the annual turnover of the government securities market was less than 1%, while their share in outstanding government securities was around 22–23% (Table 6.4 shows the amount traded in the market in ₹ Crore and the share in total turnover). However, the share of state government securities in the total turnover improved to about 7.4% in 2022–23.

Table 6.4: Liquidity (Turnover) of Government Securities.

Year	In ₹ Crore			Share in Total (%)	
	Centre	States	Total	Centre	States
2002–03	10,32,185	6,519	10,38,704	99.4	0.63
2009–10	24,80,850	69,757	25,50,607	97.3	2.73
2014–15	91,49,608	1,83,083	93,32,691	98.0	1.96
2015–16	85,57,672	3,16,479	88,74,151	96.4	3.57
2016–17	1,51,98,472	6,02,213	1,58,00,685	96.2	3.81
2017–18	98,30,117	5,63,709	1,03,93,826	94.6	5.42
2018–19	79,07,618	5,09,050	84,16,668	94.0	6.05
2019–20	**1,12,65,755**	**6,86,469**	**1,19,52,224**	**94.3**	**5.74**
2020–21	75,96,059	5,86,295	81,82,354	92.8	7.17
2021–22	66,30,083	6,78,923	73,09,006	90.7	9.29
2022–23	80,49,756	6,42,605	86,92,361	92.6	7.39

Note: Central government dated securities and state development loans considered.

Source: RBI Annual Report, CCIL.

There are many reasons for the lack of liquidity in SDLs, including the low outstanding stock, market microstructure issues, and the absence of market makers. SDLs are often new issuances, which results in fragmentation and a lack of critical mass, limiting trading volumes.

One key factor contributing to the low liquidity is the investor base structure. In FY 2018, over half of SDL ownership was held by insurance companies (34%) and provident funds (19.7%), which typically hold the bonds until maturity. These investors do not trade in the secondary market. Similarly, banks investing in SDLs tend not to trade them due to valuation norms, preferring to hold them in the "Hold to Maturity" (HTM) category. As highlighted in the previous section, insurance, pension funds, and banks together hold almost 85% of the total outstanding SDL bonds, which are not available for trading in the secondary market. Thus, SDLs remain a relatively illiquid asset.

6.2.3. Hardening of Yields

Increased market borrowing has led to a hardening of yields. As borrowings through SDLs rise, the supply of bonds in the market goes up. When the supply of any commodity increases, its price tends to fall. This holds true for SDL bonds as well. Consequently, higher borrowing leads to a decrease in bond prices, which, in turn, causes an increase in yield, as yield is inversely related to price.

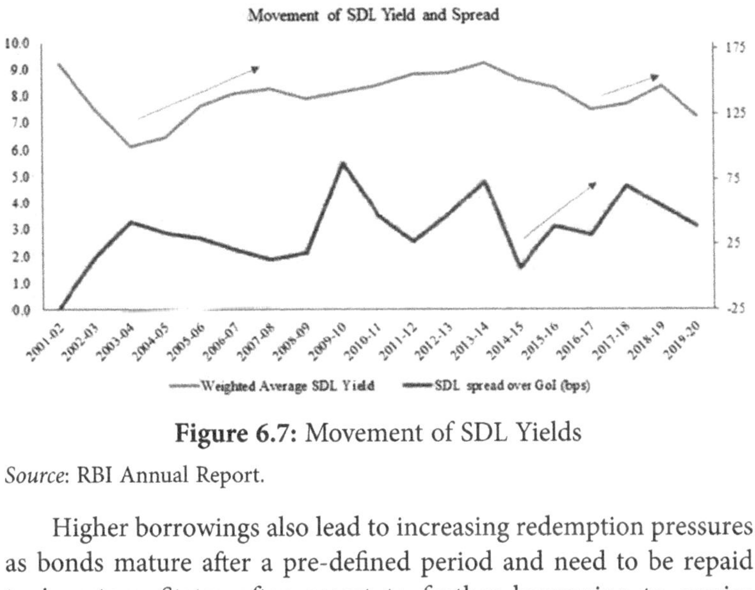

Figure 6.7: Movement of SDL Yields

Source: RBI Annual Report.

Higher borrowings also lead to increasing redemption pressures as bonds mature after a pre-defined period and need to be repaid to investors. States often resort to further borrowing to service outstanding debt (i.e., the redemption of previous bonds) and the accumulated interest burden. This creates a vicious cycle. Since the investor base for G-Secs and SDLs is almost the same, the continuous and large supply of SDLs has also contributed to the hardening of yields on central government securities.

The weighted average (cut-off) yield (WAY) of SDLs had been rising since 2016–17 till 2018–19, although it moderated in 2019–20 to 7.24%, which was about 108 bps lower than in 2018–19 (Figure 6.7). The yield of SDLs is usually higher than that of central government bonds, as SDLs are perceived to be relatively riskier. The average spread of SDL yields over central government securities of corresponding maturity increased from 39 bps in 2015–16 to 70 bps in 2017–18, indicating a rise in the cost of borrowing for the states. However, this yield spread narrowed in 2018–19 and 2019–20.

Rising yields on SDLs have a cascading effect on interest rates across other segments of the financial market, as the pricing of various products is often based on the risk-free yield curve. This leads to the crowding out of corporate bonds, as higher yields on SDLs make them more attractive to investors, reducing demand for corporate bonds.

6.3. Impact of Various Political Announcements and Reforms

6.3.1. Impact of Farm Loan Waivers

Farm loan waivers are announced by states to reduce farmers' distress by taking over their debt. In practice, banks and cooperatives waive the pending loans of beneficiary farmers upon receiving guarantees from the state. The waiver amounts are then provisioned in state budgets in a phased manner over the next few years to clear the outstanding debts. Table 6.5 gives a snapshot of the farm loan waivers announced, and the expenditures made. The farm loan waivers announced by 11 states amount to ₹2,55,260 crores.

The loan waivers have significantly increased the debt burden on these states. To manage this, states have spread the implementation of these schemes over several years to minimise the impact on their fiscal deficit. If the loan waiver is financed through borrowings, it directly increases the state's outstanding debt.

Several key points can be drawn from Table 6.5:

1. Limited Adoption: Since 2014–15, only 11 states have announced loan waiver schemes, with Jharkhand being the most recent (2020–21). Notably, these states are more prone to monsoon failures, which likely influences their decisions to announce such schemes.

Table 6.5: Farm Loan Waivers by States

Fiscal Impact of States' Farm Loan Waiver Programmes (in ₹ Crore)									
State	Announcement Year	Amount Announced	Budgeted Amount						
			2014-15	2015-16	2016-17	2017-18	2018-19	2019-20 (RE)	2020-21 (BE)
AP	2014-15	24,000	4,000	742	3,512	3,602	875	-	-
			(0.8)	-0.1	-0.5	-0.5	-0.1	-	-
Telangana	2014-15	17,000	4,250	4,250	2,957	4,016	20	6,000	6,225
			(0.8)	(0.7)	(0.4)	(0.5)	(0.0)	(0.6)	(0.6)
Tamil Nadu	2016-17	5,280	-	-	1,682	1,870	884	807	735
			-	-	(0.1)	(0.1)	(0.1)	(0.0)	(0.0)
Maharashtra	2017-18	34,020	-	-	-	15,020	3,517	-	-
			-	-	-	(0.6)	(0.1)	-	-
Maharashtra	2019-20	15,000	-	-	-	-	-	16,931	-
			-	-	-	-	-	(0.6)	-
Maharashtra	2020-21	7,000	-	-	-	-	-	-	7,001
			-	-	-	-	-	-	(0.2)
UP	2017-18	36,360	-	-	-	21,102	3,732	540	317
			-	-	-	(1.4)	(0.2)	(0.0)	(0.0)
Punjab	2017-18	10,000	-	-	-	348	4,238	2,000	2,000

Fiscal Impact of States' Farm Loan Waiver Programmes (in ₹ Crore)

State	Announcement Year	Amount Announced	Budgeted Amount						
			2014-15	2015-16	2016-17	2017-18	2018-19	2019-20 (RE)	2020-21 (BE)
			-	-	-	(0.1)	(0.8)	(0.3)	(0.3)
Karnataka	2018-19	44,000	-	-	-	3,917	12,640	5,176	441
			-	-	-	(0.3)	(0.8)	(0.3)	(0.0)
Rajasthan	2018-19	18,000	-	-	-	-	3,000	4,271	4,173
			-	-	-	-	(0.3)	(0.4)	(0.4)
MP	2018-19	36,500	-	-	-	-	-	-	-
			-	-	-	-	-	-	-
Chhattisgarh	2018-19	6,100	-	-	-	-	3,250	4,984	-
			-	-	-	-	(1.1)	(1.5)	-
Jharkhand	2020-21	2,000	-	-	-	-	-	-	2,000
			-	-	-	-	-	-	(0.5)
Total		2,55,260	8,250	4,992	8,151	49,875	32,156	40,708	22,893
Percent of states' total expenditure			0.4	0.2	0.3	1.8	1.0	1.1	0.6
Percent of GDP			0.1	0.0	0.1	0.3	0.2	0.2	0.1

RE: Revised Estimates; BE: Budget Estimates;: Not available/Not applicable.

Note: Figures in parentheses indicate loan waiver as a percentage of GSDP for the corresponding year.

Source: Budget documents of state governments, RBI report on State Finances.

2. Impressive Amounts: The quantum announced by states are impressive. A total of ₹2.55 lakh crore of waivers have been announced by all these states since FY 2015. Maharashtra alone has announced three rounds of waivers, in 2018, 2020, and 2021.

3. Expenditure Spread Over Time: The actual expenditure on these schemes is spread over a period of 3 to 5 years due to several factors: (i) non-availability of fiscal space, (ii) time needed to design and implement the schemes, (iii) time required to identify the beneficiaries, and (iv) a good monsoon in subsequent years reducing the necessity of waivers.

4. Lower Disbursements: Interestingly, the final amount disbursed is often much lower than the announced figure. For example,

(i) **Maharashtra:** The state announced a waiver of ₹34,020 crore, but only ₹ 18,540 crore was disbursed over two years, with no further expenses in the subsequent two years.

(ii) **Madhya Pradesh:** In 2018–19, the state announced ₹36,500 crore in loan waivers, yet no funds have been allocated in any of the following three budgets.

(iii) **Andhra Pradesh:** The state announced ₹24,000 crore in 2014–15, but only about 50% of this amount has been spent over the last six years.

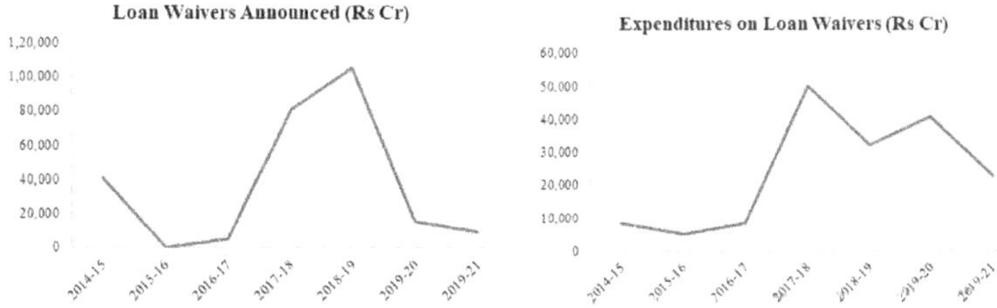

Figure 6.8: Farm Loan Waivers Announced and Expenditure

The charts above show details of the farm loan waivers announced by states and the expenditure made so far. It is seen that announcement of loan waivers by states increased significantly in the years 2017–18 and 2018–19. The expenditure, too, increased in line but by lesser amount.

It is obvious that these farm loan waivers have a strong "announcement effect" due to their large scale, as they are usually announced just before or after elections, or in response to severe farmer distress associated with droughts. However, the actual outlay or budgeted expenditure tends to be much lower.

The Agriculture Ministry has observed that loan waivers may negatively impact the credit culture by incentivising defaulters and discouraging farmers who can repay or have been making regular payments. A 2019 RBI Working Group constituted to review agricultural credit observed that loan waivers do not address the underlying causes of farm distress and can destroy the credit culture, potentially harming farmers' interests in the medium to long term. In 2019, the central government launched the Pradhan Mantri Kisan Samman Nidhi (PM-KISAN), a central income-support scheme for farmers. As farm loan waivers came under scrutiny, income support schemes for farmers, as an alternative, were for the first time announced by some state governments. The defining feature of income support schemes is that they provide cash transfers to farmers that are not linked to volume of production, factors of production employed, or market prices. Accordingly, they are categorised as Green Box payments under the Agreement on Agriculture of the World Trade Organisation (WTO). Telangana was the first state to announce an income support scheme for farmers in 2019–20.

6.3.2. Impact of Pay Commission

The wage and pension bill of the central government is about 20% of the total budgeted expenditure, while for state governments, it makes up 29% of their total expenditure. On average, roughly one-fourth of the combined budgets of state and central governments is spent on the wages, salaries, and pensions of government employees. The implementation of the Pay Commission recommendations is not always consistent across states. While some states follow their own Pay Commission rules, others adopt the central government's rules. Collectively, state governments employ more people than the central government. As a result, the fiscal impact of the Pay Commission recommendations on state budgets is substantial, leading to higher fiscal deficits and increased borrowings.

Fifth Pay Commission:

The Fifth Pay Commission was implemented in 1997–98, and as shown in the table below, its impact was spread over several years, from 1997–98 to 2000–01, rather than occurring as a one-off event (Table 6.6).

The salary, wages, and pensions of the central government (including railways) as a percentage of GDP increased from 2.7% in 1996–97 to 3.3% in 1999–00, before tapering off to 2.8% in 2001–02. On average, the fiscal impact of the Fifth Pay Commission was 0.6% of GDP per annum over four consecutive years, resulting in a cumulative impact of 2.2% of GDP for the central government. For state governments, expenditure increased from 6.8% of GSDP in 1999–00 to 7.0% in 2000–2001, before tapering off. This represented a cumulative impact of about 1% of GSDP over two years.

Table 6.6: Impact of the Fifth Pay Commission

Impact of the Fifth Pay Commission Rs Crore	1996-97	1997-98	1998-99	1999-00	2000-01	2001-02	2002-03
			Wages, Salaries and Pension				
Central Government	37,050	50,016	57,205	64,828	66,109	64,040	70,646
As % of GDP	2.7	3.2	3.2	3.3	3.1	2.8	2.8
State Governments*	91,178	99,568	1,15,576	1,35,732	1,50,776	1,52,530	1,58,812
As % of GSDP	6.4	6.3	6.4	6.8	7.0	6.5	6.3
Total	9.1	9.6	9.7	10.0	10.1	9.3	9.1

Note: For state governments, in absence of salary data, the non-plan revenue expenditure of the State government in social, economic and administrative services is taken as a proxy. * *GSDP: Gross State Domestic Products*

Source: An Economic and Functional Classification of the Central Government Budget, Government of India; RBI's report on 'State Finances: A Study of Budgets', CMIE, CPR research.

Sixth Pay Commission:

The Sixth Pay Commission was implemented in August 2008 after a delay of over two years, with the revised pay scales being applied retrospectively from 2006. This led to substantial arrear payments, along with significant salary hikes. About 40% of the arrears were paid in 2008, with the remaining 60% paid in 2009 (Table 6.7).

Table 6.7: Impact of the Sixth Pay Commission

Impact of the Sixth Pay Commission							
Rs Crore	2005-06	2006-07	2007-08	2008-09	2009-10	2010-11	2011-12
			Wages, Salaries and Pension				
Central Government	87,663	92,902	1,02,233	1,49,718	2,14,981	2,13,439	2,35,235
As % of GDP	2.4	2.2	2.1	2.7	3.4	2.8	2.7
State Governments	1,49,216	1,70,462	1,92,158	2,39,826	3,17,174	3,26,045	4,51,859
As % of GSDP	4.0	4.0	3.9	4.3	4.9	4.2	5.0
Total	6.5	6.2	6.0	7.0	8.3	7.0	7.7

Source: An Economic and Functional Classification of the Central Government Budget, Government of India; RBI's report on 'State Finances: A Study of Budgets', CMIE, CPR research.

The salary, wages, and pensions as a percentage of GDP for the central government went up to 3.4% in 2009–10 from 2.1% in 2007–08, resulting in a cumulative impact of around 1.9% over two years. Similarly, the total impact on state government was 1.4% of GSDP, spread over the same period.

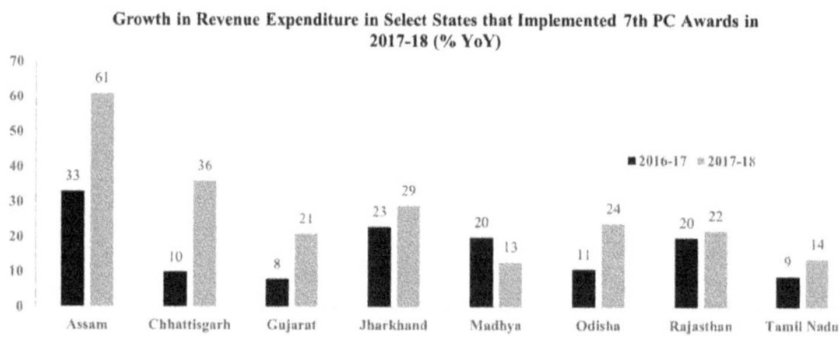

Figure 6.9: Growth in Revenue Expenditure after the Seventh Pay Commission.

Source: RBI Report on State Finances: A Study of Budgets of 2017-18 and 2018-19.

Seventh Pay Commission:

The Seventh Pay Commission recommended a 16% hike in salaries, a 63% increase in allowances, and a 24% increase in pensions, resulting in an overall hike of 23.55%, which was higher than expected. The pension hike, which amounts to 0.22% of GDP, includes an increase in the minimum pension to ₹9,000 per month from ₹3,500 and a raise of at least 2.57 times the pension for all civilians who retired or will retire prior to 1 January 2016.

Several states, including Jharkhand, Bihar, Chhattisgarh, Madhya Pradesh and Tamil Nadu, implemented the Seventh Pay Commission from 2017–18. Other states, such as Assam, Karnataka, Meghalaya, Nagaland, and Tripura, revised their emoluments as per their own Pay Commission rules. It was observed that for the states that started implementing the Pay Commission recommendations in 2017–18, there was a growth of about 28% in revenue expenditure that year.

Within revenue expenditure, the growth in wages and salaries has been particularly sharp in 2017–18 for the states that have implemented Pay Commission awards.

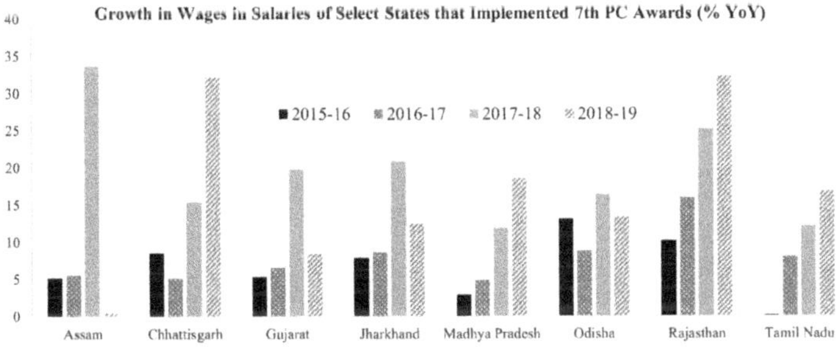

Figure 6.10: Growth in Wages and Salary after the Seventh Pay Commission.

Source: RBI Data on State Finances.

Our study suggests that the 5th CPC had a cumulative impact of 1.0% of GSDP over the two-year period from 1999–2000 to 2000–01. The impact of the 6th CPC was about 1.4% of GSDP over a similar two-year period, while the impact of the 7th CPC would be around 1% of GSDP.

6.3.3. Impact of the UDAY Scheme

Power distribution companies (DISCOMs) have continued to suffer losses primarily due to under-priced tariffs—buying power from generating companies at higher prices while selling it to consumers at lower prices set by the government—and high levels of both technical and commercial losses. As state governments own these DISCOMs, they often provide guarantees for the loans taken by them. More than 60% of the total outstanding guarantees issued by state governments are for power sector companies. If the DISCOMs default on their loan repayments, the states must either take over the loans or face negative repercussions for the banking sector.

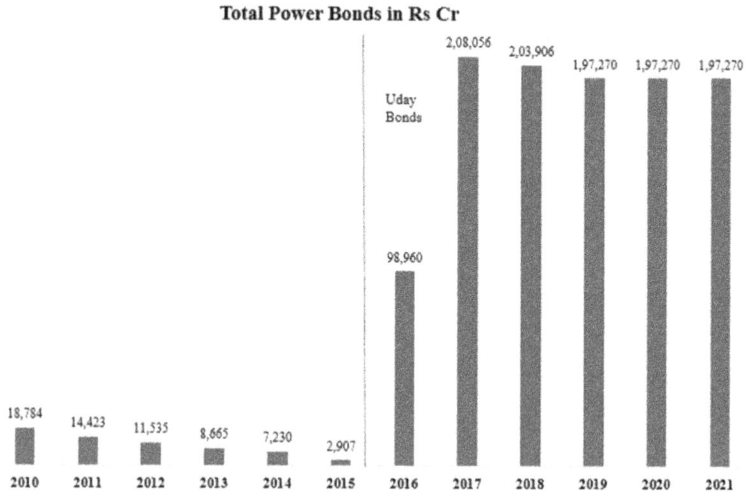

Figure 6.11: Power Bonds Issued

Source: RBI Report on State Finances.

In November 2015, the central government launched the Ujwal Discom Assurance Yojana (UDAY) to improve both the financial and operational conditions of DISCOMs. The total debt of the DISCOMs stood at ₹4.3 lakh crore as of March 2015. Under UDAY, 75% of the outstanding debt of state-owned DISCOMs was taken over by 15 state governments between 2015–16 and 2016–17. Additionally, UDAY required these states to fund a portion of the losses of DISCOMs until 2019–20. By the end of 2016–17, the share of UDAY liabilities in total outstanding debt of these 15 UDAY states on aggregate was 2.2% of their GSDP or ₹2.1 lakh crore. States were allowed to issue UDAY bonds (non-SLR) to cover these liabilities.

As shown in Figure 6.11, the issuance of UDAY bonds by states increased after 2015.

States also borrowed significantly to take over the liabilities of state power utilities under the UDAY scheme. Rajasthan, Uttar Pradesh, and Haryana are the top three issuers of UDAY bonds since FY 2016–21 (Figure 6.12).

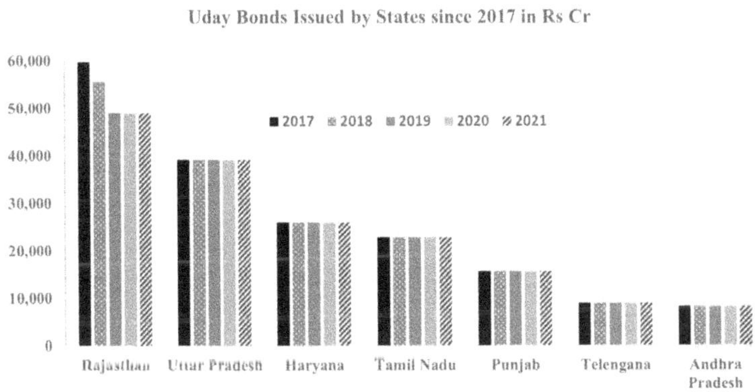

Figure 6.12: Power Bonds Issued by Select States

Source: RBI Report on State Finances.

Between 2015–16 and 2017–18, the aggregate losses of state DISCOMs declined. However, losses began to rise again after that. The overdue payments to power producers increased from ₹57,352 crores in March 2019 to ₹94,598 crores in March 2020, marking a rise of 65%.

The UDAY liabilities of states on aggregate are estimated to be 1.5% of their GSDP at the end of 2019–20 (Figure 6.13). States like Rajasthan (4.8%), Haryana (3.3%), Punjab (2.7%), and Uttar Pradesh (2.5%) have UDAY liabilities higher than the average, as a percentage of their GSDP. Together, these four states account for about 65% of the total UDAY liabilities of all states.

The lockdown, imposed because of COVID-19, further deteriorated the situation, as DISCOMs faced a severe liquidity crunch. In June 2020, the government announced a liquidity infusion scheme, offering loans worth ₹90,000 crores (0.42% of GDP), guaranteed by state governments, to help DISCOMs clear their outstanding dues to power producers. The RBI (2020) stated that while liquidity infusion schemes may provide short-term relief, another round of bailouts for loss-making DISCOMs as a result of this crisis could increase the long-term burden on state finances.

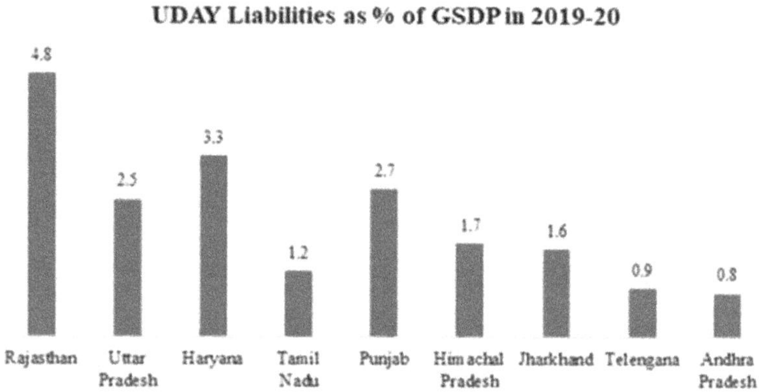

Figure 6.13: UDAY Liabilities as % of GSDP for Select States

6.3.4. GST and State Finances

The Goods and Services Tax (GST), a significant structural reform introduced in July 2017, subsumed 17 different central and state taxes, including excise duty and VAT, to bring the entire country under one indirect tax rate. With the implementation of GST, states transferred a major part of their taxation powers to the GST Council. The principle of indirect taxation for goods and services shifted from an origin-based to a destination-based system. In other words, the taxation of goods and services moved from the origin or producing states to the destination or consuming states. This shift, along with changes in the GST tax slabs compared to earlier tax rates, led to revenue uncertainty for states. This uncertainty was addressed through constitutional amendments and the GST (Compensation to States) Act, 2017. Under the GST law, states were guaranteed full compensation for any revenue loss during the first five years following the GST implementation in July 2017. Any gap between the actual revenue collected and projected revenue would be compensated by the centre. The projected revenue was estimated based on a 14% annual growth rate over the states' last tax receipts in the base year of 2015–16. The full compensation to the states was expected to be paid until FY 2022 through the compensation fund, which was financed by the levy of GST compensation cess on select items. The compensation cess, or surcharge, ranged from 12% to 200% on top of the highest GST rate of 28% for luxury and sin goods such as cars and tobacco products. Thus, this Cess would compensate the states for any revenue loss on account of the implementation of GST.

The states received full GST compensation during the first three years of GST implementation. Unlike in 2017–18 and 2018–19, the amount transferred to states in 2019–20 was higher than the collections for the year as shown in Table 6.8. GST compensation Cess for subsequent years are discussed below.

Table 6.8: GST Compensation Cess (in ₹ Crore)

	2017–18	**2018–19**	**2019–20**
Compensation Cess Collected	62,612	95,081	95,444
Compensation Cess Transferred to States	48,785	81,141	1,65,302

The centre could not provide GST compensation to the states in FY 2020–21 due to Covid-related economic slowdown, as tax collection fell short of estimates. The centre estimated that the compensation required by the states in FY 2021 would be ₹3 lakh crore, of which ₹65,000 crore was expected to be met from the cess levied, resulting in a shortfall of ₹2.35 lakh crore. Of this, ₹97,000 crore was on account of GST shortfall, while the rest was due to the impact of COVID-19 on the economy. The centre, initially, asked the states to borrow the compensation amount arising from the implementation of the GST. Many states were unhappy with the proposal and wanted the centre to borrow the entire amount. The centre eventually agreed to their suggestion and borrowed the amount to be transferred to the states. This is discussed in detail in the next section on "Impact of Covid".

The honourable Finance Minister announced that the Government of India has released ₹86,912 crore to states and UTs, clearing the entire provisionally admissible GST compensation due till May 2022. This was done to help the states in managing their resources and ensuring that their capital expenditure for the fiscal year 2022–23 is carried out without any problem. It was also highlighted that the decision to release the entire amount was taken even though only about ₹25,000 crore was available in the GST Compensation Fund. The balance of ₹62,000 crore was released by the centre from its resources, pending the collection of cesses.

The GST collections have been buoyant in recent months, driven by ongoing reforms in the GST system based on recommendations from the GST Council, as well as improving economic activities post-COVID. The average monthly gross GST collection for the first quarter of FY 2023 stood at ₹1.51 lakh crore, compared to ₹1.10 lakh crore in the first quarter of the previous financial year, reflecting an increase of 37%.

The 14th Finance Commission (2015–20) increased the share of states in the divisible pool of central Gross Tax Revenue (GTR) from 32% to 42%. Excluding the union territories of Ladakh and Jammu & Kashmir, the tax devolution share was 41% of the total divisible pool. An important point to note here is that central cesses and surcharges are not part of the divisible tax pool. In other words, states cannot claim any part of the cesses or surcharges imposed by the central government, such as the education cess. The 15th Finance Commission (FC) aimed for continuity and predictability, retaining the same tax devolution share to states at 41%. However, it has been pointed out by experts that "cess and surcharge" which was 10.4% of Gross Tax Revenue (GTR) in 2011–12, has increased to 20.2% in 2019–20. Even after deducting the GST compensation cess, it still accounts for 15%. This means that the share of cesses and surcharges is growing while the divisible pool is shrinking. As a result, only 85% of the central government's gross tax revenue in 2019–20 contributed to the divisible pool. Consequently, the states' 42% share in the divisible pool, as recommended by the 14th FC, effectively comes down to 35.7% of the centre's tax receipts in 2019–20. To change the treatment of cesses and surcharges, constitutional amendments are required.

6.4. Impact of COVID

6.4.1. Triple Whammy for States due to COVID

The COVID-19 pandemic and eventual lockdown in 2020 severely impacted state finances. States are squeezed on three fronts. First, the lockdowns and economic slowdown have significantly reduced their already limited tax revenues. Second, "health" being a state subject, state governments have been at the forefront of the pandemic response, leading to a substantial increase in COVID-related expenditures. These expenses include building healthcare infrastructure, setting up COVID centres, procuring Personal Protection Equipment (PPE), ventilators, medical kits, providing extra hospital beds and medications, and conducting large-scale testing. Moreover, states also had to take care of the migrants returning home and arrange for their travel and quarantine stay at state expense. Almost 45% of state expenditures are committed to fixed costs such as salaries, pensions, and interest payments, which cannot be slashed. Thus, there is hardly any leeway to accommodate the increased COVID-related expenditures without diverting funds from other important developmental projects. Finally, the COVID lockdown-related economic slump has reduced revenue and cess collection of the central government too. Under these circumstances, states are looking to the centre to alleviate their financial crunch, while the centre itself faces limited fiscal space.

During the COVID pandemic, state governments' expenditure on subsidies grew by 12.9% and 11.2% during 2020–21 and 2021–22, respectively, after contracting in 2019–20. Some state governments started delivering a portion of their subsidies in the form of freebies (Table 6.9). These freebies have exceeded 2% of GSDP for some of the highly indebted states, such as Andhra Pradesh and Punjab.

The RBI report published in June 2022 states that while there is no precise definition of "freebies", certain provisions such as free electricity, free water, free public transportation, waiver of pending utility bills, and farm loan waivers are often regarded as such. These freebies can potentially undermine credit culture, distort prices through cross-subsidisation, erode incentives for private investment, and disincentivise work at current wage rates, leading to a drop in labour force participation. This has increased the fiscal risks of some of the states in India.

Table 6.9: Freebies Announced by the States in 2022–23.

States	As a percentage of GSDP	As a percent of Revenue Receipts	As a percent of Own Tax Revenue
Andhra Pradesh	2.1	14.1	30.3
Bihar	0.1	0.6	2.7
Haryana	0.1	0.6	0.9
Jharkhand	1.7	8.0	26.7
Kerala	0.0	0.0	0.1
Madhya Pradesh	1.6	10.8	28.8
Punjab	2.7	17.8	45.4
Rajasthan	0.6	3.9	8.6
West Bengal	1.1	9.5	23.8

Source: Budget documents of the state government, RBI report.

As the expenditure on social welfare schemes (in the form of freebies) is often funded through additional borrowings, this exerts upward pressures on yields and increases borrowing costs. State governments need to prioritise their expenditures to achieve optimal long-term welfare benefits by ensuring that beneficiaries are empowered permanently, rather than remaining dependent on state-provided freebies. Also, states should ensure that there is a sunset clause for each social sector scheme. Reducing the quantum of non-merit subsidies will free up resources to invest in health, education, agriculture, R&D, and rural infrastructure, which will help create more jobs and reduce poverty on a sustainable basis (Gulati, 2022).

6.4.2. Policy Responses to States' Financial Stress and Hardening SDL Yields

The FRBM Act limits borrowing by the states to 3% of their Gross State Domestic Product (GSDP). In May 2020, the central government relaxed these limits for states due to revenue constraints and enhanced expenditure commitments caused by the COVID-19 pandemic. States were allowed additional borrowings of up to 2% of GSDP, subject to certain conditional reforms. The additional borrowing was structured as follows: the first 0.5 percentage point (₹1.07 lakh crore) was made available to all states unconditionally, while the next 1 percentage point was to be disbursed in four equal tranches, each tied to "clearly specified, measurable, and feasible reform actions." The remaining 0.5 percentage point was to be accessed by states, subject to their "completely achieving" the milestones in at least three out of the four reform areas. These areas included the one-nation-one ration card scheme, ease of doing business, reforms of power sector distribution companies, and reforms of urban local bodies. However, not many states were able to achieve the reform targets within the short time frame.

In the GST Council's 42nd meeting in October 2020, the centre accepted the states' estimate of the GST shortfall amount at ₹1.10 lakh crore to be filled by market borrowing. The GST Council also decided to extend the surcharge on taxes on luxury goods beyond the originally mandated date of June 2022 to repay the borrowings. As a result, the central government notified a four-year extension of the GST compensation cess until June 2026. The honourable Finance Minister announced that the interest on the borrowed amount would be paid from the cess collected. Fifty percent of the remaining funds would be used towards paying the principal amount borrowed, while the other fifty percent would be towards COVID-affected compensation. However, the centre's suggestion that states should borrow to cover the shortfall was not accepted by the states.

Finally, the centre decided to borrow an additional ₹1.1 lakh crore in tranches during the second half of FY 2020–21 to provide compensation to states for the shortfall in their revenue due to the GST implementation. This amount would be passed on to the states as a loan, instead of GST compensation cess releases, and would reflect as capital receipts in state governments' finances, contributing to their respective fiscal deficits. The centre borrowed ₹1.1 lakh crore in 2020–21 and ₹1.59 lakh crore in 2021–22 as back-to-back loans to meet a portion of the shortfall in cess collection.

The revenue collected through the levy of GST Compensation cess on luxury goods is expected to cover the entire shortfall and service the back-to-back loans released to the states to meet their shortfall in compensation.

The SDL yields and spreads started rising in the second quarter of FY 2021, driven by concerns over higher state government borrowings due to revenue shortfalls. To address these concerns in the bond market, the RBI, in its Monetary Policy Statement in October 2020, broke new ground and allowed OMO in SDLs to improve secondary market liquidity and lower SDL yield spreads over corresponding G-Secs. The first ever SDL OMO of ₹10,000 crore was conducted on 22 October 2020.

6.5. Risk Asymmetry in SDLs

Following the recommendations of the 12th Finance Commission, states were allowed to borrow directly from the market. It was hoped that the investors would scrutinise the fiscal health of the states, which would, in turn, encourage better fiscal management by offering lower borrowing costs. However, surprisingly until FY 2017, the cut-off yields of SDLs in primary auctions remained narrowly clustered, despite variations in fiscal performance. States with better fiscal parameters had expressed disappointment that the market did not provide any incentive for better performance on fiscal front. This issue regarding risk asymmetries across states eventually attracted policy attention.

The Economic Survey 2016–17 highlighted a lack of correlation between the yield on state government bonds and their debt or deficit positions. Moreover, the FRBM Review Committee Report titled "Responsible Growth: A Debt and Fiscal Framework for 21st Century India," published in January 2017, stated that despite SDL borrowing rates being market-determined, it is felt that risk asymmetries across states are not adequately reflected in the cost of borrowings. The report observed that several well-managed states with strong fiscal performance expressed dissatisfaction, stating that they are not adequately compensated for better management of their fiscal discipline. Furthermore, it pointed out that there seems to be an element of cross-subsidisation, with financially stronger states effectively subsidising weaker ones, which is akin to financial repression.

A 2017 study on SDL yields by Ghose, Padhi, and Parida (group chief economic adviser and economists in SBI) found that market variables related to market microstructure were significantly correlated with SDL yields. The study revealed that states that frequently borrowed from the market with larger ticket sizes were able to attract better yields compared to those states that relied less on SDLs.

Mr. B.P. Kanungo, former Deputy Governor of RBI, in his speech[2] in August 2018, highlighted several measures taken by the RBI to address credit risk asymmetry. These measures included:

- Conducting weekly auctions of SDLs since 24 October 2017, to prevent the bunching of issuances.
- Publishing high-frequency data in the RBI Monthly Bulletin, relating to the buffers that state governments maintain with the RBI, their market borrowings, and the outstanding SDLs, thereby enhancing transparency essential for deepening the SDL market.
- Incentivising state governments to have their SDLs rated by credit rating agencies by allowing lower initial margin requirements for rated SDLs. The margin for rated SDLs would be set at 1% lower than that for unrated SDLs within the same maturity buckets.

The RBI has been actively working with state governments to address risk asymmetries across states. In recent years, states with better fiscal indicators have been rewarded by the market in terms of lower borrowing costs (or lower yields).

2. Keynote Address by Shri B.P. Kanungo, Deputy Governor, Reserve Bank of India, at the Financial Market Conclave of the Bengal Chamber of Commerce and Industry, Mumbai, on 31st August, 2018.

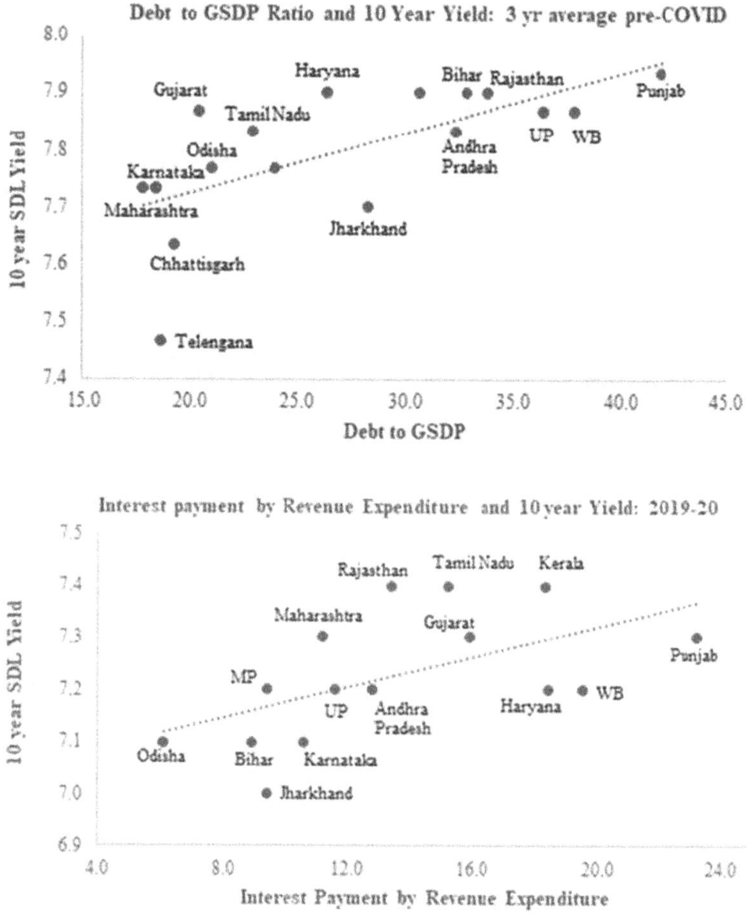

Figure 6.14: Key Fiscal Indicators and 10-Year SDL Yields

Source: Reserve Bank of India.

It has been observed that there is a direct relationship between the fiscal performance of states and their SDL yields, even though the yields across different states remain closely clustered. We have plotted fiscal indicators, such as the Debt-to-GSDP ratio and interest payments as a percentage of Revenue Expenditure, against 10-year SDL yields, as shown in Chart 7.14. A higher Debt-to-GSDP ratio indicates fiscal unsustainability, while a high interest payment to revenue expenditure ratio suggests that a large part of the state's expenditure is dedicated to servicing outstanding debt, leaving less for developmental work and potentially harming long-term growth prospects. It is seen that both scatter plots have an upward trend, indicating that fiscally weaker states—those with higher Debt-to-GSDP ratios and higher interest payment to revenue receipts ratios—tend to have higher SDL yields (Chart 6.14). The first chart uses a three-year average data set prior to the COVID-19 pandemic, while the second is based on data from the post-COVID year of 2019–20. In other words, states with higher deficits, growing liabilities, and poor debt sustainability tend to face higher borrowing costs (higher SDL yields).

Since SDLs do not have credit ratings, these debt ratios play an important role and are used by market participants to determine SDL yields. Therefore, it is essential for states to consolidate their fiscal position in order to reduce their borrowing costs.

6.6. Current Status of State-Level Debts

A recent report by the RBI (A Study of Budgets of 2024–25) highlights that State governments have made commendable progress after pandemic towards fiscal consolidation by containing their aggregate gross fiscal deficit within 3 percent of GDP for three consecutive years (2021–22 to 2023–24), while restricting revenue deficit at 0.2 percent of GDP in 2022–23 and 2023–24. This has allowed the States to scale up their capital spending and improve the quality of expenditure. However, several Indian states are experiencing significant economic stress. As shown in Table 6.9, Punjab, Himachal Pradesh and Andhra Pradesh had the highest revenue deficits in FY 2023, at 3.8%, 3.3%, and 3.3% of their Gross State Domestic Product (GSDP), respectively (excluding the special states of the Northeast and Union Territories). Additionally, Himachal Pradesh, Bihar and Punjab are among the states with high gross fiscal deficits. Punjab is also notable for having high Non-Development Expenditures and low Development Expenditures as a share of total expenditures.

Another important indicator is the proportion of a state's revenue receipts spent on servicing debt—specifically, the ratio of interest payments to revenue receipts. On the whole, 12.6% of the revenue receipts of all states and UTs in FY 2023 were spent to pay interest on their debt. Among the major states, Odisha performed the best, paying only 3.7% of its revenue receipts on interest payments in FY 2023. On the other hand, the worst-performing states—those that allocated about a fifth of their revenue receipts to service debt—included Punjab, Haryana, Kerala and West Bengal. The data, moreover, shows that Punjab has the highest share of interest payments in its revenue expenditure. In 2022–23, the interest payment of Punjab was almost double the national average of 12.6%, reaching 22.7%. Other states above the national average included Haryana (22.5%), West Bengal (20.5%), Tamil Nadu (19.2%), Kerala (19.0%), and Andhra Pradesh (16.2%).

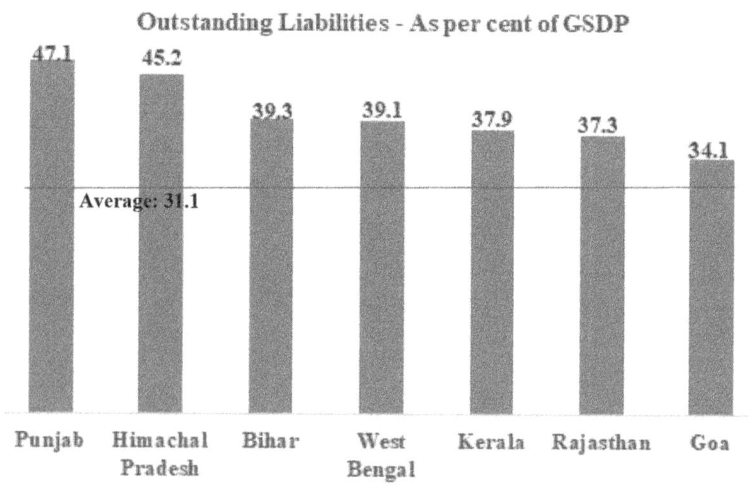

Figure 6.15: States with higher than National Average of Outstanding Liabilities (FY 2022–23)

Source: RBI Data.

Table 6.9: Fiscal Indicator of States (FY 2022-23).

No	States	RD/ GSDP	GFD/ GSDP	Development Expenditure/ Total Exp.	Non-Developmental Expenditure/ Total Exp.	Interest Payment/ Revenue Receipt
1	Andhra Pradesh	3.3	4.0	64.8	28.3	16.2
2	Arunachal Pradesh	-18.1	5.0	71.6	26.3	3.5
3	Assam	2.5	5.9	67.2	30.1	7.7
4	Bihar	1.5	6.0	68.2	25.6	8.8
5	Chhattisgarh	-1.9	1.0	68.3	21.8	6.8
6	Goa	-2.7	1.2	63.5	30.2	10.5
7	Gujarat	-0.9	0.8	64.5	26.0	12.7
8	Haryana	1.7	3.2	52.8	29.0	22.5
9	Himachal Pradesh	3.3	6.5	60.3	33.5	12.7
10	J & K	-2.7	2.2	53.4	41.4	12.3
11	Jharkhand	-3.2	1.1	66.3	26.3	7.8
12	Karnataka	-0.6	2.1	67.9	25.3	12.4
13	Kerala	0.9	2.5	43.8	39.6	19.0
14	Madhya Pradesh	-0.3	3.3	68.0	20.8	9.5
15	Maharashtra	0.1	1.9	59.2	25.9	10.3
16	Manipur	-4.3	4.4	58.2	37.3	5.5

No	States	RD/ GSDP	GFD/ GSDP	Development Expenditure/ Total Exp.	Non-Developmental Expenditure/ Total Exp.	Interest Payment/ Revenue Receipt
17	Meghalaya	0.1	6.0	63.3	26.8	6.9
18	Mizoram	-0.6	3.6	63.8	33.3	4.8
19	Nagaland	-1.9	4.2	52.3	43.0	7.0
20	Odisha	-2.6	2.0	64.0	27.4	3.7
21	Punjab	3.8	5.0	35.6	30.4	22.7
22	Rajasthan	2.3	3.8	65.1	27.1	15.7
23	Sikkim	-1.1	4.5	65.4	32.0	8.9
24	Tamil Nadu	1.5	3.4	58.4	28.3	19.2
25	Telangana	-0.5	2.5	69.1	25.1	13.7
26	Tripura	-0.8	2.1	57.9	35.8	7.5
27	Uttar Pradesh	-1.6	2.8	62.5	29.5	10.3
28	Uttarakhand	-1.7	1.0	56.2	32.9	10.4
29	West Bengal	1.8	3.3	60.0	29.0	20.5
30	NCT Delhi	-1.4	-0.4	71.9	14.0	5.2
31	Puducherry	-1.5	-0.8	59.0	27.3	8.2

Source: RBI report.

With revenue falling due to slowing growth during FY 2020 and FY 2021, many state governments were being forced to compromise on welfare schemes to meet committed expenditures, such as interest payments, pensions, and salaries. Additionally, two years of COVID-related expenditures further added to their liabilities. However, states have managed to perform better fiscally post-COVID.

According to RBI data, the total outstanding liabilities of six states (excluding the Northeastern states)—Punjab, Himachal Pradesh, Bihar, West Bengal, Kerala, and Rajasthan (Figure 6.15)—exceeded the national average of 31.1% in FY 2022–23. Too much debt restricts the state's ability to take up welfare or development works.

It has already been observed that several states allocate higher capital outlay or development expenditure. Higher capital expenditure helps states to develop assets that can increase revenue receipts in the future. On the other extreme, Punjab and Kerala have higher non-development expenditures.

Many state finances are showing signs of severe distress, particularly due to populist measures. It has been highlighted by the RBI that the precarious fiscal position of Punjab is a result of such measures. In certain states, a major share of subsidies is provided for supplying free or low-cost electricity. For instance, over 95% of the total subsidies in Punjab and Rajasthan were provided for the electricity sector. In a report by the chief economic adviser of the State Bank of India, it has been specified that the freebies offered by these states are "economically unsustainable," and that some states are "living beyond their means".

In 25 July 2024, Supreme Court granted States the authority to impose taxes on minerals and land containing minerals as well as to claim royalty payments retrospectively from 1 April 2005. These tax payments would be spread over 12 years starting from April 2026. This is expected to significantly benefit mineral-rich States such as Andhra Pradesh, Chhattisgarh, Jharkhand, Karnataka, Odisha, Madhya Pradesh, Maharashtra, Tamil Nadu and Telangana. Jharkhand was the first State to levy taxes following the order, proposing a cess of ₹100 per tonne for coal and iron ore, ₹70 for bauxite, and ₹50 for manganese ore and other minerals.

It is worth mentioning that Odisha stands out among states in managing to improve its fiscal health significantly in the last two decades. It was one of the most fiscally stressed States in the early 2000s, with a debt-GSDP ratio at 57.3% in 2002–03 (vs. 32.1% for all States) and the interest payments to revenue receipts ratio (IP/RR) at 34.2 percent. Strategic revenue and expenditure management have strengthened Odisha's public finances, with the debt-GSDP ratio declining to 16.0% in 2023–24, the lowest among the Indian States. The interest payments to revenue receipts ratio in FY 2023–24 declined to 3.6%. The state of Odisha has a Budget Stabilisation Fund. The fund is administered by the RBI and is funded from the surplus in Odisha's revenue account. It is designed to act as a strategic reserve to offset any decline in mining revenue. This is expected to help Odisha in maintaining financial stability and a certain level of expenditure. As on 31 March 2023, the fund had a corpus of more than ₹13,000 crore.

6.7. Way Forward

According to International Monetary Fund (IMF), India's GDP in 2025 is likely to be $4.2 trillion, marginally higher than that of Japan. Thus, India is the fourth largest economy of the world in 2025 after the US, China and Germany. It is expected to be the third largest economy of the world in 2028. Development and reforms are continuous and iterative processes. Since 2003, state governments have taken various steps to improve fiscal and debt management. All states have enacted the FRBM Act and even managed to achieve the mandated targets. There is an institutional commitment to fiscal prudence that helped achieve debt sustainability. However, we have witnessed fiscal slippages in the past in several states. During the 2017–21 period, 14 states, on average, crossed the prescribed 3% limit for fiscal deficit (FD) as a percentage of GSDP. Rising fiscal deficits and increased state government borrowings, coupled with low liquidity and a narrow investor base, against the backdrop of already high central government borrowings, can have significant macroeconomic implications. The situation worsened since 2020. The burden of high COVID-19-related expenditures of states with declining revenues has stretched fiscal space significantly. The fiscal health of states and their increased market borrowings (SDLs) can have an adverse impact on investment and the growth of the economy.

It is well-known that SDLs carry no credit risk, as they are considered sovereign, and states have the power to impose taxes to increase revenues. The absence of credit risk is reflected in the zero-risk weight assigned to SDLs held by commercial banks in the calculation of their Capital to Risk Assets Ratio (CRAR) under the Basel III capital regulations, just like central government bonds. There has been no default on SDLs to date. In addition, states are required to maintain a consolidated sinking fund (CSF) with the RBI to provide a cushion for the amortisation of market borrowings. These factors help enhance investor confidence in SDLs, which may explain why their yields are clustered within a narrow band.

In a statement issued by the RBI in June 2022, the central bank underlined the fiscal risks confronting several state governments in India. The RBI even referred to the economic crisis in Sri Lanka, pointing to warning signs of rising fiscal stress in state finances. Factors such as the slowdown in own tax revenue, a high share of committed expenditure, ballooning overdue of DISCOMs, and rising subsidy burdens—including rising expenditures on non-merit freebies—have further strained state government finances, which were already exacerbated by COVID-19. The RBI specifically warned that for the five most indebted states—Bihar, Kerala, Punjab, Rajasthan and West Bengal—their debt stock is no longer sustainable, as debt growth has outpaced their Gross State Domestic Product (GSDP) growth over the last five years.

There was a need to bring states back onto the fiscal consolidation path after the pandemic. States were provided encouragement, incentives, and hand-holdings to get adjusted to the new normal. Economic development depends on effective debt management by the states. Risk should be assessed in its entirety, taking into account debt sustainability, the reforms initiated, and the fiscal prudence indicators of the states.

The RBI is already working with states to build a robust SDL market and streamline debt management to address emerging risks. The RBI has started publishing SDL-related and other state-specific fiscal data regularly. Stakeholders, including both domestic and foreign investors, need to actively utilise these data to make informed investment decisions. Fiscally prudent states need to be rewarded with lower borrowing costs.

While these are top-down approaches, there is also a need for bottom-up strategies. State governments should proactively engage with both domestic and foreign investors by holding investor meetings. The effort by the Odisha government to bring in more transparency by acknowledging, assessing, and preparing for unforeseen credit risks is a welcome move. In addition, fiscally prudent states can take the lead by getting their state SDLs rated by reputed credit rating agencies. These ratings should be made public, allowing states to benefit from lower cut-off yields in auctions based on higher ratings. There should be a clear distinction between developmental and non-developmental expenditure. A few states should adopt a long-term perspective and avoid falling for populist measures for short-term gains. For example, P. Thiaga Rajan, the former and dynamic finance minister of Tamil Nadu, quickly recognised the state's biggest challenge—its debt—and began working on restructuring it.

The RBI has stated that "Overall, while the State governments have made progress in fiscal consolidation, there is scope for further improvement in expenditure efficiency, outcome and climate/green budget, uniform and more transparent data reporting and use of modern techniques like artificial intelligence and machine learning."

CHAPTER 7

Growing Popularity of Municipal Bonds in India

Municipal bonds (commonly referred to as "Muni bonds") are debt instruments issued by municipal corporations, local government bodies, provinces, cities, districts, and other associated bodies to raise funds. Just like other debt instruments, Muni bonds, too, have a fixed maturity period, and investors can earn a fixed interest rate on them. These bonds can either be short-term, with a maturity of one to three years, or long-term, with a maturity of up to ten years. The local bodies repay the interest and principal on these bonds using revenues collected from sources such as property taxes, professional taxes, or the revenues generated from specific projects.

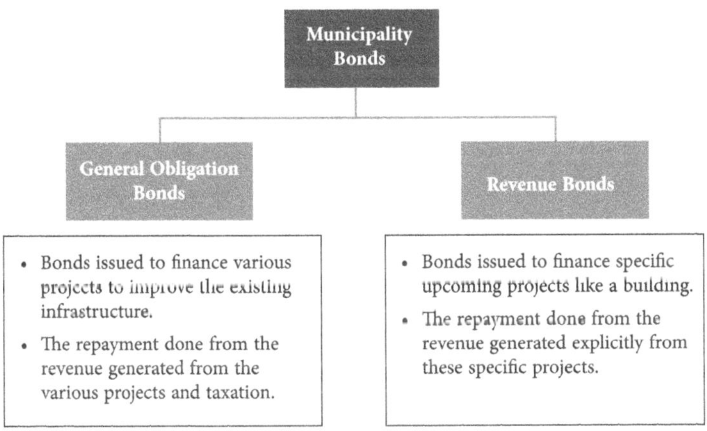

Figure 7.1: Types of Municipality Bonds

In India, there are generally two types of municipal bonds: General Obligation Bonds and Revenue Bonds.

Local government bodies, such as urban municipalities, can issue municipal bonds to raise funds for socio-economic development projects like roads, airports, railway stations, schools, hospitals, parks, bridges, and more within their jurisdiction. The Muni bonds in India are rated by credit rating agencies prior to being issued to the public, making them a relatively safe investment option. In India, municipal bonds can be purchased by investors through dealers, banks, brokerage firms, or sometimes directly from the municipality.

The advantages of investing in municipal bonds are:

1. **Transparency**: These bonds are rated by credit rating agencies, enhancing their transparency and credibility. These bonds must have a rating above the investment grade for the public issue. The primary motive of credit rating is to substantiate and popularise the bonds' credibility, building investors' confidence in them.
2. **Low Risk**: Issued by municipal authorities and often backed by state guarantees, these bonds tend to have lower risks.
3. **Tax Benefits**: In India, municipal bonds are exempted from taxation, provided the investor complies with certain stipulated rules. Additionally, the interests generated from these bonds is also tax-exempt.
4. **Predictable Income:** Most municipal bonds pay interest twice a year, giving investors a clear understanding of how much income to expect and when.
5. **Opportunity to Invest Locally:** Municipal bonds allow investors to support projects that directly benefit their community. Investors may have more information about the issuing municipality or feel personally connected to the funded projects.

However, there are a few disadvantages of investing in municipal bonds:

1. **Long Maturity**: Municipal bonds typically have a lock-in period of three years, which reduces liquidity for investors.

2. **Slow Secondary Market**: The secondary market for municipal bonds is not very active, making it challenging to sell these bonds prematurely. Additionally, there exists uncertainty about their yielding capacity.
3. **Low Returns**: The returns generated by municipal bonds are generally lower than those from other market-linked instruments.

Investors in municipal bonds face risks similar to those of other bond investors, including credit risk, interest rate risk, currency risk, liquidity risk and call risk.

7.1. Evolution of Municipal Bonds in India

Municipal bonds were first issued in India in 1997, five years after the 74th Constitutional Amendment, which decentralised urban local bodies (ULBs), granting them autonomy, accountability to citizens, and financial reforms that enabled them to access capital markets and FIs. Thus, we can say that the municipal bonds have only been in existence in India since 1997.

Between 1997 and 2010, city corporations in Bengaluru, Ahmedabad, Nashik, and Madurai experimented with bond issues, raising only about ₹1,400 crores. The poor investor response was due to the fact that these bonds were privately placed, not tradable in the secondary market, and lacked regulatory clarity. As a result, no new issues were made after 2010.

To revive the municipality bond market and attract investors by making these bonds safer for investment, the SEBI issued detailed guidelines for the issuance and listing of municipal bonds in March 2015, clarifying their regulatory status. The guidelines include:

1. **No History of Defaulting**: The Municipal body must not have a history of defaulting on loan repayments or debt securities acquired from banks or FIs in the past year.
2. **Positive Net Worth**: The municipal body must possess positive net worth for each of the three years preceding the issuance of municipal bonds.

3. **Wilful Defaulters' List**: Municipal entities, their group companies, directors, and promoters must not be mentioned in the wilful defaulters' list published by the RBI. Also, such entities or individuals should not have defaulted on any payments of interest or principal on public debt instruments.
4. **Rating:** The bonds should have a minimum investment-grade rating and a minimum tenure of 3 years.
5. **Minimum Subscription:** In case of non-receipt of the minimum subscription, all application money must be refunded within a time period of 12 days.
6. **Contribution to Project Cost:** Municipalities need to contribute at least 20% of the project cost. They must also ensure full asset coverage to repay the principal amount if required.
7. **Escrow Account:** Revenues generated by the municipalities must be deposited into a separate escrow account, which is to be supervised by banks or FIs.

The amended regulations of SEBI allow SPVs set up for implementing smart city projects to raise funds through municipal bonds (Muni Bonds). This move will facilitate investment in the public infrastructure of the 100 smart cities proposed by the Government of India (GOI). The SEBI regulations define the terms, conditions, and requirements for social issues, including employment standards, credit rating, minimum registration, accounting, auditing, reporting obligations, and other disclosures.

In 2017, the Pune Municipal Corporation (PMC) became the first local body in India to issue municipal bonds in nearly one and a half decades, raising ₹200 crores for its smart city project. Since then, several urban municipalities have successfully raised funds through Muni bonds.

Figure 7.2 summarises the important points in the evolution of municipality bonds in India.

Figure 7.2: Inflection Points in the History of Municipality Bonds in India

7.2. Municipal Bonds Issued by Few Cities in India

The Bangalore Municipal Corporation (BMC) was the first city council in India to issue municipal bonds, raising Rs 125 crores in 1997. The Ahmedabad Municipal Corporation (AMC) followed in 1998 with its first public offering, raising ₹100 crores—making it the first municipal bond issue in Southeast Asia.

Table 7.1 below highlights some of the major municipal bonds issued by various urban municipal bodies following the SEBI guidelines in 2015. A new era dawned in 2017 with the launch of the Pune Municipal Corporation (PMC) bonds.

Table 7.1: Municipal Bodies and Muni Bonds Issued.

Municipal Body		Amount (in ₹ Crores)	Description
Pune Municipal Corporation (PMC)	June, 2017	200	History created by PMC as it launched India's largest municipal bond program (rated AA+) after a long break in 2017, raising ₹200 crores for its smart city project. Listed in BSE. It was oversubscribed six times, with domestic insurers, pension funds, and large state-owned banks invested. PMC proposes to increase water tax to raise revenue. The scheme aims to provide water for all the citizens of Maharashtra's second-biggest city. ₹300 crores will be invested for a reservoir, ₹700 crores for putting meters, and ₹1,800 crores for getting the distribution network.
Greater Hyderabad Municipal Corporation (GHMC)	Feb, 2018	200	GHMC successfully raised ₹200 crores as the first tranche to fund the Strategic Road Development Plan (SRDP). Bonds listed on BSE.
Indore Municipal Corporation (IMC)	June, 2018	140	IMC, rated as AA (SO), or two notches lower than the top grade, raised about ₹140 crores by selling bonds, which offered 9.25% with 10-year maturity. Funds were raised for new-generation urban clusters under the smart city programme.
Greater Hyderabad Municipal Corporation (GHMC)	Aug, 2018	195	GHMC successfully raised ₹195 crores as the second tranche to fund the Strategic Road Development Plan (SRDP). Bonds listed on BSE.
Andhra Pradesh Capital Region Development Authority (APCRDA)	Aug, 2018	2,000	APCRDA floated bonds worth ₹2,000 crores to raise funds to build its capital city Amravati. The issue was oversubscribed by 1.53 times. Listed on BSE.

Municipal Body		Amount (in ₹ Crores)	Description
Bhopal Municipal Corporation (BMC)	Sept, 2018	175	BMC listed its bonds on the NSE, becoming the second municipal corporation in Madhya Pradesh to lists its debt instrument. The funds mobilised to be used for implementation of projects identified under government's Atal Mission for Rejuvenation and Urban Transformation (AMRUT).
Greater Vishakhapatnam Municipal Corporation (GVMC)	Dec, 2018	80	Visakhapatnam made it into the league of top six creditworthy urban local bodies in the country with a credit rating of AA+.
Ahmedabad Municipal Corporation (AMC)	Jan, 2019	200	The issue was oversubscribed 10 times in one hour. With this offering, AMC successfully mobilised funds for the fifth time from the bond market.
Surat Municipal Corporation (SMC)	Feb, 2019	200	SMC issued bonds for the first time worth ₹200 crores to fund its project of sewage treatment plant.
Greater Hyderabad Municipal Corporation (GHMC)	Aug, 2019	100	GHMC, on 20th August, 2019, raised ₹100 crores through an issue of municipal bonds, through the BSE's electronic bidding platform, as a part of its ₹300 crores fund-raising plan. The corporation already raised ₹395 crores in the first two tranches. The proceeds were used to develop flyovers and underpasses under the Strategic Road Development Plan.
Lucknow Municipal Corporation (LMC)	Nov, 2020	200	On 2nd December, 2020, LMC bonds became the first municipal bonds from North India to be listed on BSE. Lucknow became the ninth city in India to have issued municipal bonds and the first city to issue such a bond after the launch of AMRUT scheme.

Municipal Body		Amount (in ₹ Crores)	Description
Ghaziabad Municipal	March, 2021	150	The first city in India to issue a 'green bond' for an environmentally sustainable project of wastewater reuse. Ghaziabad became the second city in Uttar Pradesh and 10th in India to raise municipal bonds.
Vadodara Municipal Corporation (VMC)	March, 2022	100	The civic body successfully raised ₹100 crores through its maiden municipal bond issued on a Private Placement Basis on the BSE for 14 projects under the AMRUT scheme.
Indore Municipal Corporation (IMC)	Feb, 2023	244	Issued India's first retail-focused municipal bond, marking a significant step in broadening the investor base for these instruments. This issuance was specifically targeted for sustainable projects.
Municipal Bond Index of NSE	Feb, 2023		NSE launched the first Municipal Bond Index tracking the performance of 28 municipal bonds issued by 10 issuers, The bonds have an investment-grade credit rating of the AA category.

In 2024, several Indian cities issued municipal bonds to finance various projects. These include:

1. **Vadodara Municipal Corporation:** Issued India's first certified green municipal bond in March 2024, worth ₹100 crore, earmarked for building and enhancing liquid wastewater management infrastructure. This bond was also Asia's first green municipal bond.
2. **Ahmedabad Municipal Corporation:** Following Vadodara, Ahmedabad Municipal Corporation (AMC) issued the first municipal green bonds in Gujarat worth ₹200 crore that was oversubscribed by 6.8 times.
3. **Ghaziabad Municipal Corporation:** Issued Certified Green Municipal Bond in 2025, raising ₹150 crore for a state-of-the-art Tertiary Sewage Treatment Plant (TSTP).

7.3. Why Municipality Bonds are Needed in India?

In developed countries like the United States, municipal bonds are a major source of funding for urban local bodies to meet infrastructure needs. In India, the traditional sources of revenue of Urban Local Bodies (ULBs) include property tax, professional tax, advertisements, user charges, fees/charges for usage of municipal assets and facilities, assigned revenues (such as a share of entertainment tax or stamp duty), and grants-in-aid. The dependence of these ULBs on the grants and subsidised funds of the Central and State governments, for providing basic urban services, has always been high. These bodies also borrow funds from development FIs, as well as multilateral and bilateral funding agencies for their projects.

It is a well-known fact that the revenues earned by municipal bodies in India have not been buoyant; the rate of growth of per capita municipal revenue, from 2012–13 to 2017–18, was only half that of the rate of growth of GDP during the same period. The health pandemic has further strained the balance sheet of both the centre and the states. As a result, the share of tax devolution to the states from the total central revenue pool has fallen to 26% in 2020–21, compared to nearly 30% during the 2015–19 period. This decline has squeezed the funds available to ULBs for their development projects.

On the other hand, rapid migration from rural to urban areas has led to a sharp increase in city populations, putting a serious strain on basic infrastructure such as water supply, roads, and transport. Most civic bodies have no major revenue generation sources other than traditional resources. According to the Economic Survey of 2019–20, India requires a $1.4 trillion investment in infrastructure by 2024–25, with a significant portion earmarked for urban areas. The COVID-19 pandemic has further exposed the gaps in healthcare infrastructure, highlighting the need for higher investment in this sector as well.

Due to the large investment need in India, the Urban Local Bodies (ULBs) must tap into the market to efficiently deal with the increased demands of a growing population, while also reducing their dependence on a state or central grants. It can be a feasible alternative in the coming years. Moreover, as infrastructure projects have long gestation periods, municipal bonds are well-suited to align with the asset-liability structure.

Although some Indian cities have started tapping the market for funding their infrastructure projects, a mere 1% of urban bodies' financial needs are met through municipal bonds in India as against 10% in the US.

Therefore, the Municipal Bond Market in India is important because:

- There is a huge need for new infrastructure development and the upgradation of existing infrastructure in India to support potential growth at various levels (State/Centre).
- Traditional sources of revenues for ULBs, including taxes, non-tax revenues, and grants from the state and central governments, are insufficient to meet the demands.
- The development of smart cities would entail substantial expenditure for the creation of urban infrastructure, such as water supply, sanitation, public health, and road transportation. A major challenge in upgrading smaller

towns into smart cities is securing the necessary financing. Municipal bonds can play an important role in funding key government initiatives like smart cities and Amrut.

- Indian cities can use municipal bonds to revitalise their creaking infrastructure.
- Given the large investment requirements, access to the market for ULBs to raise funds has become both necessary and a feasible alternative for the future.

7.4. Challenges Faced by Urban Bodies and the Way Forward

It is clear that municipal bonds can play an important role in financing infrastructure development for smart cities and contribute to India's ambitious goal of building 100 smart cities. However, there are several challenges faced by smaller urban bodies in issuing such bonds. The most significant one, while accessing capital markets, is the low creditworthiness due to slow governance reforms, poor accounting standards, and low institutional capabilities. As a result, only financially strong and large municipal corporations can directly access capital markets.

Most urban local bodies lack the institutional capacity to raise funds, maintain proper accounting standards, and develop bankable projects. To tackle these issues, the 15th Finance Commission suggested reforms, including making it mandatory for urban local bodies to submit audited accounts to access grant disbursements. This will increase transparency, improve creditworthiness, and making it easier to attract investors to Muni bonds.

In recent years, there has been a concerted policy push from both the centre and regulatory agencies (such as SEBI) to encourage the issuance of municipal bonds.

- In 2019, the government decided to implement a uniform reporting system based on international standards.
- For the first time, the Ministry of Housing and Urban Development is creating a database of audited annual accounts for local bodies.

- › The ministry has tied up with an external agency that has culled data from 2,000 current and past balance sheets of thousand local bodies to promote financial transparency.
- › The availability of audited accounts will help local bodies build credibility, improve financial transparency, and attain higher credit ratings, making them more attractive to investors.

- State governments are also being incentivised through economic stimulus measures to push forward various reforms that would improve governance and enhance the financial health and creditworthiness of urban local bodies.

These initiatives will enable urban bodies to contribute towards building resilient infrastructure. The Ministry of Housing and Urban Development has assigned credit ratings to local bodies, which assess the credit risk of prospective debtors (in this case, the urban local bodies) based on their assets, liabilities, revenue streams and available resources for capital investments. A better rating of a ULB means a good financial condition to repay the funds, which it mobilises from various funding. Highly rated ULBs can easily tap the capital market to raise funds, as Investors have greater confidence in their repayment capacity.

New Delhi Municipal Council (NDMC), Navi Mumbai, and Pune are the cities with the highest credit rating of AA+ (AA Plus). They are followed by Visakhapatnam, Ahmedabad, and Greater Hyderabad Municipal Corporation, each holding a credit rating of AA. The Government has incentivised Municipal bonds through initiatives like AMRUT and Urban Missions. AMRUT 2.0 grants ₹13 crore per Rs 100 crore raised (capped at ₹26 crore/ULB), driving credit-worthy cities to bond markets. Incentives are tied to reforms like audited financials, credit ratings, and Structured Payment Mechanisms (SPMs), ensuring fiscal responsibility. According to a study by CareEdge Ratings, between 2017 to 2024, around Rs 3,000 crore was raised through Municipal bonds, with one-third of these issuances occurring in 2023–2024. It is projected that municipal corporations could raise an additional debt of about ₹28,000 crore, indicating the municipal bond market can grow approximately 15 times from FY 2026–2034.

Infrastructure projects are generally capital-intensive with long gestation periods, often leading to a funding gap. Therefore, strengthening the bond market and boosting public investment are both viable and necessary solutions. The successful issuance of Muni bonds by a few ULBs will encourage other local bodies to adopt sound financial practices, maintain audited accounts, and enhance financial transparency.

CHAPTER 8

Comparison of Bond Markets of Few Asian Economies vs India

We have already seen that, historically, the government bond markets grew with the need to finance government budget deficits. Countries exhibit significant differences in terms of the degree of involvement of central banks in the government bond market. On one end of the spectrum are developed economies such as Japan, the USA, Australia, the UK and South Korea, where the finance ministry is solely responsible for deciding fiscal policy, issuing government debt, and overseeing the operation of the government bond market. In these economies, the governments do co-ordinate with central banks which independently pursue monetary policy and liquidity management in the secondary market.

On the other end of the spectrum are countries like Thailand, where central banks assume dual responsibilities—conducting independent monetary policy and managing public debt. Furthermore, in some countries, such as Malaysia, central banks, being statutory bodies under the jurisdiction of the Ministry of Finance, operate the government bond market at the behest of their governments.

The experiences of these countries highlight that the degree of independence of the central bank may be a necessary but not a sufficient condition for the development of the bond market. A comparison of India's bond market, both government and corporate, with select Asian economies is crucial to understanding India's stands and identifying important lessons that can help develop a more robust corporate bond market.

In this section, the Indian bond market is compared with those of other major Asian economies.

8.1. Size of Bond Market of Select Asian Economies

As of March-end 2021, India ranks seventh in bond market size among select Asian peers, with a strong presence of government bonds, which make up 57.8% of GDP (including central government, state government bonds, and treasury bills). In contrast, the corporate bond market remains relatively small, accounting for just 18% of GDP. Corporate bonds account for only 27% of the total outstanding bonds in India (Table 8.1).

Table 8.1: Size of Bond Market in Asian Economies (% of GDP)

Country	Government	Corporate	Total Bond Market
India	57.8	18.0	75.8
China	62.7	35.3	98.0
Indonesia	28.2	2.8	31.0
Japan	223.2	16.8	239.9
S. Korea	60.7	85.1	145.7
Malaysia	66.2	56.5	122.7
Philippines	42.2	8.8	51.0
Singapore	72.8	34.9	107.8
Thailand	65.3	23.7	89.0
Vietnam	19.3	4.2	23.5

Note: Data for Asian Bond Market as of March 2021.
Source: Asia Bond Monitor; CCIL.

Interestingly, in nearly all countries, the bond market is dominated by government securities. It is not surprising, as a well-developed government bond market is often considered a necessary condition for the growth of the corporate bond market.

As of March 2021, four Asian economies had a bond market size exceeding 100% of GDP—the highest in the region was that of Japan at 240%, followed by South Korea (146%), Malaysia (123%), and Singapore (108%). On the other hand, Vietnam had the smallest share at 24%, though this has been increasing in recent quarters.

Japan tops the list with a very large government bond market, representing 223% of GDP. In comparison, corporate bond market of Japan is minuscule, accounting for just 16.8% of GDP. China ranks as the fifth-largest bond market, with net outstanding debt at 98% of GDP. Similar to Japan, the Chinese market is also dominated by government securities.

However, unlike other economies, South Korea, ranked second, has a much larger corporate bond market. Corporate bonds in South Korea account for around 85% of GDP, indicating a highly developed bond market relative to the size of the economy. The table also shows that countries like Indonesia and the Philippines have considerably smaller bond markets. Notably, countries such as South Korea, Malaysia, and Singapore—where corporate debt forms a larger share of GDP—also have higher GDP per capita compared to India.

8.2. Turnover in the Secondary Market in Asian Economies

While the size of the bond market continues to be a key determinant of liquidity in the securities market, liquidity is more accurately measured by the bid-offer (or bid-ask) spread and trading volume. The turnover ratio, which is the total value of bonds traded in the secondary market relative to the total outstanding bonds, indicates market activity. In other words, a higher turnover ratio reflects a more active secondary market. Table 8.2 below summarises the turnover ratios for government and corporate bonds in Asian countries as of March 2021.

Table 8.2 also indicates that India has a comparatively healthy turnover in its bond market. Despite having a larger bond market, China and South Korea exhibit a more passive secondary market compared to India, which stands seventh in terms of the size of the bond market.

Table 8.2: Turnover Ratio in Asian Economies

Country	Turnover Ratio	
	Government Bond	Corporate Bonds
India	1.3	0.5
China	0.4	0.2
Indonesia	1.13	0.2
Japan	0.3	0
S. Korea	0.4	0.2
Malaysia	0.3	0.1
Philippines	0.2	NA
Thailand	0.4	0.1

Note: Data as of March 2021.

Source: Asia Bond Monitor; CCIL.

8.3. Foreign Holding in Government Bonds

Countries follow different policies regarding foreign investments in government bonds. On one hand, China maintains a very strict policy, while on the other hand, Indonesia and Malaysia encourage Foreign Institutional Investment (FII) with more favourable policies.

Table 8.3: Foreign Holding in Government Debt Securities in Asian Economies

Country	Foreign Holding % of Total
India	1.9
China	10.1
Indonesia	22.9
Japan	13.2
S. Korea	14.6
Malaysia	26.0
Philippines	2.34
Thailand	12.9
Vietnam	0.82

Note: The data as of March 2021.

Source: Asia Bond Monitor; RBI.

It is reported that non-resident investors do not require any approvals or registration for investing in government issuances in Indonesia. Therefore, it is not surprising that FII in government bonds is high in both Indonesia and Malaysia, at 23% and 26%, respectively (Table 8.3).

Thailand too allows FII in government securities with no restrictions, with foreign investors holding around 13% of government bonds.

In contrast, foreign holdings in Indian government bonds remain relatively low, at around 2%. As discussed in the previous section, this is due to strict investment limits set by the RBI for FPIs. Moreover, caps on total foreign investment, as well as limits by investor class, maturity, and issuer, have been implemented through a complicated mechanism by the SEBI. In recent years, the interest of FPIs in Indian bonds has gone down.

8.4. Investor Profile of Government Securities

The ownership pattern of government securities among major Asian economies, as of March 2021, shows that investors can be broadly classified into categories: Central Banks, Governments, Banks, Contractual Saving Institutions (such as insurance companies, pension funds, etc.), and others (which include FIIs).

In Japan, a substantial portion of government securities (44%) is held by the Central Bank, largely due to large-scale bond purchases (quantitative easing) undertaken in recent years to boost growth. India ranks second after Japan, with 16% of government securities held by the RBI as part of liquidity operations. Other Asian countries show significantly lower holdings of government securities by their central banks. On the other hand, China stands out, as the People's Bank of China does not invest in government securities (Table 8.4).

Banks are the second-largest investors in government securities in most countries, primarily due to regulatory requirements. China tops the chart, with banks holding 66.8% of government securities, followed by Indonesia, India, and Malaysia. In Thailand, contractual saving institutions—such as insurance companies, pension funds, and state and local government retirement funds—hold the largest share of government securities. In China, however, these institutions hold only 3.4% of the total government securities. Indonesia shows the highest investment by "others," largely due to the inclusion of FIIs in this category.

Table 8.4: Ownership Pattern of Government Securities in Asian Economies

Country	Investors (% of Total)				
	Central Bank	Government	Banks	Contractual Savings Institutions	Others
India	16.2	0	37.6	29.7	16.5
China*	0	0	66.8	3.4	29.9
Indonesia	10.7	0.0	37.9	14.1	37.4
Japan	44.4	3.5	14.4	20.4	17.3
S. Korea	3.0	16.3	18.3	34.7	27.6
Malaysia	1.9	0.0	34.0	32.1	32.0
Thailand	3.8	1.3	19.0	50.0	25.9

Note: Data as on March 2021; *for China, as of September 2017.

Source: Asia Bond Monitor; RBI.

A comparison with Asian peers indicates that outstanding government bonds in India, at 57.8% of GDP as of March 2021, are in line with other Asian countries, such as China (62.7%) and South Korea (60.7%). However, the share of corporate bonds outstanding in India, at only 18% of GDP, is very low compared to China (35.3%) and South Korea (85.1%). Interestingly, the corporate bond market in India, despite being relatively smaller in comparison with other Asian economies, plays a crucial role in satisfying the financing needs of the economy along with higher liquidity. Foreign investments in Indian government securities are far lower than those in other Asian economies like Indonesia and Malaysia, which, despite having smaller markets, attract more foreign capital.

The Korean bond market is one of the most robust bond markets in Asia, both in terms of size and growth. It shows that government policy reforms and the development of a vibrant government bond market are essential for the development of the corporate bond market. The Asian financial crisis of 1997–98 underscored the limitations of a well-managed, regulated, and supervised banking system in countries like Hong Kong and South Korea. It emphasised that banking systems alone cannot be the sole source of long-term investment in an economy.

However, the South Korean corporate bond market has gone through several boom-and-bust cycles over the years. There is a lot to learn from Korea's experience, particularly its experiment with the bond guarantee scheme, how it evolved after the 1998 crisis, and the moral hazard it created. In 2008, the Reserve Bank specifically discouraged banks from guaranteeing bonds, citing the potential to distort the risk-return trade-off and hinder the development of the bond market as an effective alternate source of funds. Moreover, the South Korean experience showed that a financial crisis could trigger the collapse of the guarantee system. There are also the positive takeaways like the development of a credit rating system, credit enhancements, and asset-backed securities to help grow its corporate bond market. We take a closer look at the South Korean experience in the box below.

Box 8.1: Case Study of South Korean Corporate Bond Market

Evolution of Corporate Bond Market in South Korea—A Case Study

The Korean corporate bond market is the second largest in Asia in terms of outstanding bonds, amounting to 146% of GDP as of March 2021, following Japan at 240%. However, in terms of market depth measured as the ratio of outstanding bonds to GDP, South Korea boasts the largest corporate debt market in the region, with corporate bonds making up 85% of its GDP. In comparison, the Chinese corporate bond market is relatively smaller at 35% of GDP, while India's is even more limited at just 18% of GDP during the same period.

It is, therefore, interesting to understand how South Korea's large corporate debt market evolved over the years.

The Korean government, realizing the benefits of the corporate bond market, started an ambitious bond market development strategy by the late 1960s. The Capital Market Promotion Act was enacted in 1968 to promote both equity and bond markets, followed by the Securities Investment Trust Business Act (SITBA) in 1969, which aimed to stimulate contractual-type investment trusts to mobilise domestic capital. In 1974, the Korea Investment Trust Company (KITC) was established as the first investment trust company (ITC). By 1997, there were 23 new Investment Trust Management Companies (ITMCs) with large assets under management, helped by increasing household savings and increased interest in trust products. Pension funds and insurance companies also played significant roles as institutional investors in the corporate bond market.

The development of the Korean government debt market did not take place until the Asian financial crisis in 1997. Prior to this, the yield on the three-year corporate bond was used as the benchmark bond yield.

However, significant structural changes occurred in the Korean debt market following the Asian crisis:

- **Government Bond Market Expansion**: The government bond market started to grow rapidly, with large issuances of treasury bonds (KTBs), as the government urgently needed huge public funds for financial restructuring and fiscal pump-priming to boost the economy.
- **Private Sector Financing Challenges:** FIs, in the process of restructuring, became risk-averse and hesitant to lend to the corporate sector. As a result, private companies were compelled to raise non-guaranteed funds from the bond market.
- **Increased Issuance of Asset-Backed Securities (ABS):** To facilitate both financial and corporate sector

restructuring, a significant volume of ABS needed to be issued.

As a result, the proportion of funds raised by corporates from the bond market relative to their total borrowings increased to 22% in 1998 from 16.7% in 1997.

Following the crisis, interest rates plunged, driving funds into investment trust companies (ITCs) and their bond-type certificates in search of attractive yields. The amount of funds in these certificates surged from 65 trillion won at the end of 1997 to 203 trillion won by the end of February 1999. The ample liquidity in ITCs was subsequently channelled into the corporate bond market, enabling many private companies to issue large quantities of non-guaranteed bonds.

However, the corporate debt market in Korea suffered several crises in quick succession:

Daewoo's Collapse, July 1999

The abundant liquidity following the crisis helped many firms, including the Daewoo Group, the second-largest corporate conglomerate in Korea, to aggressively expand their businesses by raising funds through corporate bonds. However, this rapid growth proved unsustainable. The collapse of the Daewoo Group in mid-July 1999 resulted in a complete reversal of the corporate bond market. ITCs suffered huge losses due to dishonoured bonds of Daewoo, which triggered a large withdrawal of funds from ITCs and created a severe liquidity crisis. This set off a vicious cycle. The Daewoo crisis showed the importance of a credit rating system and greater transaction transparency.

The government responded by introducing a "Bond Market Stabilisation Fund" of 3 trillion won by November 1999, with contributions from banks and insurance companies, which helped soften corporate bond yields. To restore investor confidence in ITCs, several measures were implemented, including strengthening balance sheets, increasing transparency, cleaning up nonperforming assets held by ITCs, and mandating the adoption of the mark-to-market accounting principle.

Crisis at Maturity in 2000

The large-scale corporate bonds issued just after the Asian crisis had short durations, and these began to mature in the second half of 2000. This raised a need to roll over those debts. During the same time, the Daewoo Group collapsed, and financial conditions in the corporate bond market sharply deteriorated. Moreover, liquidity conditions of large firms, such as Hyundai subsidiaries, also worsened, further damaging sentiment. Firms with lower credit ratings found it extremely difficult to roll over their maturing bonds, with increasing fears of defaults.

The funds held by ITCs' bond-type certificates decreased sharply due to withdrawals, dropping from 181 trillion won at the end of June 1999 to just 45 trillion won by the end of June 2000.

In response, the authorities introduced a 10 trillion won "Bond Fund", raised through subscriptions from 15 banks and other FIs to address the crisis. The "Korea Development Bank (KDB) Prompt Underwriting Scheme" was also introduced at the end of 2000, which facilitated the issuance of corporate bonds. Additionally, the government adopted a securitization and credit guarantee system through the Korea Credit Guarantee Fund (KCGF). Three new Credit Rating Agencies (KIS Pricing, Korea Bond Pricing, and NICE) were launched. These initiatives helped stabilise financing conditions in the corporate bond market.

Accounting Scandal of SK Group and Credit Card Insolvency, 2003

In 2003, the accounting scandal involving SK Global, a large firm in Korea, created significant turmoil in the financial market. At the same time, the slowing economy squeezed consumers who were heavily indebted to credit card firms. Many individuals defaulted on their debts, leading to a serious liquidity problem for credit card companies. As risk-aversion increased, there was a widespread "flight-to-quality" in the local bond market, worsening fundraising conditions in the corporate bond market. However, the bond-type funds of ITCs suffered only mild outflows this time around. To soothe market anxieties, both the government and the Central Bank of Korea introduced a series of measures to improve liquidity in the system.

Thus, the South Korean corporate bond market went through a number of boom-and-bust cycles. Weak institutional setups, including poor accounting practices by FIs, the absence of credit-rating agencies, limited investor protection, and an inefficient liquidation process, all contributed substantially to the market turmoil.

The South Korean government introduced the Bond Market Stabilisation Fund to stabilise bond yields, with contributions from banks and insurance companies. The government also provided incentives to encourage investment in ITC products and launched new products with tax breaks. To promote investor confidence, ITCs were re-capitalised using public funds and NPAs held by ITCs were permitted to be written off. These timely measures helped avert the crisis, but they also raised questions about the moral hazard associated with high-risk lending.

It is well known that a healthy government bond market provides a benchmark for the reasonable valuation of corporate bonds. However, in South Korea, the issuance of government bonds increased sharply only after the 1998 crisis, as the government borrowed funds to support the restructuring of the financial, public and corporate sectors. Before that, the government had maintained a balanced budget. By the end of 2002, government and public bonds accounted for 73% of the total outstanding KSE-listed bonds, totalling 614 trillion won, while corporate bonds accounted for 27% (down from 40% in 1997). As a result, government bonds began to serve as the benchmark for corporate bond yields.

After 2005, reforms in South Korea focused on reducing issuance costs by meeting more diverse and sophisticated investment demands. This included the introduction of STRIPS, the issuance of 20-year bonds, inflation-indexed bonds, and products aimed at retail investors (Park, 2008). Following the 2008 global financial crisis, Korean corporate bond issuance increased due to lower interest rates. However, despite the market's large size and depth, several challenges persist.

8.5. Conclusion

Based on the above discussions, we can draw some comparisons with the Indian corporate bond market:

1. Unlike India, where the government bond market developed much ahead to finance government borrowings, the Korean government debt market did not develop as it tried to have a balanced fiscal policy prior to the Asian crisis. However, South Korea's corporate bond market developed quite early.
2. Indian corporate bond market is currently facing issues similar to those that South Korea experienced in the early 2000s, such as corporate governance problems, concerns over the credibility of credit rating agencies, liquidity issues, defaults, and the need for stronger investor protection. These issues highlight the need for a strong institutional framework.
3. The size and depth of South Korea's corporate bond market (as % of GDP) are much larger than that of India. However, the turnover ratio (ratio of the volume of bonds traded in the secondary market to the total outstanding bonds) of the corporate bond market in India, which

stands at 0.50, is higher than South Korea's 0.2 as of March 2021. This indicates that the secondary market for corporate debt in India is relatively more active.

4. The Korean corporate debt market, just like the Indian market, faces challenges such as the dominance of large corporates and issuance of only highly rated bonds.
5. South Korea's corporate bond market is larger than its government bond market, accounting for nearly 60% of outstanding bonds. In contrast, the government bond market in India accounts for around 80% of total outstanding bonds. The need for budget deficit financing in India might have resulted in crowding out of the corporate bond market. It is important to explore whether India's large PSBR is one of the primary reasons for hurting the development of the corporate bond market.

PART II

A. Sovereign Bond Market

In Part II, we will dive deeper into the **why, what,** and **how** of the bond market through econometric analysis. This section consists of two parts: Chapters 9, 10, 11 and 12, which focus on Sovereign Bonds, and Chapters 13 and 14, which examine Corporate Bonds.

These chapters include the introduction, research questions, literature review, and interpretation of empirical results. A technical section is also included (wherever needed) in the chapters.

The following research questions are explored in this part.

Sovereign Bond Market:

- What macroeconomic factors influence bond yields? Specifically, do short-term interest rates drive long-term government bond yields in India, after accounting for various key economic factors such as inflation and economic activity?
- Is there a relationship between the slope of the yield curve (the difference between long- and short-term rates) and future economic activity in India? Can the slope of the yield curve be used to forecast future GDP growth in India?
- What is the impact of various macroeconomic shocks (such as demand, supply, policy rates, liquidity and exchange rates) on the entire yield curve? Is it possible to understand how monetary policy changes transmit to long-term interest rates?

Corporate Bond Market:

- What are the key determinants for the development of the corporate bond market?
- Do government borrowings through the bond market crowd out private investment? Does the quality of government expenditure matter?

CHAPTER 9

Sovereign Bond Yields and Macro Factors

9.1. Bond Price, Coupon Rate and Yield

Bonds are essentially loans provided by investors to bond issuers, which can be either government or corporate entities. In return, investors earn interest—paid annually or semi-annually—throughout the life of the bond and receive the face value upon maturity.

Bond yield is the return an investor realises on a bond over its lifetime, and it differs from the coupon rate. We have already discussed various interest rates associated with bonds. The coupon rate is the annual interest rate specified at the time of issuance of the bond, and the cash flows from a bond, which occur annually, are determined by this coupon rate.

The current yield of a bond depends on its price and coupon (or interest payment). Bond prices can vary based on market conditions, much like share prices in the equity market. A bond may be purchased for more than its face value (at a premium) or for less than its face value (at a discount).

The market price, or current value, of a bond is calculated by dividing the bond's cash flows by the yield rate. As a result, bond price and yield are inversely related. If bond prices go up, yields go down, and vice versa. Investors follow the bond yields instead of bond prices. This can be a little confusing for some, which is why direct retail investment in the bond market is generally lower compared to the equity market.

Let's take an example to better understand the relationship. Suppose an investor purchases a bond with a face value of ₹1,000, maturing in five years, and with an annual coupon rate of 10%. This means the bond will pay 10% or ₹100 in interest annually for 5 years and ₹1,000 at maturity. Now, if interest rate rises to 12% after a year, all new investments will earn higher interest of ₹120 for similar investments. But the original bond will still pay an interest of ₹100, making it less attractive to investors who can now buy bonds that pay ₹120 in interest. If the investor wants to sell the original ₹1,000 bond, its price will be lower (sold at a discount) to adjust the yield to 12%, so that the coupon payments and maturity value align with the new market rate. Thus, we can see that when interest rate increases, the market price of a bond declines. Conversely, if interest rates fall, the bond's price would rise because its coupon payments become more attractive.

It is the norm to look at bond yields to understand the variation of bond prices due to different market conditions. To fully grasp this, we need to explore what factors impact bond yields.

Do macroeconomic factors have an impact on bond yields?

9.2. What Moves the Yield

We try to observe the movement of bond yields for sovereign bonds (central government securities or G-Secs) over different periods. The 10-year central government bond is considered the benchmark bond due to its high liquidity, with other financial instruments often calibrated relative to this benchmark bond.

The government bond yields are found to react to both domestic and international macroeconomic news. Figure 9.1 below charts the trend of the 10-year benchmark G-Sec yield and its reactions to numerous macroeconomic events in 2012–13. During 2012, India's growth was slowing, and authorities attempted to adopt accommodative policies to support the economy. However, in 2013, the US Federal Reserve, which had maintained very low interest rates after the Global Financial Crisis in 2008, suddenly shifted its approach.

In response to the 2008 financial crisis and the ensuing recession, the Federal Reserve executed a policy known as quantitative easing (QE), which involved large-scale purchases of Treasury bonds (federal government bonds) and other securities. By purchasing a significant amount of bonds, the Federal Reserve kept the demand for government bonds high, which in turn kept prices high and yields low. This buying of bonds, moreover, infused liquidity into the financial sector, helping to maintain low borrowing costs throughout the economy, as these costs are often tied to government bond yields. This was done by Federal Reserve to maintain financial stability and promote economic growth in the aftermath of the 2008 crisis. In 2013, the Federal Reserve suddenly announced that it would be reducing or tapering the pace of its Treasury bond purchases to limit the amount of money it was feeding into the economy. This event, known globally as the "Taper Tantrum", triggered panic among investors, resulting in a sharp spike in US Treasury yields. This move had a ripple effect, causing a sudden jump in all bond yields around the world, including in India. Thus, this time frame offers an interesting opportunity to examine the impact of both national and international macroeconomic news on domestic benchmark bond yields.

The benchmark bond yield moved up at the start of the fiscal year in April 2012, following the government's announcement of higher borrowing. Increased borrowing meant a larger supply of bonds, which typically results in lower bond prices and higher yields. At various points, the central bank, the RBI, tried to keep bond yields lower through both Repo Rate cuts and Open Market Operations (OMOs). The bond yields fell in line with Repo or policy rate cuts. The RBI also used direct policy instruments like OMOs, where it bought bonds in the open market. This led to two effects. First, demand for bonds increased due to RBI's intervention, which raised bond prices (just like any commodity) and consequently lowered yields. Second, the RBI bought bonds and infused liquidity into the financial system, increasing the money supply and driving down interest rates.

Lower-than-expected inflation, driven by softening commodity prices, positively impacted bonds as yields came down. This was due to the expectation of potential RBI policy rate cuts fuelled by lower inflation. Additionally, weaker growth projections and heightened global risk aversion helped keep bond yields low. Increased risk aversion made investors prefer low-risk government bonds over volatile equities, resulting in higher demand for bonds and a further drop in yields.

The reaction of bond yields to the US Federal Reserve's taper tantrum post-May 2013 is most clearly illustrated in Figure 9.1. As soon as the first hint of "tapering" emerged in May 2013, the selling of bonds by the FIIs commenced, and yields started inching up. In response, the RBI raised interest rates and tightened liquidity to defend the exchange rate and curb outflows. The strategy was based on the assumption that higher interest rates would attract FIIs back to purchase domestic bonds.

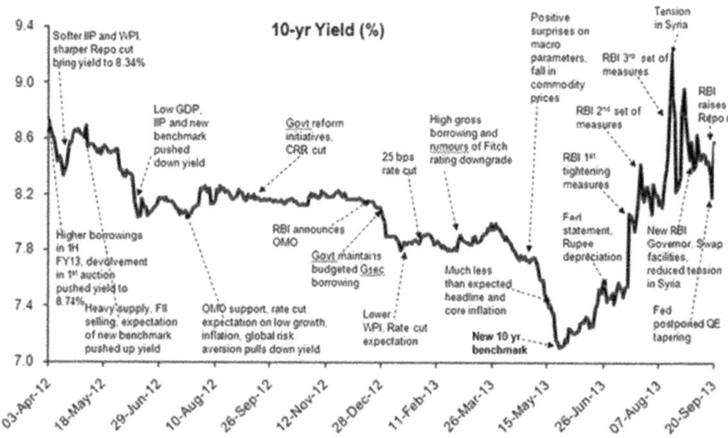

Figure 9.1: Trend of 10-Year Benchmark Bond Yield from April 2012 to September 2013.

Source: RBI database.

However, higher interest rates failed to attract FIIs, and the 10-year benchmark yield surged from 7.55% in mid-July to as high as 9.23% by mid-August 2013. Domestic macroeconomic vulnerabilities got exposed. India's twin deficits—fiscal and current account—were reaching critical levels, inflation was spiking, and the growth (gross domestic product) rate was crashing. India was at the forefront of the "fragile five" club, alongside Brazil, Indonesia, Turkey, and South Africa, all grappling with poor macros. Bond yields reflected these challenging conditions.

From the high fiscal deficit to favourable growth-inflation dynamics, government reform initiatives, RBI policy, rising international risk aversion, capital outflows, sharp currency depreciation, and domestic macro vulnerabilities, yields reacted to "each and every" piece of news.

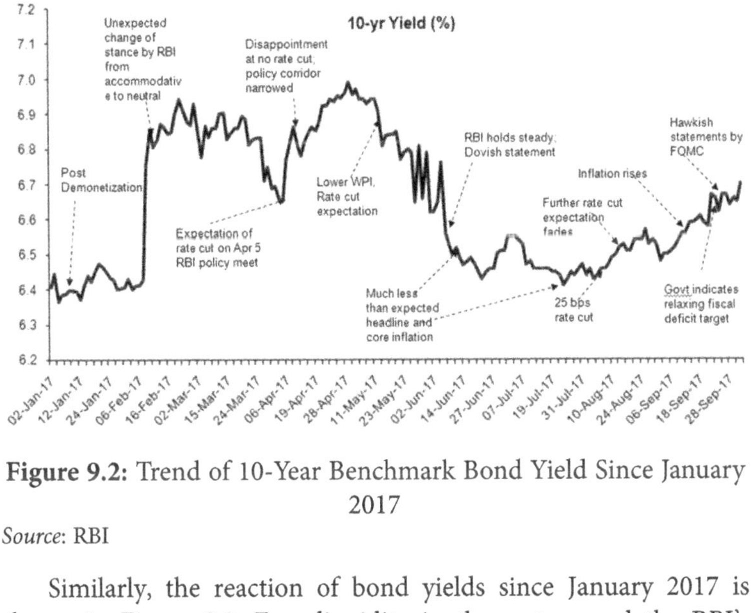

Figure 9.2: Trend of 10-Year Benchmark Bond Yield Since January 2017

Source: RBI

Similarly, the reaction of bond yields since January 2017 is shown in Figure 9.2. Easy liquidity in the system and the RBI's accommodative policy stance following demonetisation kept bond yields soft at around 6.4%. However, an unexpected shift in policy by the RBI in mid-February 2017 caused yields to jump to almost 7%. Later, lower-than-expected headline and core inflation helped the benchmark yield soften in June–July 2017, bringing it back to previous levels. However, yields started to gradually rise again after August, driven by three main factors: (i) higher oil prices, which pushed up inflation and reduced the likelihood of further rate cuts by the RBI, (ii) lower revenue collection, leading to higher-than-expected government borrowings (and a larger fiscal deficit), and (iii) the US Federal Reserve raising interest rates in December 2017.

Figure 9.3: Trend of 10-Year Benchmark Bond Yield Since January 2017.

Source: RBI.

Finally, let's look at the movement of the 10-year benchmark yield from March 2021 to March 2022 (Figure 9.3). In the first quarter of FY 2022, from April to June 2021, the benchmark yield softened in response to the dovish stance of monetary policy. The central bank also introduced a new Government Securities Acquisition Programme called G-SAP 1.0. It was the same as the OMO purchase of government securities, but instead of surprise announcements, the RBI announced an advance calendar for purchasing G-Secs. The idea was to keep yields on long-term G-Secs, which had spiked beyond 6% earlier, to cool down. By committing to buy older G-Secs from market participants, the RBI achieved two things—it created room for these players to buy new bonds in upcoming auctions and signalled to the market participants that if bond prices fall (and yields rise), it would step in to support them. As a result, the 10-year G-Sec yield softened by 12 bps from April to June, closing at 6.05%, trading within a range of 5.96% to 6.19%.

In the second quarter of FY 2022, from July to September 2021, the 10-year generic yield rose by 17 bps to close at 6.22%. Several factors contributed to this rise: (i) rising global crude oil prices heightened concerns about inflation, (ii) the RBI resorted to increased quantum variable rate reverse repo (VRRR) auctions to absorb surplus liquidity from the system, and (iii) the Monetary Policy Committee's upward revision of its inflation forecast. In August 2021, yields further hardened, reaching 6.26%. By the end of September 2021, hawkish signals from the most central banks around the world, coupled with a sharp rise in crude oil prices, put upward pressure on yields.

The 10-year yield continued its upward trend through October 2021 and closed at 6.45% in December 2021 in line with rise in US Treasury yields and international crude oil prices. It rose by 23 basis points between October to December 2021. The yield hardened further in February and March 2022 due to rising international crude oil prices and higher expected gross borrowing by the central government for the next financial year. Yields remained elevated in March amid a rally in commodity prices following the escalation of the geopolitical conflict (Ukraine-Russia war). The 10-year benchmark G-Sec yield closed at 6.84% on 31 March 2022, marking a rise of almost 84 bps for the year.

The bond yields move almost in tandem with the RBI repo rate. However, the yields react to high-frequency news much ahead of RBI policy actions. This is because the market is forward-looking, whereas the RBI policy decisions are based on macro data that is typically announced with a delay.

It is obvious from the above discussion that domestic macroeconomic variables influence the bond yields. In the upcoming chapters, we will not only empirically examine the impacts of macroeconomic factors but also analyse the information embedded in bond yields.

CHAPTER 10

Long-Run Determinants of Sovereign Bond Yields in India

The Government Securities (G-Sec) market, or Sovereign Bond market, is an important component of the financial sector, serving multiple roles within the economy, as discussed in the previous section. For the government, the bond market is the primary source to raise funds, while for investors, sovereign bond yields act as the benchmark risk-free yields in the market. The Central Bank of India (RBI) operates the government bond market by deciding the auction calendar and conducting auctions, among other tasks. In this capacity, the RBI functions both as the debt manager for the government and as the regulator of the government bond market, including its key participants—PDs and banks.

The multifaceted roles played by the RBI give it the ability to influence the nominal yields of government bonds through adjustments to its policy rates. According to Keynes (1930), the central bank can drive long-term interest rates primarily through the policy actions on short-term interest rates and other monetary policy tools at its disposal. He further acknowledges that investors' liquidity preferences based on psychological, social, and other expectations, can influence the interest rates.

This chapter aims to examine whether Keynes's hypothesis—that short-term interest rates can drive long-term government bond yields—holds true in India, after accounting for key economic factors such as inflation and economic activity. It also explores whether government borrowings, represented by the fiscal deficit as a percentage of nominal GDP, influence long-term bond yields. Several studies have found that fiscal deficits do not significantly impact bond yields, contrary to prevailing beliefs in policy circles.

From a policy perspective, understanding the determinants or drivers of government bond yields in India is very important. It helps assess the impact of fiscal and monetary policies on bond yields. Additionally, it is important to examine whether the influence of the short-term interest rates on the long-term bond yields remained true during the period of globalisation, the unconventional monetary policies of developed economies, and the divergent monetary policies of various economies in 2017–18.

We begin by establishing a theoretical framework and identifying the macroeconomic variables most likely to influence long-term yields, alongside short-term rates. The empirical analysis gives us some interesting results.

10.1. Literature Review: Influence of Macro Variables on Long-Term Yields

A significant amount of literature is available that looks into the macroeconomic determinants of bond yields. Poghosyan (2012) studies the determinants of sovereign bond yields for 22 advanced economies over the period 1980–2010. The study finds that, in the long-run, government bond yields are influenced by the government debt-to-GDP ratio and the potential growth rate, while in the short-run, yields are affected by inflation and short-term interest rates.

Kinoshita (2006) develops a theoretical model linking government bond yields to government debt, using a panel of 19 advanced economies. His findings suggest that a 1% point increase in the government debt-to-GDP ratio results in a 2-5 basis point rise in real long-term government bond yields. Similarly, Laubach (2009) and Engen and Hubbard (2004) report an impact of 3-5 basis points for the US.

In an interesting study, Hauner and Kumar (2009) explore the "conundrum" of low government bond yields despite high fiscal imbalances observed in G-7 advanced economies following the global financial crisis. The study suggests that the upward pressures on government bond yields due to ballooning fiscal deficits is more than offset by foreign inflows triggered by "safe heaven" considerations.

Existing studies on Euro area government bond yields, or their spread against Germany, fall into two broad categories—one covering the period prior to the global financial crisis and the other examining the post-crisis period. Both groups of studies follow the general literature on government bond yields based on three main factors: international risk, credit risk, and liquidity risk. Prior to 2007, the international risk factor was an important determinant of bond yields and spreads (Codogno et al., 2003; Geyer et al., 2004). However, many studies find that a country's domestic macroeconomic fundamentals, such as the debt-to-GDP ratio, fiscal deficit, current account deficit, and unemployment rate, are the primary determinants of government bond yields (Bernoth et al., 2004; Pagano & von Thadden, 2004).

Studies focusing on government bond yields after the recent financial crisis suggest that, prior to 2008, the majority of the Euro area sovereign spreads were influenced by a common factor, such as global risk appetite (Zoli, 2013; Sgherri & Zoli, 2009). However, since 2008, the results point to a significant increase in the influence of domestic factors on bond yield spreads during the crisis (Barrios et al., 2009).

In 2017, the short end of the US yield curve moved up as the Federal Reserve raised rates, while long-term rates softened, raising doubts about whether central banks can actually influence the longer end of the curve. This could be due to several factors: (i) Investors' perception of lower inflation risk in the future, leading to a decline in risk premiums and, consequently, softer long-term yields; (ii) Despite low US yields, they remained higher than those in Europe, Japan, and the UK, prompting global savings to flow into US Treasuries in search of higher and safer returns, which contributed to falling yields; and (iii) The market believed the Federal Reserve might refrain from raising rates too quickly, as doing so could harm the nascent revival of the US economy.

In the Indian context, a study by Shivam and Jayadev (2004) finds that the Expectation Hypothesis (EH) holds for the Indian money market, suggesting that the market efficiently facilitates the implementation of monetary policy. Similarly, empirical evidence shows that the rational expectation hypothesis is valid for the government securities market in India (Kanjilal, 2014). This means that the return on long-term instruments is equal to the expected average return of short-term instruments over the life of the long-term instrument.

Macroeconomic variables such as the Bank Rate, Repo Rate, Reverse Repo Rate, WPI, Index of Industrial Production (IIP), GFD, and GDP have a significant impact on yield rates in India (Himachalapathy & Rakshitha, 2015; Akram, 2014). A similar significant impact of monetary policy on both the level and curvature of the bond yield curve is observed by Bhattacharyya (2012). This indicates that the government bond market is strongly influenced by policy measures, highlighting the central bank's distinct role in market development. The study also finds that the exchange rate plays a significant role in determining the slope of the yield curve. However, several studies have found evidence suggesting that the fiscal deficit does not influence interest rates in India, contrary to the debates within policy circles (Chakraborty, 2012).

Tanweer Akram has done extensive work on the impact of macro variables on government bond yields in India, Japan, and other advanced economies. In the Indian context, it has been empirically proven that long-term interest rates on government bonds are primarily driven by short-term interest rates and inflation.

This empirical study is based on Akram and Das's paper on the determinants of government bond yields by extending the time frame of the study to the present period and including a few new variables in the study. The accuracy of the results is further enhanced by accounting for structural breaks.

10.2. Theoretical Framework and Model for Government Bond Market

It is well-established that interest rates are influenced not only by central bank's actions but also by human psychology, social conventions, and liquidity preference. Keynes (1936) articulated his views on interest rates in terms of "the degree of liquidity preference." He stressed that "the rate of interest is a measure of the unwillingness of those who possess the money to part with their liquid control over it." For Keynes, the necessary condition for liquidity preference was "the existence of uncertainty regarding the future of the rate of interest."

He observes that "expectations about the future rate of interest" depend on liquidity preference. Investors who believe future rates will be higher than the expected rate of interest will prefer to hold cash, while those with the opposite view will borrow to purchase debts of longer maturity. Furthermore, according to the liquidity preference theory, interest rates on short-term securities are lower as investors sacrifice less liquidity and assume less risk compared to investing in medium-term or long-term securities. Thus, the demand for money is a function of the interest rate.

Higher interest rate lowers the demand for cash due to the higher opportunity cost—the amount lost today by holding cash, which does not bear interest, compared to interest-bearing bank deposits. If the interest rate is above the normal rate, people will expect it to fall in the future, leading to a rise in bond price. Hence, to earn capital gains (due to speculative motive), they will hold more bonds and less cash at higher interest rates. It is, in fact, the liquidity preference driven by the speculative motive, along with the quantity of money, that determines the rate of interest.

Keynes holds that the primary influence of monetary policy is on short-term interest rates. However, he states, "experience shows that, as a rule, the influence of the short-term rate of interest on the long-term rate is much greater than anyone would have expected." We try to understand whether the short-term interest rates can be the primary driver of long-term government bond yields in India, after controlling for various key macroeconomic factors.

We consider a simple model based on Akram and Das's (2015b) interpretation of Keynes's views to explore the impact of macroeconomic variables on long-term interest rates of government bonds. This model uses a two-period horizon: time periods t = 1 and 2.

r_{LT}: long-term interest rate on a government bond in period 1;

r_1 and r_2: short-term interest rates on a Treasury bill in period 1 and period 2, respectively;

Er_2: expected short-term interest rate in period 2;

$f_{1,1}$: 1-year, 1-year forward rate;

z: term premium;

π_1, π_2: current inflation rates in periods 1 and 2, respectively;

$E\pi_2$: expected rate of inflation in period 2;

g_1, g_2: current growth rates in periods 1 and 2, respectively;

Eg_2: expected growth rate in period 2;

fd_1, fd_2: government fiscal deficit in periods 1 and 2, respectively; and

Efd_2: expected government fiscal deficit in period 2.

The interest rate on the 2-year government bond will depend on the short-term interest rate in period 1 and the 1-year, 1-year forward rate (as shown in equation 1).

$$\left(1+r_{LT}\right)^2=\left(1+r_1\right)\left(1+f_{1,1}\right) \tag{1}$$

The 1-year, 1-year forward rate will be based on the investor's expectations of the short-term interest rate on Treasury bills in period 2, as well as the inclusion of the term premium, z (as shown in equation 2).

$$f_{1,1} = Er_2 + z \tag{2}$$

The term premium that influences long-term yields can include several factors, such as inflation expectations, risk premium, and investor preferences. Hautsch and Ou (2008) observed that capacity utilisation and industrial production are important long-term predictors of the risks associated with the level and slope of the yield curve. Both growth and inflation variables can influence the term premium. Therefore, the expected short-term interest rate on Treasury bills in period 2, along with the term premium, will be a function of the investor's expectations of growth and inflation during that period (as shown in equation 3).

$$Er_2 + z = F^1(Eg_2; E\pi_2) \tag{3}$$

Hence, the 1-year, 1-year forward rate is the sum of the expected short-term interest rate on the Treasury bill in period 2 and a function of the investor's expectations regarding the growth rate and inflation in period 2 (as shown in equation 4). Thus, the forward rate is a function of the expected short-term interest rate, the expected growth rate, and the expected rate of inflation in period 2 (as shown in equation 5).

$$f_{1,1} = Er_2 + F^2(Eg_2; E\pi_2) \tag{4}$$

$$f_{1,1} = F^3(Er_2; Eg_2; E\pi_2) \tag{5}$$

It follows that the long-term interest rate is a function of the short-term interest rate in period 1, as well as the expected short-term interest rate, growth rate, and inflation rate in period 2 (as shown in equation 7).

$$r_{LT} = F^4(r_1, f_{1,1}) \tag{6}$$

$$r_{LT} = F^4(r_1, F^3(Er_2; Eg_2; E\pi_2)) \tag{7}$$

According to Keynes, an investor forms expectations of the long-term future based on his current experience and the immediate past, as it is not truly possible to have a proper mathematical expectation of the unknown and uncertain future. The expected future values of macroeconomic variables are based on present conditions. Therefore, for an investor, the expected short-term interest rates in period 2 will be based on the actual short-term interest rates in period 1 (as shown in equation 8). Similarly, the expected growth rate in period 2 will be dependent on the actual growth rate in period 1 (as shown in equation 9), the expected rate of inflation in period 2 will be based on the actual rate of inflation in period 1 (as shown in equation 10), and the expected government fiscal deficit in period 2 will depend on the fiscal deficit in period 1 (as shown in equation 11).

$$Er_2 = r_1 \tag{8}$$

$$Eg_2 = g_1 \quad (9)$$

$$E\pi_2 = \pi_1 \quad (10)$$

$$Efd_2 = fd_1 \quad (11)$$

An investor's expectations of key economic variables depend largely on current conditions, or on the investor's assessment of those conditions. By incorporating Keynesian assumptions into the model, we arrive at the following:

$$r_{LT} = F^4(r_1, F^3(r_1, g_1, \pi_1)) \quad (12)$$

$$r_{LT} = F^5(r_1, g_1, \pi_1) \quad (13)$$

Extending the model to include a government fiscal deficit, we get:

$$r_{LT} = F^6(r_1, g_1, \pi_1, fd_1) \quad (14)$$

In contrast, under rational expectations, where investors are expected to have perfect foresight, the investor's expected short-term interest rates, growth rate, inflation rate, and government fiscal deficit in period 2 would be equal to the actual short-term interest rates, growth rate, inflation rate, and fiscal deficit, respectively, in period 2 (as shown in equations 15, 16, 17, and 18).

$$Er_2 = r_2 \quad (15)$$

$$Eg_2 = g_2 \quad (16)$$

$$E\pi_2 = \pi_2 \quad (17)$$

$$Efd_2 = fd_2 \quad (18)$$

This would result in long-term interest rates being a function of the current short-term interest rate, growth rate, rate of inflation, and government finance variables in period 2 (as shown in equation 19).

$$r_{LT} = F^7(r_1, r_2, g_2, \pi_2, fd_2) \quad (19)$$

10.3. The Variables Considered and the Methodology

Data Source

For this study, nominal yields on 10-year Indian government bonds (IGBs), 3-month treasury interest rates, and other macroeconomic variables are used. The Consumer Price Index (CPI)-IW index is used as a proxy for consumer prices, as India did not have a single consumer price index until 2012. A summary of the variables used in the study and their descriptions is given in Table 10.1. The quarterly data spans from March 2005 to June 2017, with a total of 50 data points.

Table 10.1: The Data and The Variables

Variables	Description	Frequency	Source
Indian Short-term Interest Rates			
ST Yield	Government benchmarks, auction rate, 3 month Treasury yield, %	Daily, converted to quarterly	CCIL
Repo	Quarter-end policy repo rate	RBI policy	RBI Handbook
Indian Long-term Interest Rates			
LT Yield	Government bonds, benchmark G-sec 10-year yield, %	Daily, converted to quarterly	RBI Statistical Data
Inflation			
CPI	India, consumer price index, total, base 2012, % YoY change	Monthly, converted to quarterly	Central Statistical Organisation (CSO), RBI Database
CPI-IW	India, consumer price index for industrial workers, total, base year 2001, % YoY change	Monthly, converted to quarterly	CSO, RBI Database
WPI	India, wholesale price index, total, base 2011-12, spliced series, % YoY change	Monthly, converted to quarterly	CSO, RBI Database
Oil Price	International crude oil price, USD/barrel	Daily, converted to quarterly	CMIE
Economic Activity			
GDP	Gross domestic product, change in real GDP, %YoY	Quarterly	CSO, RBI Database
IIP	Industrial growth, % YoY	Monthly, converted to quarterly	CSO
Other Variables			
FD	Fiscal deficit as % of nominal GDP	Quarterly	Budget Document
Fed Fund	Fed fund rate of USA	Quarterly	US Fed

Methodology

Unit Root Test: As most time series are non-stationary and affected by temporary or permanent shocks, unit-root/stationarity tests are performed on both the levels and the first differences of all data series. Both the ADF and Phillips-Perron (PP) unit root tests are used to check the stationarity of the series. Table 10.2 below shows the unit root results for all the series considered in this study.

Table 10.2: Results of the Unit-Root Test

Variables	ADF		PP		Inference
	Level	First Difference	Level	First Difference	
LT Yield	-3.311623	-9.200702***	-3.170989	-11.59927***	I (1)
ST Yield	-1.66015	-5.75207***	-2.06562	-5.77087***	I (1)
Repo	-2.849247	-4.310994***	-2.086327	-4.186795***	I (1)
WPI, π_{wpi}	-3.225672	-4.709827***	-2.284622	-4.373405***	I (1)
π_{cpi}	-3.566737	-2.161807	-3.238709	-5.648529***	I (1)
CPI-IW, π_{cpiiw}	-0.524167	-4.186251***	-1.422105	-6.653707***	I (1)
Oil Price	-2.434229	-5.846537***	-1.943463	-5.64405***	I (1)
IIP	-2.699841	-6.364295***	-3.058358	-6.366625***	I (1)
GDP	-3.191315	-7.072281***	-3.344697	-7.074333***	I (1)
FD	-1.722931	-13.11274***	-6.999723***		I (1)
Fed Fund	-3.391820***		-1.207731	4.671114***	I (1)

Notes: a) ADF: Augmented Dickey-Fuller test; PP: Phillips-Perron test; T-stats are given.

b) The *, **, and *** indicate significance at the 10, 5, and 1% levels.

Source: Author's calculations.

The results show that the series LT Yield, ST Yield, Repo, WPI, CPI, CPI-IW, Oil Price, IIP, GDP, FD, and Fed Fund Rate are non-stationary at the level and are integrated to order 1.

We aim to assess the impact of short-term interest rates, inflation, growth, fiscal deficit, and other factors on long-term government bond yields. As most of the macroeconomic variables are announced with a delay, their impacts on bond yields are observed after a lag. A lag of one quarter is used for GDP, FD, and inflation variables.

Cointegration Test

After performing the unit root test for each variable, cointegration analysis is carried out to examine whether a long-term relationship exists among the variables and, if so, to identify the nature of that relationship. Since all the variables are integrated of order 1, the Engle and Granger (1987) method is used to analyse cointegration among the variables. Engle-Granger estimates the long-run equation:

$$y_t = \delta_0 + \delta_1 x_t + u_t$$

where, y is the dependent and x is the independent variables.

The OLS residuals from the above equation are a measure of disequilibrium:

$$\bar{u}_t = y_t - \bar{\delta}_0 - \bar{\delta}_{1xt}$$

A test of cointegration is a test of whether residual is stationary. This is determined by ADF and PP tests on the residuals.

Stepwise Regression

A stepwise regression procedure is used to build the regression model by systematically entering and removing predictors. In order to find a useful regression model, it is desirable to include all variables that truly predict the response. Failing to do so may result in an underspecified model, which could be misleading. Several equations are constructed in accordance with the model presented in the earlier section, and these equations are subsequently tested empirically.

Equation (19) serves as the base equation, which examines how the long-term interest rate on government bonds depends solely on the short-term interest rate. The subsequent equations are then constructed by incorporating additional independent variables, such as inflation, growth, and the fiscal deficit.

$$\text{LT Yield}_{\text{G-sec10}} = a_1 + a_2\text{*ST Yield} + a_3\text{*IND Variable} + c \qquad (20)$$

The dependent variable is the LT Yield, representing the 10-year G-sec yield, while the primary independent variable is the ST Yield, which refers to the 3-month Treasury yield. Other independent variables related to inflation include WPI, CPI, CPI-IW, and Oil Price. Similarly, the independent growth variables are IIP and GDP. The equations explore the relationship between the long-term interest rate and the short-term interest rate, along with inflation (WPI, CPI, CPI-IW, Oil Price), growth (IIP, GDP), and fiscal deficit, using stepwise regression.

10.4. Empirical Results

The results for the linear specifications using Ordinary Least Squares (OLS) estimation are provided in Table 10.3, columns 1 to 8. Without any additional controls, the estimated coefficient for ST Yield is positive, equal to 0.313, and statistically significant at less than 1% level (column 1). This indicates that a unit increase in ST Yield is associated with an increase of 0.31 in LT Yield. In other words, a 1% point increase in the ST Yield level corresponds to a 31 bps increase in the LT Yield level.

The results in columns 2 to 5 show that controlling for inflation variables such as WPI, CPI-IW, CPI, or Oil Price—either individually or jointly—does not alter our initial findings. Due to the high correlation between CPI and other inflation variables, CPI is excluded from the model when other inflation variables are included. Similarly, oil price is not included in the model with other inflation variables due to its high correlation with them. The estimated coefficient for ST Yield remains positive, economically large, and statistically significant at the 1% level. While the impact of oil prices is statistically significant, its economic effect is very small. Including CPI in the equation reduces the number of data points to 20, but ST Yield remains significant and large.

The short-term yield remains significant even after controlling for GDP and IIP (column 6). Moreover, the coefficient increases in magnitude from 0.31 (column 1) to 0.36 (column 6). However, the growth variables (IIP and GDP) do not appear to have any significant impact.

Interestingly, when controlling for the fiscal deficit (as % of GDP) and the US Fed Fund Rate in column (7), the estimated coefficient for ST Yield remains significant and positive, with its magnitude increasing further. Similar to GDP, neither the fiscal deficit nor the US Fed Fund Rate is significant.

Next, we control for almost all variables by adding CPI and removing the other inflation variables from the analysis. The regression results in column (8) show that the coefficient for ST Yield remains positive, with its magnitude nearly doubling from 0.31 (column 1) to 0.59.

The significance level of the estimated coefficient for ST Yield remains high throughout as we control for other variables, and the magnitude of ST Yield continues to increase. The R-square value also improves significantly, reaching 64% as seen in column 8. However, with the inclusion of the new CPI series, the total number of observations decreases to 20. This results in a limitation, as the findings are based on a smaller sample size.

It is worth noting that the R-square value increased continuously as new variables were added. In the final regression, R-square increased significantly, as shown in Table 10.3. This indicates that almost 64% of the variation in the long-term yield is described by the independent predictor variables. Furthermore, the inclusion of the independent variable "CPI" improves the R-square value, suggesting that CPI has a greater influence on determining bond yields compared to WPI.

The OLS residuals for each of the 8 equations are tested for unit roots using the ADF and PP tests. It was found that all the residuals (Residual 1 to Residual 8) are I(0), or stationary, indicating that the model is stable. The stability of the model is also tested through the CUSUM test, which shows that the residuals remain well within the five percent level, indicating stability.

These results are in line with findings in other studies, which suggest that changes in short-term interest rates are important drivers of changes in long-term government bond yields.

Table 10.3: Basic Regression Results

Dependent variable: Long Term Government Bond Yield (Benchmark G-sec 10-year yield, LT Yield).

All variables are I (1) or integrated of order 1.

Variables	1	2	3	4	5	6	7	8
ST Yield	0.313***	0.348***	0.468***	0.353***	0.448***	0.360***	0.405***	0.592***
WPI		-0.107***		-0.112***		-0.111***	-0.110***	
Oil Price			-0.023***					
CPI-IW				-0.023		0.024	0.011	
CPI					-0.042			-0.029
GDP					0.066	-0.016	-0.026	0.083
IIP						0.001	0.022	0.022
FD							0.029*	-0.024
Fed Fund							-0.310	
R-Square	0.13481	0.2477	0.30821	0.24974	0.56905	0.25212	0.33622	0.63872
No of Observations	48	48	48	48	20	47	47	20

Note: The *, **, and *** indicate significance at the 10%, 5%, and 1% levels.

10.5. Validation of the Output

Based on the regression results and the equation obtained above, the dependent variable "LT YIELD" is forecasted in Figure 10.1 below.

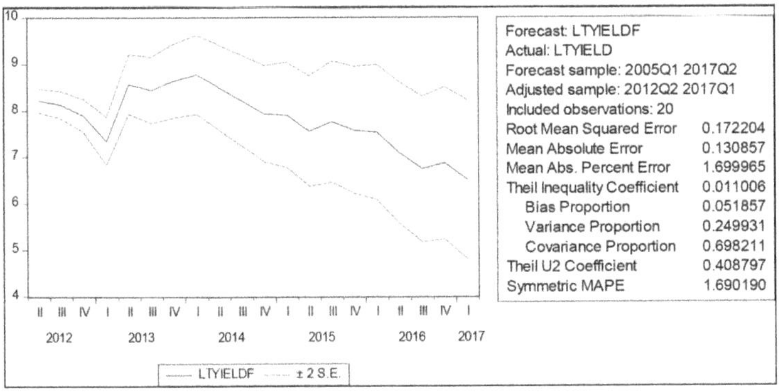

Figure 10.1: Movement of estimated LT YIELD

Source: EViews

The estimated values for LT YIELD are plotted against the actual values of yields of 10-year G-Sec (Figure 10.2). It is seen that the two graphs almost move together, which demonstrates that the model is capable of accurately estimating the dependent variable.

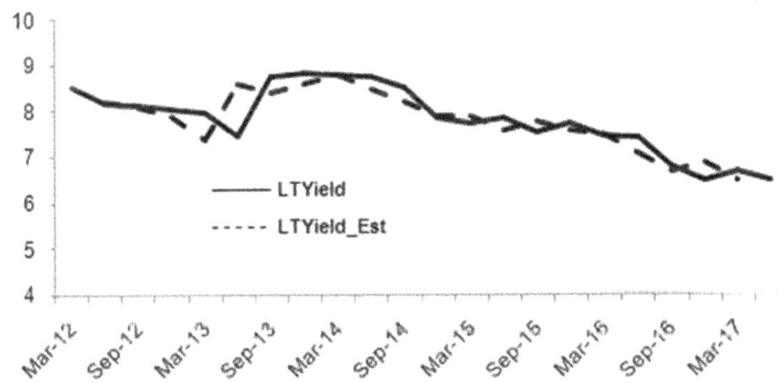

Figure 10.2: Trend of actual 10-year yield and the estimated values from the model.

Source: RBI database, Estimated Yield.

10.6. Policy Implications and Future Research Opportunities

The empirical results of this study support our initial hypothesis that a central bank's (RBI's) actions, through its monetary policy tools, influence treasury yields (short-term interest rates), which, in turn, primarily affect long-term interest rates in India. The interest rates on longer-maturity government bonds in India are positively correlated with short-term treasury bill interest rates, even after controlling for various macroeconomic variables, such as inflation, the growth rate of industrial production, and the debt ratio.

Higher (or lower) long-term interest rates on government bonds are influenced by higher (or lower) short-term interest rates, higher (or lower) inflation rates, a faster (or slower) rate of growth of industrial production, and a higher fiscal deficit. Moreover, the results indicate that the impact of government indebtedness (fiscal deficit as a percentage of GDP) is not as high as the influence of short-term interest rates and inflation.

As the times series data of the dependent and primary independent variables exhibit a change in their pattern at a certain point, fitting a single linear regression model may not be appropriate. These changes are referred to as structural breaks. To account for this, a dummy variable needs to be incorporated. Incorporating a structural break improves the results, as observed in our study (refer to the technical section at the end).

The results of this study contribute to the on-going policy debates on monetary-fiscal coordination, policy mix during boom-and-bust cycles, and the sustainability of government debt. The findings suggest that the RBI's policy can have a strong influence on long-term government bond yields through short-term interest rates. The central bank's credibility and its ability to effectively communicate its intentions to the market will determine its ability to keep short-term interest rates within its policy band.

The results also show that in the model using CPI as the inflation variable, the fiscal deficit has a negative correlation with bond yields, but the impact seems to be very small. In other words, a higher level of fiscal deficit of the government surprisingly does not have an adverse effect on government bond yields, contrary to the conventional view. This might be due to an inadequate number of quarterly data points available. With other inflation variables, the impact of fiscal deficit is positive but not statistically significant. These findings are consistent with studies by Akram & Das (2015a, 2015b) and Chakraborty (2012, 2016).

It is to be noted that during the recent period of globalisation, with the unconventional monetary policies of developed economies and the divergent monetary policies across various nations, the relationship between short-term and long-term bond yields has remained consistent in the Indian context. This study will help policymakers develop appropriate models and make informed policy decisions.

This study explores the relationship between macro variables and the benchmark 10-year G-Sec bond yield. This analysis can be extended to other short-term and long-term bonds, such as the 1-year, 5-year, and 30-year sovereign bond yields. Moreover, by considering the new CPI, the number of data points can be increased by considering monthly data for high-frequency variables and their impact on bond yields. While this study primarily explores the overall relationship between short-term and long-term government bond yields in India, it does not look into the different shapes of the yield curve during various periods, nor does it investigate whether the relationship holds across these periods. Future research could extend this study to explore whether short-term interest rates fail to predict long-term yields during periods of an inverted yield curve in India.

Box 10.1: Technical Section: Structural Break

There might be a structural break in the data series used during 2013 that needs to be accounted for reliable results. It would be interesting to conduct cointegration analysis while accounting for this structural break.

Unit root tests with breaks for both the LT Yield and ST Yield variables indicate structural breaks in both series in Q1 of

2013 (Table 10.4). As shown in Chart 3.2, the structural break in Q1 of 2013 can be attributed to a sharp rise in the 10-year bond yield after May 2013. Just prior to this, bond yields had softened due to easing commodity prices. However, the US Fed's sudden announcement to taper down bond purchases resulted in large FII outflows, leading to the continued depreciation of Rupee. As the RBI tightened liquidity and raised interest rates to defend the currency, India's macroeconomic vulnerabilities got exposed (high fiscal and current account deficits, with high inflation and low growth). The 10-year benchmark yield jumped by 168 bps to 9.23% in just one month. Hence, the bond yield's initial dip followed by a sharp rise resulted in a structural break, which has been found to be statistically significant.

Table 10.4: Results of Unit-Root Test with Break-Point

Break Selection: Minimize Dickey-Fuller t-statistics		
	Level	**First Difference**
LT Yield	-5.341653	-9.038601***
ST Yield	-3.196048	-7.087826***

Break Date: 2013Q1;
Source: Author's calculations.

In order to incorporate the structural break at Q1 of 2013, a dummy variable (Dum) is generated such that

$$\text{Dum} = \begin{cases} 0, \text{ for } 2005{:}Q1 \text{ to } 2013{:}Q1 \\ 1, \text{ for } 2013{:}Q2 \text{ to } 2017{:}Q2 \end{cases}$$

The last two regression equations from Table 10.3 (column 7 and 8) are used again along with the dummy variables for incorporating the structural break.

So, we get four models now:

Model 1:

$$\text{LT Yield}_{G\text{-sec10}} = a_4 + a_5{*}\text{ST Yield} + a_6{*}\pi_{wpi} + a_7{*}\pi_{cpi\text{-}iw} + a_8{*}\text{GDP} + a_9{*}\text{IIP} + a_{10}{*}\text{FD} + c \quad (21)$$

Model 2: (incorporating Structural Break)

$$LT\ Yield_{G\text{-}sec10} = a_{11} + a_{12}{*}ST\ Yield + a_{13}{*}Dum + a_{14}{*}(Dum{*}ST\ Yield) + a_{15}{*}\pi_{wpi} + a_{16}{*}\pi_{cpi\text{-}iw} + a_{17}{*}GDP + a_{18}{*}IIP + a_{19}{*}FD + c \quad (22)$$

Model 3: (with CPI)

$$LT\ Yield_{G\text{-}sec10} = a_{20} + a_{21}{*}ST\ Yield + a_{22}{*}\pi_{cpi} + a_{23}{*}GDP + a_{24}{*}IIP + a_{25}{*}FD + c \quad (23)$$

Model 4: (incorporating Structural Break)

$$LT\ Yield_{G\text{-}sec10} = a_{26} + a_{27}{*}ST\ Yield + a_{28}{*}Dum + a_{29}{*}(Dum{*}ST\ Yield) + a_{30}{*}\pi_{cpi} + a_{31}{*}GDP + a_{32}{*}IIP + a_{33}{*}FD + c \quad (24)$$

The results for the linear specifications using the Newey-West Regression estimation are provided in Table 10.5.

Table 10.5: Regression Results with Structural Break

Dependent variable: Long Term Government Bond Yield (Benchmark G-sec 10-year yield, LT Yield).

All variables are I (1) or integrated of order 1.

Newey-West Regression is used.

Variables	Model 1	Model 2	Model 3	Model 4
ST Yield	0.359***	0.409***	0.592***	0.944***
WPI	-0.109***	-0.120		
CPI-IW	0.016	0.021		
CPI			-0.029	0.020
GDP	-0.017	-0.010	0.083	0.081
IIP	0.003	0.005	0.022	0.032
FD	0.032	0.037	-0.024**	-0.024**
Dummy		-0.045		0.022
Dummy * ST Yield		-0.237		-0.323
R-Square	0.30421	0.31425	0.63872	0.64673
No of Observations	47	47	20	20

Note: The *, **, and *** indicate significance at the 10%, 5, and 1% levels.

Including the structural break improves the R-square value in Model 2 from 30% to 31%. This implies that the independent variables can now predict almost 31% of the variation in the dependent variable.

The coefficients of ST Yield remain positive, significant, and above 40%. The new retail inflation series, CPI, has a significantly greater influence on bond yields compared to other measures of inflation. This may be due to RBI's flexible inflation targeting mandate, which was adopted a couple of years ago, with headline CPI serving as the anchor for inflation. However, the number of observations decreases to 20 due to the new series using the base year 2011–12. The growth variables do not show as much significance. The fiscal deficit remains significant at the 5% level.

Overall, the results reinforce the finding that short-term interest rates are important determinants of variations in long-term government bond yields in India. Predictability increased after incorporating the structural break.

CHAPTER 11

Information Within the Slope of the Yield Curve

Sovereign bond yields form the backbone of term structure theories because the government bond market is the most liquid debt market in any country, and government securities are considered default-free. As a result, government bond yields represent the risk-free rates in the country.

A yield curve is a line that plots yields (interest rates) of bonds having equal credit quality but different maturities at a particular point of time. For example, plotting the yields of government bonds with maturities of 1 year, 5 years, 10 years, etc., on 22 September 2022, would give the yield curve for that day. The graph displays the bond's yield on the vertical axis and the time to maturity on the horizontal axis. It represents the yield (or interest rate) an investor expects to earn if he lends his money for a given period. The curve may take different shapes at different points of time based on the macroeconomic outlook or business cycle (refer to the box). However, it is typically upward sloping, as an investor is expected to earn higher interest rate for investment of longer tenure. The yield curve helps in determining the pricing of fixed-income instruments—both sovereign and corporate.

It is important to have a well-developed sovereign bond market so that a reasonably good sovereign yield curve can be constructed. The financial instruments in the market are calibrated with reference to sovereign yield curve by adding an appropriate risk premium or credit spread. Since bond yields for different maturities fluctuate daily in response to market variations, the "shape" of the yield curve also keeps changing. These changes provide valuable insights into the economic outlook.

The yield curve is said to be "steepening" when the yields on long-term bond rise faster than those on short-term bond (Figure 11.1). This typically indicates expectations of stronger growth ahead. On the other hand, when yields on short-term bond are moving up faster than the yields on long-term bond, the yield curve is said to be "flattening," often indicating a slowdown in growth. In rare cases, the yield curve can even become "inverted," where short-term yields exceed long-term yields, indicating a likelihood of a recession.

The slope of the yield curve is expressed as the difference between the long- and short-term interest rates. It provides valuable information regarding the future expectations for the economy's interest rate scenario and has long been used as a leading indicator to predict economic slowdowns. This has been successfully used by both policymakers and market participants to understand the state of the economy and the likelihood of a slowdown. This relationship has been tested across various time periods and geographies, dating back to the late 1980s.

Since the mid-1990s, the relationship between the slope of the yield curve (the difference between long- and short-term rates) and future economic activity has proven to be accurate in many economies.

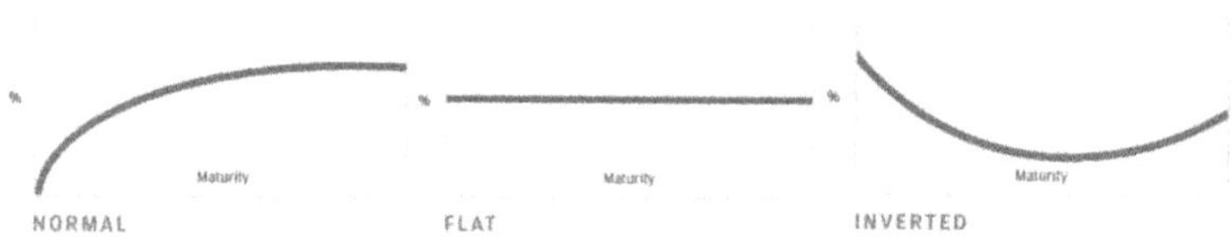

Figure 11.1: Different Yield Curve Shapes

Although economic theory suggests that the yield curve can help forecast real output, no theory specifically establishes a clear connection between yield curve inversions and recessions. In practice, however, since 1960, a yield curve inversion (measured by the difference between ten-year and three-month Treasury rates) has preceded the last seven recessions in the USA, as identified by the

National Bureau of Economic Research (NBER). It is reported that, in terms of monthly averages, the ten-year rate was at least 12 basis points below the three-month rate before every recession during that period. One of the recessions predicted by the yield curve was in 2008. The yield curve inverted in August 2006, a little more than a year before the recession started in December 2007. However, there have been a couple of false positives, such as the inversion in late 1966 and a very flat curve in late 1998. A recent yield curve inversion in March 2019, in USA, raised concerns among many recession watchers.

Spot yield curves can be used to construct forward interest rates for other maturities. These forward rates reflect the market's expectations of future interest rates and inflation levels. This implies that the shape of the spot yield curve is likely to mirror market participants' expectations of future interest rates. Even central banks use these indicators in framing the monetary policy. The informational content and predictive power of the yield curve stem from the above premise.

The yield curve spread consists of two components: the expected real interest rate and expected inflation, both of which are helpful for forecasting. The expected real rate is based on expectations of future monetary policy and, hence, of future real growth. Furthermore, inflation is positively related to economic activity and, hence, may also contain information about future growth. So, the spread (the difference between short- and long-term yields) gives expectations about future interest rate movements and can be a valuable tool for policymakers in shaping policies and taking corrective measures to influence the economy.

The shape of the spot yield curve most likely reflects market participants' expectations of future interest rates. Estrella and Hardouvelis, in the early 1990s, empirically demonstrated that the yield curve could be used to predict real growth in consumption, investment, and aggregate GNP, as well as NBER-dated recessions. Similarly, in India, it has been found that the yield on Treasury bills with a residual maturity of 15–91 days in the secondary market serves as the best economic indicator of the economic business cycle (RBI, 2006; Bordoloi & Rajesh, 2007).

This chapter explores whether the yield curve spread in the government fixed-income market can predict future economic activity in India. Can the mysteries and information held within the yield curve be used by policy makers?

The key contribution of this empirical study to the literature is that, instead of simply showing the predictive power of the yield curve, an attempt has been made to compare the predictive power of a Composite Index of Leading Indicators (CILI) with that of the slope of the yield curve.

Since the Central Bank (RBI) does not announce a Lead Indicator Index and no publicly available indices exist for India, a CILI is first constructed with available potential high-frequency indicators, based on the methodology prescribed by the NBER and preferred by the RBI (RBI, 2006). Non-Agricultural GDP (NAGDP) is used as the reference series. The study looks, for the first time, at the predictive ability of both CILI and the slope of the yield curve during the key periods, including the global financial crisis of 2008, domestic macroeconomic problems of 2013, and the unexpected and forced disruption caused by demonetisation at the end of 2016.

Policymakers often have to make decisions based on expected future economic conditions. The motivation of this study is to show that the movement of the yield curve in India can serve as a simple, additional, and reliable tool for validating or detecting early signs of reversal, even though policymakers have access to a wide range of high-frequency economic variables and standard models for forecasting.

11.1. Classical Business Cycles, Growth Cycles and Growth Rate Cycles

Classical business cycles are defined as recurring phases of expansion and contraction in the levels of various economic and financial time series. The classical definition of business cycles, as proposed by Burns and Mitchell (1946), is as follows:

> "Business cycles are a type of fluctuations found in the aggregate economic activity of nations that organise their work mainly through business enterprises. A cycle consists of expansions

> occurring at about the same time in many economic activities, followed by similarly general recessions, contractions, and revivals, which merge into the expansion phase of the next cycle. This sequence of changes is recurrent but not periodic. The business cycles vary from more than one year to ten or twelve years; they are not divisible into shorter cycles of similar character with amplitudes approximating their own."

These observations form the core of the definition of classical business cycles in market economies, as outlined by Mitchell in 1927. The key features include:

- Business cycles are recurrent sequences of alternating phases of expansion and contraction across a wide range of economic time series.
- A cycle consists of simultaneous expansions in many economic activities, followed by general recessions.
- This sequence of changes is recurrent but not periodic; cycles typically last from one to ten or twelve years.
- Business cycles cannot be divided into shorter cycles of similar magnitude and character.

This characterisation of the business cycle is also highlighted by Moore (1982) and Zarnowitz and Boschan (1975). Moore (1982) observed:

> "No single measure of aggregate economic activity is called for in the definition because several such measures appear relevant to the problem, including output, employment, income, and trade, and no single measure is either available for a long period or possesses all the desired attributes".

In "classical" business cycles, the sequence of up and down phases that make up the business cycle must be repetitive and not periodic (Zarnowitz & Ozyildirim, 2002). Unlike in physics, the cycles of economic activity are not even or smooth to show regularity in terms of periodicity over a long-time horizon.

During the 1960s, frequent alternating periods of expansion and slowdowns in the economic activities in major industrial countries raised questions about the practical use of classical business cycles in analysing cyclical movements in economic activities. There was a need for a concept of the business cycle more in line with real economic activity. This led to the emergence of the concept of the growth cycle (Mintz, 1969). The growth cycle is defined as the movement or deviations of the actual growth rate of the economy from the long-run trend growth rate.

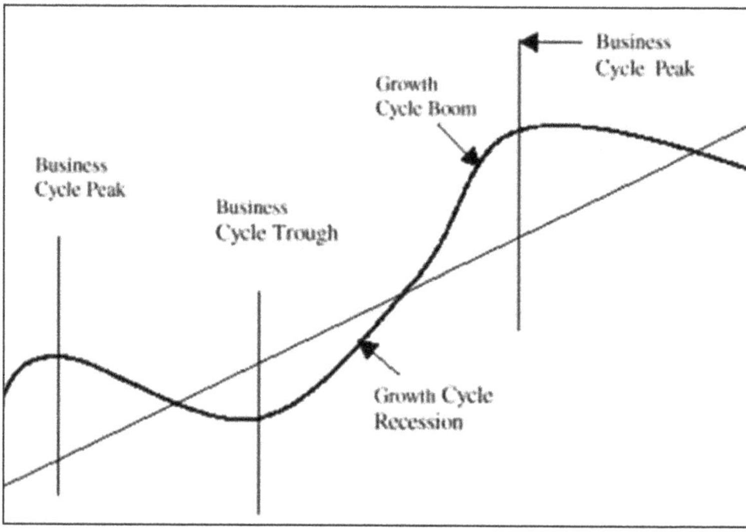

Figure 11.2: Classical Business Cycle and Growth Cycle

Source: Business cycles and leading indicators of industrial activity in India (2003).

The high-growth phase in a growth cycle coincides with the recovery phase of the business cycle, rather than the peak, while the low-growth phase corresponds to the later stages of expansion that eventually lead to a recession. However, some slowdowns continue to exhibit positive growth rates and result in renewed expansions rather than recessions. As a result, while all classical cycles are linked to growth cycles, not all growth cycles align with classical cycles. The peaks in the growth cycle tend to precede the peaks in the business cycle (Figure 11.2).

Mintz's pioneering work on growth cycle chronology (1969, 1972, 1974) was instrumental in helping the Organisation for Economic Co-operation and Development (OECD) develop leading indicators for its member countries to monitor growth cycles. In the early 1970s, growth cycle analysis formed the basis for the International Economic Indicators (IEI) project (Klein & Moore, 1985) at the NBER.

A key criticism of the growth cycle approach is that the growth rate is subject to frequent and sometimes significant revisions, especially near the end of the series. In other words, while growth cycles are not hard to identify in a historical time series, it is difficult to measure them accurately on a real-time basis (Boschan & Banerji, 1990). This difficulty arises because the trend in the most recent year or two cannot be accurately measured and must be estimated. As a result, the trend becomes highly unstable towards the end (Cullity & Banerji, 1996). So, it is difficult to determine growth cycle dates with precision, at least in real-time.

This limitation of growth cycle analysis led to the use of growth rate cycles to measure economic cycles. The growth rate cycles are nothing but the cyclical ups and downs in the growth rate of economic activity. The most common representation of the growth rates is through month-to-month changes or the same-month-year-ago changes. Alternatively, the growth rate can be represented by the six-month smoothed growth rate, a concept introduced by Moore. This method eliminates the need for extrapolating past trends, which was a key requirement in growth cycle analysis. The Economic Cycle Research Institute (ECRI) adopted the growth rate cycle concept to monitor economic activity in real time across various economies.

Over time, different concepts emerged for measuring business cycles. While business cycle and growth rate cycles were more suited for real-time monitoring and forecasting of economic activity, growth cycles were better suited for historical analysis (Klein, 1998).

11.1.1. Leading, Coincident and Lagging Indicators of Business Cycles

To examine the repetitive sequences of business cycles/growth cycles/growth rate cycles, the indicator approach consists essentially of classifying economic indicators into three categories—leading, coincident, and lagging. The next step is to combine the relevant components into corresponding composite indexes.

Leading indicators are those economic time series that precede the turning points of the reference series and hence can provide useful information regarding the future movement in the reference series a priori.

Coincidental indicators, however, move in tandem with the reference series. Usually, an index, called a coincidental index, is constructed using indicators from different sectors of the economy to represent current economic activity.

The lagging indicators, on the other hand, reach their turning points after the peaks and troughs of the reference series, meaning they lag behind overall economic activity. These indicators help to classify and confirm the underlying patterns of economic activity.

11.1.2. Composite Index of Leading Indicators

To track business cycles, a composite index of a group of economic time series is preferred rather than an individual series. The group of time series need to have similar characteristics (timing) as the reference series but represent different sectors of the economy. This is because the movement of an individual series may vary across different business cycles. Furthermore, it is difficult to predict in advance which individual variable will be most effective at identifying each turning point. Therefore, a composite index helps reduce the measurement error associated with a given cyclical indicator. As Moore (1982) noted:

"Virtually all economic statistics are subject to error and, hence, are often revised. Use of several measures necessitates an effort to determine what is the consensus among them, but it avoids some of the arbitrariness of deciding upon a single measure that perforce could be used only for a limited time with results that would be subject to revision every time the measure was revised."

Furthermore, Zarnowitz and Boschan (1975) point out that "To increase the chances of getting true signals and reduce those of getting false ones, it is advisable to rely on all such potentially useful (series) as a group."

The Composite Index of Leading Indicators (CILI) is a combination of various indicators that peak and trough earlier than the reference series. It serves as a useful forecasting and planning tool for policymakers, financial analysts, investors and businesses.

11.2. Literature Review

11.2.1. Identifying Macro Indicators for Constructing CILI

A significant body of literature exists on business cycle analysis and the construction of lead indicator indices. However, a review of all such studies is not feasible here.

Interest in business cycle theory began to grow in the 1970s, as major industrial economies experienced fluctuations in their real growth rates following a period of sustained and almost constant growth after the Second World War. Given the importance of the industrial sector in developed economies, using lead indicators of industrial output to predict economic conditions became increasingly popular. Most empirical studies focused on industrial production data, available monthly, as the reference series for leading indicator analysis. This approach gained acceptance among policymakers, investors, and the business community, as it provided early signals of recessions or recoveries.

The NBER did some early empirical work on leading indicators in the 1930s. Since then, the NBER has developed several versions of its leading series over the years and constructed a Composite Index of Leading Indicators (CILI). According to NBER, the CILI, being an aggregate of multiple indicators, can predict turning points more effectively than any single indicator, as no individual indicator can fully explain the cyclical fluctuations in overall activity over time.

The seminal work by Mitchell and Burns identified key business cycle indicators in the 1940s. Later, in 1950, Moore published a new list of 21 business cycle indicators, classified into three groups—leading, coincident, and lagging—based on their tendency to reach cyclical turning points before, at the same time as, or after the business cycle peaks and troughs. The Organization for Economic Co-operation and Development (OECD, 2005) later framed a methodology to construct the series on leading indicators for its member countries.

Recent empirical studies on leading indicators have developed new methods based on new economic theories, more refined statistical methods to test the forecasting reliability of the indicators, fine-tuning the determination of timing of turning points of the business cycle, etc. Different countries use a variety of leading indicators, such as the index of overtime hours, average work-week, new companies registered, new orders, applications for unemployment compensation, vendor performance, construction activity, stock prices, money supply, changes in raw material prices and the index of consumer expectations, among others.

11.2.2. Empirical Studies on Measuring Indian Business Cycles

A significant number of empirical studies have been conducted on business cycles in the Indian economy. While most of these studies have used the growth cycle methodology, a few have also explored the growth rate cycle approach.

Thorpe and Mitchell conducted pioneering work on business cycles in the Indian economy as early as 1926 at the NBER. Their study identified the chronology of cyclical fluctuations in the Indian economy from 1890 to 1925. The economists empirically proved that, even in an economy largely dominated by agriculture, distinct business cycles existed.

The seminal work on growth cycles in India by Chitre (1982) established synchronous movements in a large number of key economic indicators around their respective long-term trends, including non-agricultural net national product, industrial production, capital formation, money stock, and bank credit. The study involved constructing a diffusion and composite index comprising 15 indicators representing overall economic activity and identified five growth cycles during the period 1951–75. Using the net national product (NNP) series as the reference cycle, Nakamura (1991) identified coincident indicators for the Indian economy. The stylised facts about the business cycle in the Indian economy for the period 1951–1985 were investigated by Hatekar (1994) using the Hodrick–Prescott (HP) filter. While studies during this period (pre-1991 reform) identified cyclical behaviour in a wide range of economic activities, they were unable to isolate leading and lagging indicators, as the number of turning points in the GDP cycle was too few.

Dua and Banerji (1999) constructed an index of coincident economic indicators for the Indian economy starting from the mid-1950s, using the traditional NBER methodology with some modifications. The index was based on five economic indicators: real GDP at factor cost, the IIP, wages in the factory sector, registered unemployment, and industrial production of consumer goods. The study found that business cycles in India averaged over six years, with recessions lasting just under a year on average, while expansion cycles averaged less than three years, with downturns typically lasting around two years.

Mall (1999) used the growth cycle methodology to construct a composite index of leading indicators (CILI) based on 14 economic indicators, aimed at tracking the movement of the IIP-manufactured product from Q1 of 1989 to Q1 of 2000. The CILI was found to have a lead period of two quarters. Later, Dua and Banerji (2001) also constructed a composite index of leading indicators (CILI) that covered three broad sectors of the economy: monetary, construction, and corporate. This CILI had an average lead of 12 months at business cycle peaks and zero months at troughs. Additionally, the growth rate of the CILI had an average lead of three months at growth rate cycle peaks and zero months at troughs.

Chitre (2001) extended the earlier study and investigated 94 monthly indicators to understand the business cycles in India for the period 1951–1982. The eleven economic indicators, covering different segments of the economy, were used to construct the reference series using three different techniques: the Diffusion Index, the Composite Index, and the First Principal Component. All three methods yielded nearly identical reference dates. The study identified five leading indicators for business cycle peaks: production of pig iron, electricity production, cheque clearance, production of radio receivers, and the ratio of manufactured product prices to industrial raw materials prices. For business cycle troughs, seven leading indicators were identified: production of pig iron, electricity production, cheque clearance, ratio of manufactured product prices to industrial raw materials prices, aluminium production, production of capital goods, and motorcycle production.

A study by the OECD (2005) found that industrial production in India had registered 7 growth cycles (measured from trough to trough) over the period 1978 to 2004. The average duration of the complete cycle was 38 months, with an average expansion phase of 20 months and an average contraction phase of 18 months. From an initial set of 30 economic indicators, eight were identified as leading indicators for constructing the Composite Index of Leading Indicators (CILI). These indicators included: the Business Confidence Index, imports, money supply, exchange rate (Rupee per US Dollar), deposit interest rate, stock prices (SENSEX), production of basic goods, and production of intermediate goods. The CILI was found to have a median lead of four months over the two cycles registered in industrial production since 1995.

The RBI study (2002) recommended quarterly non-agricultural GDP as the reference series for business cycle analysis in India. It also pointed out some of the constraints in constructing the CILI, including the unavailability of time series data that are critical for the early-stage indicators (like new orders, order books, and construction approvals) and expectation-sensitive indicators (like capacity utilisation).

In 2006, the RBI published a detailed draft on leading indicators for Indian business cycles, analysing the cycles using both quarterly and monthly data. Between April 1993 and December 2000, the report identified six indicators for the Indian business cycle: narrow money, non-food credit, WPI raw materials, production of aluminium, rail goods traffic, and coal production. Two non-linear techniques, probit model and Artificial Neural Network method, were used to analyse the monthly growth rate cycle of industrial output. The study empirically found that the average duration of expansion and recession phases was 16 months and 14 months, respectively. Additionally, the yield of Treasury bills with a residual maturity of 15–91 days in the secondary market emerged as the most reliable economic indicator for predicting future business cycle movements.

Mohanty, Singh, and Jain (2003) used the IIP as the reference series and constructed a CILI comprising of non-oil imports, exports, US GDP, bank deposits, non-food credit, currency demand, money supply growth, prices of industrial raw materials, prices of manufactured products, treasury bill yields, stock prices, railway freight, and cargo handled at major ports. The study identified 13 growth cycles in the Indian economy from 1970–71 to 2001–02, each with varying durations. On average, the expansion phase lasted 12 months, while the recession phase lasted 16 months. The CILI was able to forecast the turning points of the reference series with a lead period of about 6 months.

Using the same reference series, Bordoloi and Rajesh (2007) identified 8 growth rate cycles in the Indian economy from April 1980 to March 2006. The average duration of both the expansion and recession phases was found to be 14 months each. Through a probit model, the study identified several leading economic indicators with forecast horizons of 3 months and 6 months. Notably, the study found that the yield on Treasury bills with a residual maturity of 15-91 days was the best single leading indicator of the economic cycle.

Sharma (2016) showed that the exchange rate was a significant leading indicator in the post-reform period in India, leading the turning points of business cycles (with GDP as the reference series) by three months. Paramanik and Kamaiah (2017) constructed a monthly CILI for the Indian business cycle between April 1994 and December 2015, using various economic indicators, such as narrow money, WPI, exchange rate, Sensex, imports, exports, and business cycle indicators from the US and the euro area. The IIP was taken as the reference series, and Principal Component Analysis (PCA) technique was applied to assign appropriate weights to each leading variable for constructing the CILI. The resulting CILI could accurately predict two major troughs in the Indian business cycle with lead times of six and eleven months, respectively.

Table 11.1 summarises the business cycles of India as identified in the studies mentioned above.

Table 11.1: Troughs and Peaks of Indian Business Cycle from Various Literature

Trough	Peak
Mall (1999), growth cycle approach	
	1951–52
1953–54	1956–57
1959–60	1964–65
1967–68	1969–70
1974–75	1978–79
1980–81	1989–90
1992–93	1995–96
Patnaik and Sharma (2002), classical approach	
	1956–57
1957–58	1963–64
1965–66	1978–79
1979–80	1990–91
1991–92	
Mohanty (2003), growth cycle	
1971 November	1972 December
1973 October	1974 July
1976 January	1976 August
1978 March	1979 March
1980 September	1982 May
1983 September	1984 September
1986 December	1987 July
1988 April	1989 January
1989 November	1990 September
1993 March	1993 November
1994 September	1995 May
1995 December	1996 August
1998 March	2000 November
2001 September	
Chitre (2004), growth cycle	
	1952 January
1953 November	1956 June
1958 June	1961 March
1962 February	1965 March

Trough	Peak
1968 January	1970 April
1970 November	1972 February
1975 January	1976 November
1977 October	1978 May
1980 April	
Dua and Banerji (2012), classical approach	
	1964 November
1965 November	1966 April
1967 April	1972 June
1973 May	1973 November
1975 February	1979 April
1980 March	1991 March
1991 September	1996 May
1996 November	
OECD (2016), growth cycle	
1997 October	1999 December
2003 January	2007 September
2009 March	2010 December
2013 April	
Pandey, Patnaik, and Shah (2017), growth cycle	
1999 December	2003 March
2007 June	2009 September
2011 June	2012 December

11.2.3. Predictive Ability of the Yield Curve

Although empirical studies have shown the significance of the slope of the yield curve in predicting economic slowdowns, these works are predominantly focused on developed economies, such as the US and Europe. Similar work in emerging economies has been much less common, as domestic bond markets in these regions have only started to deepen significantly after the turn of the millennium (IMF, 2002, 2003, 2005, 2006; Mehl & Reynaud, 2005).

Although Mitchell (1913) was the first to analyse the behaviour of interest rates across different maturities over the business cycle, it was Kessel (1965) who made specific, though not quantitative, references to the behaviour of term spreads. He highlighted that the spreads between long- and short-term rates remain low at the start of recessions, around the business cycle peak. Later, Butler (1978) used the yield curve as a predictor of economic activity. The late 1980s saw a surge in research on the yield curve as a leading indicator. Laurent (1988, 1989) used the term spread to predict GNP growth in the USA. The study by Harvey (1988) came up with a theoretical relationship between the real term spread and real consumption growth and presented some confirming empirical evidence. Estrella and Hardouvelis (1989, 1990, 1991) empirically demonstrated that the yield curve could be used to predict real growth in consumption, investment, and aggregate GNP, as well as NBER-dated recessions.

For forecasting real activity, Mishkin (1990) suggested that the best results could be empirically obtained by taking the difference between two Treasury yields with maturities that are far apart. Therefore, at the long end, the clear choice was the ten-year rate, as it is the longest maturity available in most countries consistently over a long period. At the short end, there were several options, ranging from overnight rates to 2-year bond rates. Estrella and Mishkin (1997) suggested the three-month Treasury rate as a reasonable choice. Furthermore, they compared the term structure (or yield curve) as a predictor of recessions with a wide range of other indicators and concluded that the yield curve is one of the best predictors, particularly at horizons of around one year.

Bernard and Gerlach (1996) found that domestic term spreads were useful for forecasting future recessions in eight countries, with a forecast horizon of at least five quarters, except for Japan and Belgium. The predictive power, measured through a Probit model, was highest in Germany, followed by Canada and the US. Foreign spreads were also found to contain information about the future movement of the domestic economy, especially of the German spread on the Japanese economy and the US on the UK economy.

Mensah and Tkacz (1998) examined the ability of several financial indicators over the period Q1 of 1957 to Q4 of 1996 to forecast Canadian recessions and found that the spread between the yield on Canadian long bonds and the 90 day Commercial Paper (CP) rate was particularly useful for this purpose. Stock and Watson (2003) examined a large number of competing indicators in forecasting output growth and concluded that, although none of them exhibited ideal properties, the term structure "came closest" to achieving those goals within the given limitations.

There have also been studies focused on the Euro area. Bernard and Gerlach (1998), in their paper, empirically showed for eight European countries that the slope of the yield curve is a good predictor of real economic activity. Berk and van Bergeijk (2001) examined 12 euro-area countries from 1970 to1998 and found that the term spread contained only limited information about future growth. Their work was based on the previous theoretical research of Estrella and Hardouvelis (1991) and Estrella and Mishkin (1996). Interestingly, it was found that the predictive power of the yield curve in the Euro area held until the end of 20th century, which almost disappeared by the beginning of 21st century and reappeared during the financial crisis (from 2008) and in the years following (Giacomini & Rossi, 2006; Chinn & Kucko, 2010; De Pace, 2011). Hvozdenska (2015) studied the relationship between the slope of the yield curve and economic activity in selected countries between the years 2000 and 2013. The results confirmed that the 10 years and 3 months yield spread had significant predictive power for real GDP growth after the financial crisis.

Arnaud Mehl (2006) found that the domestic yield curve in emerging economies contained in-sample information at both short and long forecast horizons and often improved out-of-sample forecasting performance. He further found that, for emerging economies with an exchange rate peg to the US dollar, the US yield curve was often a better predictor than the domestic curves for explaining their economic movements.

Studies have also provided strong empirical evidence of the yield curve's ability to predict economic slowdowns in India. Kanagasabapathy and Goyal (2002) used a probit model and found that the yield spread—worked out as the difference between the monthly average of secondary market yield on government securities with 10 years residual maturity and those with 2–3 months residual maturity—contained significant information about the future movement in the industrial sector in India over the period from April 1996 to July 2001, with a lead period of nine months.

Nath, Singh, and Dalvi (2012) showed in their study that the yield curve spread, measured by the difference between the spot rates of 10 years and 3 months securities, could effectively estimate economic activity in terms of the IIP. Using Probit and Logit models with data from 1997 to 2011, the results suggested that the yield spread can have significant predictive power for forecasting industrial production growth over a one-year time horizon.

Hemal Khandwala (2015) fitted a duration model to estimate the conditional probability of an economic recession, using the slope of the yield curve as a predictor for India. The focus was on determining the conditional probability of a recession rather than quantifying the general probability of an impending recession. The study found strong empirical evidence supporting the yield curve's ability to predict economic slowdowns in India.

11.3. Standard Methodology

11.3.1. Identifying Reference Series

The construction of a composite leading indicator starts with the selection of a reference series that suitably represents the whole economy. The reference series could be a single economic indicator or a combination of several economic indicators. Moore observed that the reference series should represent four key sectors of the economy, viz., output, employment, income, and trade. Accordingly, some studies construct a coincidental composite index of multiple indicators as the reference series. However, it is also common to use a single series as a reference series.

Ideally, GDP is adopted as the reference series, as it encompasses all economic activities. Alternatively, Non-Agriculture-GDP (NAGDP) may also be used as the reference series. However, if it is necessary to track the movement of the economy at a higher frequency, the monthly industrial production series is considered as the reference series as GDP or NAGDP are available only on quarterly basis.

After selecting the reference series, the following steps are performed, as shown in Figure 11.3. The series is seasonally adjusted and then passed through HP and BP filters to identify the business cycles. The peaks and troughs indicated by the reference series are then compared with those indicated by the CILI and the yield curve spread to find which one serves as the better lead indicator.

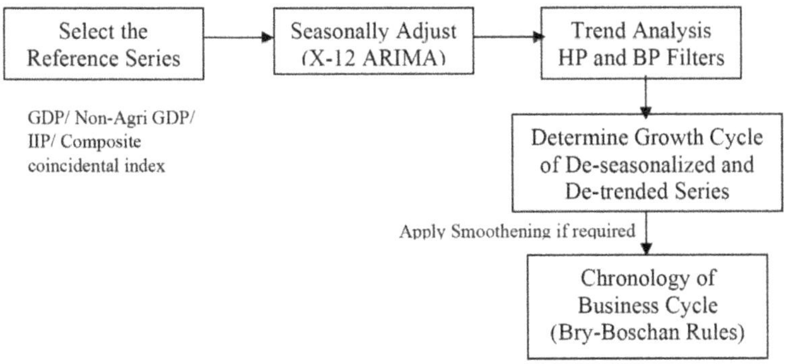

Figure 11.3: Selection of Reference Series

As the goal of the study is to predict changes in the economic cycle, the GDP series of India seems to be the most appropriate reference series, as it covers all sectors of the economy. The quarterly series is taken instead of annual data to allow for higher frequency analysis.

In India, the agriculture sector is highly volatile and heavily dependent on the monsoon. Keeping this into account, the study opts to use Non-Agriculture GDP (NAGDP) as the reference series, as suggested by the Working Group on Economic Indicators of the RBI (2002).

From a policy perspective, it might be better to have a series with high-frequency monthly data. The usual monthly reference series used in various studies is the IIP. However, since the industrial sector accounts for only 25% of NAGDP, the IIP is not considered for this study.

The time period considered for the study must be carefully determined. Until the 1970s, the agricultural sector accounted for more than 40% of India's GDP, and recessions during that time were largely triggered by the failures of monsoons. The agricultural sector played an important role in determining economic growth until the early 1990s. However, weather-related shocks, stemming from the dominance of agricultural, were not the only factors influencing exogenous shocks over endogenous ones as drivers of the Indian business cycle. During this period, the Indian economy was largely dominated by the government. It is said that the government owned roughly half of the economy's productive capacity in the first four decades following India's independence in 1947. As a result, the endogenous factors driving cyclical processes in free-market economies were hindered. Consequently, the functioning of leading indicators of the business cycle in market economies was distorted until the 1990s.

The Indian economy underwent a structural transformation following significant reforms after the unprecedented macroeconomic crisis of 1991, which was triggered by the Gulf crisis. By the late 1990s, the agricultural sector contributed about 25% to GDP, down from 40% in the late 1970s. With the increased use of irrigation and the growth of agri-allied activities, the economy has become much less vulnerable to weather-related shocks. Far-reaching economic liberalization helped mitigate the extreme distortions caused by free-market mechanisms. The economy, as a whole, was influenced by global trade cycles due to a relatively open trade regime and increased capital inflows. Hence, after the 1991 reforms, cyclical variations in economic activities in India were majorly influenced by the internal dynamics of the economy, along with supply shocks. The leading indicators began to function as expected only after the 1990s. Therefore, it is not relevant to consider data points before 1991 for this study.

Quarterly GDP numbers are available since the 1990s, but the rupee yield curve in the gilts market only started emerging in 1996. Therefore, the data series after 2000 seems most appropriate for this study. Some major economic series (such as GDP, IIP, WPI, etc.) have been revised with a new base year of 2011–12. To ensure a longer series, spliced data can be used, combining the old series with a base year of 2004–05. So, the study will consider data from 2005 to 2018.

Unfortunately, the Ministry of Statistics and Programme Implementation (MoSPI) had not released the back data of the quarterly GDP series with the 2011–12 base year by the time of this study. In August 2018, MoSPI announced the release of a back series for GDP data, provided by an expert panel. However, it was not possible to use this data as: (1) the series is just indicative and not final; and (2) only annual, not quarterly, data was made available. By the end of November 2018, NITI Aayog, along with MoSPI, announced the release of the official back series data for GDP. However, this data was not publicly available at the time the study was being completed.

Hence, for the quarterly NAGDP series, the difference between the old series and the new series is calculated and then sliced backward to arrive at a longer time series starting from 2005. This adjusted series is used as the reference series.

11.3.2. Determination of Turning Points

The initial detection of turning points is carried out using the procedures and rules developed by the NBER (Bry & Boschan, 1971), supplemented by experienced judgment. The following criteria must be met for the selection of a turning point:

- The peaks and troughs must alternate.
- Alternating peaks and troughs must be followed by five months of opposite movement to qualify as a turning point.
- Harding and Pagan (2002) identify that the minimum duration of a phase should be two quarters, with a complete cycle lasting at least five quarters.
- In terms of monthly data, the minimum duration for a phase is five months, and for a complete cycle, it is 15 months.
- If the data at the turning point is flat, the most recent period is selected as the turning point.

These rules of thumb, applied by the Economic Cycle Research Institute (ECRI), trace their roots to the 1946 study by Burns and Mitchell.

11.3.3. Construction of CILI

The choice of economic indicators for CILI is very important, as the forecast performance heavily depends on the quality of the selected indicators. These indicators should cover all broad sectors of the economy, such as the real sector, financial sector, government sector, and external sector, among others.

De Leeuw (1991) highlights five rationales for the selection of a leading indicator:

1. **Production Time:** This refers to the time taken from the decision to produce until actual production occurs.
2. **Ease of Adaptation:** Certain economic factors have lower costs for short-run variations than others (e.g., weekly hours compared to employment).
3. **Market Expectations:** Some time series are particularly sensitive to future economic activity, reflecting or responding to market expectations.
4. **Prime Movers:** Changes in economic activity are basically driven by a few measurable forces, such as monetary and fiscal policies.
5. **Change-versus-Level:** Variations in economic time series tend to occur before changes in levels, signalling upward or downward movements earlier.

The traditional NBER approach uses the following six criteria for selecting a series:

1. **Economic Significance:** How important is the indicator in reflecting business cycles?
2. **Statistical Adequacy:** How well does the series measure the economic variable?
3. **Timing:** How consistently has the series led the economy at turning points?
4. **Conformity:** How regularly has the indicator conformed to the business cycle as a whole?
5. **Smoothness:** How easily can non-random movements of the series be distinguished from the irregular component?
6. **Timeliness:** How promptly is the series made available?

As stated in the RBI report (2006), each criterion is assigned a score, and an overall score for each indicator is then calculated. The indicators selected for forecasting overall economic activity are chosen based on their overall scores.

The first step is to prepare an exhaustive list of time series, each representing a broad sector of the economy. These series are then evaluated based on their relevance, cyclical behaviour, and practical considerations. Predicting cyclical turning points is one of the most challenging exercises in economic forecasting.

The steps involved are as follows (Figure 11.4):

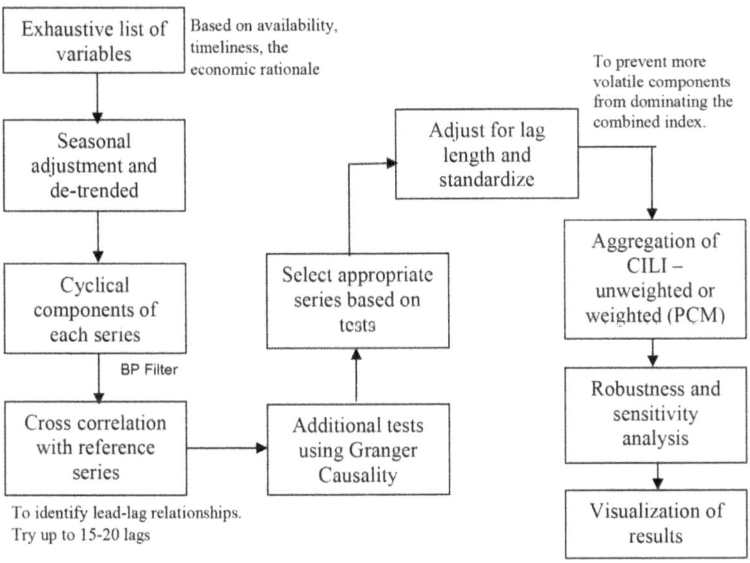

Figure 11.4: Construction of CILI

Let's first look at various economic series and decide on the lead indicators that can be used to predict changes in the reference series. Based on factors such as availability, timeliness, and economic rationale—such as production time, ease of adaption, market expectations, and prime movers—an exhaustive list of potential leading indicators is compiled (Table 11.2). These indicators are chosen to cover the five key sectors, viz., monetary, banking, financial market, real sector, and external sector (Paramanik and Kamaiah, 2017). The quarterly data of these indicators are sourced from CSO, RBI and CMIE, covering the period from Q2 of 2005 to Q1 of 2018.

Table 11.2: Choice of Lead Indicators

No.	Indicator	Type	Description
1	Bank Credit (CREDIT)	Prime Mover	Sharp growth in overall credit indicates higher output growth. Bank credits are disbursed to meet investment and consumption needs—this helps in raising economic activities (Chitre, 1991).
2	Non-food Credit (NONFOODCREDIT)	Prime Mover	Non-food credit growth indicates higher investment demand in the economy and, hence, higher expected growth. (RBI, 2006; Mohanty, Singh, & Jain, 2003).
3	Exports (EXPORTS)	Prime Mover	Within the external sector indicators, rising exports causes manufacturing or producing firms that are directly or indirectly related to exports, to produce more. This leads to higher output in the economy (Chitre, 1991; Mohanty, Singh, & Jain, 2003; Paramanik & Kamaiah, 2017).
4	Government Expenditure (GOVTEX)	Prime Mover	Increased government expenditure gives an immediate fiscal boost to the economy (Nomura, 2018).
5	Money Supply (M3)	Prime Mover	The monetary indicator, broad money is necessary for smooth transactions. Easy liquidity plays a vital role in determining output. A rise in the money supply is expected to help increase the output in an economy in the future. However, in the long run, it may adversely impact, leading to inflation (Mohanty, Singh, & Jain, 2003).
6	Money Supply (M1)	Prime Mover	The narrow money is also a monetary indicator that helps boost growth. (Paramanik & Kamaiah, 2017).
7	Currency with Public (CWP)	Prime Mover	More currency with the public leads to higher consumption which increases growth. However, just like other monetary indicators, in the long run, a sustained high currency with the public may lead to inflation (RBI, 2006; Mohanty, Singh, & Jain, 2003).

No.	Indicator	Type	Description
8	Repo Rate (REPO)	Prime Mover	An increase in the policy rate increases the cost of credit and is expected to lead to a reduction in the investment rate, which may lead to fall in the output in the future (Chitre, 1991; Nomura, 2018).
9	US Gross Domestic Product (USGDP)	Prime Mover	The external sector of an economy, particularly the exports, depends on the movement of the global economy. Higher global growth leads to higher exports and higher investment inflows. The growth of the US economy can be used as a leading indicator (RBI, 2006; Mohanty, Singh, & Jain, 2003; Paramanik & Kamaiah, 2017).
10	Exchange Rate: Rupee/ US Dollar (RSUSD)	Other	Sharply depreciating exchange rate indicates a macro vulnerability of the economy (Sharma, 2016; Paramanik & Kamaiah, 2017).
11	Cargo Handled at Major Ports (CARGO)	Other	Cargo handled in the major ports reflects the transactions done by an economy with the rest of the world (RBI, 2006; Mohanty, Singh, & Jain, 2003).
12	Foreign Tourist Arrival (FORTOURIST)	Other	Increase in foreign tourist arrival means increased gains in tourism/ services sector within the economy.
13	Freight Revenues of the Railways (FREIGHT)	Other	Freight revenues reflect the economic activities within the economy (Chitre, 1991; Mohanty, Singh, & Jain, 2003).
14	Index of Industrial Production (IIP)	Other	The production of capital goods, intermediate goods, consumer goods, cement, and electricity are expected to push up the overall output further (RBI, 2006; Chitre, 1991).
15	IIP Electrical (IIPELEC)	Other	Same as above. (RBI, 2006, Chitre, 1991).
16	IIP Manufacturing (IIPMAN)	Other	Same as above.
17	Commercial Vehicle Sales (CMV)	Other	Higher sale in commercial vehicle represents higher investment in the economy (RBI, 2006).
18	Passenger Car Sales (PASSENGER)	Other	Increased sale in passenger cars indicates higher consumption (Nomura, 2018).

No.	Indicator	Type	Description
19	2- and 3-Wheeler Sales (WHEELER)	Other	Increased sale in 2- and 3-wheelers indicates growing rural economy.
20	Rural Wage (RURALWAGE)	Other	Wage growth indicates higher demand and higher activities.
21	Imports (IMPORTS)	Expectations Sensitive	Increase in the imports indicates high domestic demand for the imported items, either for consumption or investment purposes. These are reflections of a growing economy (Chitre, 1991; Paramanik & Kamaiah, 2017).
22	Non-oil Imports (NONCRUDEIM)	Expectations Sensitive	Non-oil imports include items of capital goods and many others, which are re-exported and, thus, signal higher investments and the possibility of an enhanced economic activity in the economy (RBI, 2006; Mohanty, Singh, & Jain, 2003).
23	Wholesale Price Index (WPI)	Expectations Sensitive	Rising cost of the industrial raw materials may be the result of increasing demand from the industrial sector due to higher demand/economic activities. However, in the long run, sustained higher cost of the production may decrease profitability of the firms and adversely affect the economy (RBI, 2006; Mohanty, Singh, & Jain, 2003).
24	WPI of Manufactured Goods (WPIMAN)	Expectations Sensitive	Same as above.
25	WPI of Primary Goods (WPIPRI)	Expectations Sensitive	Same as above.
26	Brent Oil Price (BRENTOIL)	Expectations Sensitive	Macro stability of Indian economy is highly dependent on oil prices as India imports almost 80% of its requirements. High oil prices lead to higher inflation, higher CAD, and higher fiscal deficit.

No.	Indicator	Type	Description
27	Stock Prices-BSE Sensex (SENSEX)	Expectations Sensitive	Several studies on business cycle have found stock price as an important leading indicator for future growth. According to Estrella and Mishkin (1996), Stock prices incorporate views regarding both the future profitability of the firm and future interest or discounting rates. Thus, a stock price reflects profit expectations and incorporates the market psychology. A rising stock price reflects the positive expectation about the economy. (Nomura, 2018; Mohanty, Singh, & Jain, 2003; Paramanik & Kamaiah, 2017).

The cross-correlation between various lagged cyclical indicators and the reference series is calculated. The number of months or quarters at which the correlation coefficient is the highest indicates the average lead of the indicator over the reference series. However, there are a few limitations to this method. The presence of outliers can affect the estimate of the cross-correlation coefficient. Despite this, the composite indicator constructed from a selection of series provides reliable information about the turning points of the reference series.

The CILI is constructed as the simple average of selected leading indicators, using the traditional NBER methodology with some modifications. Each series is first detrended. Next, to prevent more volatile components from dominating the index, as prescribed by the NBER, the cyclical components of the series are divided by the standardisation factor, which is the standard deviation of the detrended trend-cycle component. After that, the standardised series are simply averaged across all components in the index. This scaling process implicitly provides a weighing scheme, meaning no explicit weights need to be assigned. Finally, a trend adjustment is applied to the combined index by multiplying it by a suitable factor to scale the trend up or down to align with the reference series, the NAGDP.

11.3.4. Slope of The Yield Curve

To analyse the advantage of the slope of the yield curve in India as a predictor of domestic growth, a standard methodology outlined by Stock and Watson (2003) is applied. The slope of the yield curve, denoted as X_t, is defined as the difference at the time-period t between the yield on the long-term (domestic) government bond (in local currency), denoted r^l_t, and that on the short-term (domestic) treasury bill (in local currency), denoted r^s_t.

$$X_t = r^l_t - r^s_t \qquad (1)$$

This slope of the yield curve is then analysed to determine whether it can predict turning points in the reference series.

The ten-year benchmark bond is used as the long-term government bond, while the three-month (91 days) government bill serves as the short-term series. The yields of ten-year government bonds and three-month (91 days) government bills, as traded in secondary markets, have been obtained from CCIL and NSE for the period from Q2 of 2005 to Q1 of 2018. The difference between these two bond yield series is used as a leading indicator.

Until 1991, interest rates were controlled by the government, and the RBI monetised government debt. The Indian currency was pegged to the value basket of currencies of major trade partners. The balance of payment crisis in 1991 forced India to bring in several significant reforms, including the adoption of market-based interest rates and the public auction of government bonds. These reforms led to the opening up of the economy, the introduction of a market-determined, free-floating currency, and the abolition of the License Raj. The rupee yield curve in the gilt market started to emerge since 1996 only. Since the spliced GDP growth series starts from 2005, the yield rates are considered for that period as well.

In India, short-term rates usually track long-term rates. However, when examining the chart of the 10-year benchmark G-Sec bond rate versus the 3-month T-Bill rate (Figure 11.5), we see that, in 2017, the long-term rate did not track the short-term rate as closely as it had in previous years. The graph shows that during periods when the RBI conducts OMOs to release excess liquidity—artificially lowering short-term rates—and tighten liquidity in response to inflationary pressure, the 10-year rate diverges from the short-term rate. Furthermore, the 10-year rate appears to fluctuate less compared to the short-term rate since about April 2009. This shift in the relationship between the 3-month rate and the 10-year rate indicates that the fundamental information conveyed by the yield spread may have changed as well.

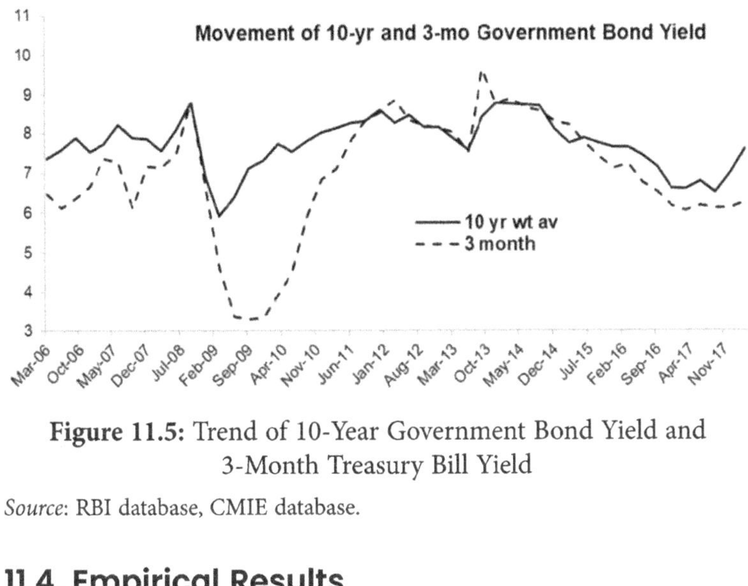

Figure 11.5: Trend of 10-Year Government Bond Yield and 3-Month Treasury Bill Yield

Source: RBI database, CMIE database.

11.4. Empirical Results

11.4.1. Reference Series

As explained in the previous section, the quarterly GDP series (spliced series) is used to identify the chronology of business cycle turning points. First, we adjust the Non-Agricultural GDP series for seasonality. Next, the seasonally adjusted series is filtered through the HP filter to extract the cyclical component. The NBER suggests a business cycle periodicity of 2 to 8 years for extracting the cyclical component. The standardised cyclical component is then subjected to the dating algorithm developed by Bry and Boschan (1971).

Figure 11.6 and Table 11.3 given below show three episodes of recession in the economy during the period from 2005 to 2018.

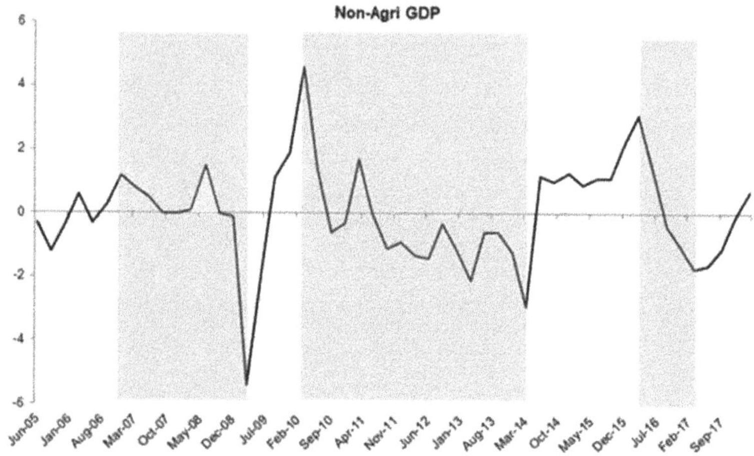

Figure 11.6: Turning Points in Cyclical Component of Seasonality Adjusted NAGDP

Table 11.3: Results of Bry-Boschan Dating Algorithm Bry-Boschan Output Business Cycles

Turning Points for NAGDP	
Peaks	Troughs
2006Q4	2009Q1
2010Q1	2014Q1
2016Q1	2017Q1

Source: Author's calculations.

December 2006 to March 2009 Recession: India's growth rate decelerated during this period as the global financial crisis affected the country through various channels, including trade and financial markets. Export growth sharply decelerated, and both credit growth and investment followed suit, in line with the global economic downturn.

March 2009 to March 2010 Expansion: India's growth rebounded swiftly after the financial crisis, driven by coordinated efforts from the government and the central bank. On the monetary front, the RBI slashed the policy rate by a substantial 425 basis points between September 2008 and April 2009. The government suspended the Fiscal Responsibility and Budget Management (FRBM) Act, 2003, which mandated a reduction of the fiscal deficit to 3% of GDP, to accommodate fiscal stimulus. As a result, the fiscal deficit widened to 6% of GDP in FY 2008–09, up from 2.5% in the previous fiscal year.

March 2010 to March 2014 Recession: Economic growth started to falter after 2010, with the GDP growth rate plummeted to 5.4% in 2012–13 due to a combination of factors. The delay in withdrawing the fiscal and monetary stimulus intended to cushion the economy during the financial crisis resulted in high inflation and a widening current account deficit. Macro instability became more apparent as the US Federal Reserve announced the gradual winding down of its liquidity measures (the so-called "tapper-tantrum").

March 2014 to March 2016: The growth picked up again, supported by improved macroeconomic stability and subdued oil prices. The GDP growth rate touched 8.1% in 2015–16.

March 2016 to March 2017: The growth slowed as investment did not pick up as expected. The twin balance sheet problem—non-performing assets (NPAs) on banks' balance sheets and over-leveraged corporates, particularly in the infrastructure sector—hurt growth. Additionally, the demonetisation in November 2016 squeezed liquidity in the cash-driven informal sector of the economy.

11.4.2. The Lead Indicators and Construction of CILI

The technical advisory group of the Reserve Bank of India (RBI Report, 2006) recommends that the lead period for the composite index should be at least two quarters ahead for quarterly data (e.g., NAGDP) and four months ahead for monthly data (e.g., IIP).

Table 11.4, given below, presents the set of potential leading indicators initially selected based on the cross-correlation analysis (Appendix I). From the table, cargo at major ports and M1 (narrow money) emerge as the most promising leading indicators, with a correlation coefficient of 0.68 with NAGDP at a lead of 1-quarter. Similarly, the correlation coefficient between IIP and NAGDP at a lead period of 1-quarter is found to be 0.47. But from the policy point of view, it is necessary to have some idea about the future movement of the economy at least 2-quarters ahead. It can be observed from the cross-correlation table that, even at a lead period of 2-quarters, the correlation coefficients between cargo at major ports and M1 with NAGDP are found to be 0.41 and 0.39, respectively.

Table 11.4: Potential Leading Indicators for NAGDP—Growth Rate Cycle

Indicators	Lead Period	Correlation Coefficient
IIP	1	0.47
IIP Manufacturing	1	0.42
M3	1	0.34
M1	1	0.68
Cargo at Major Ports	1	0.68
Revenue from Railway Freight	1	0.43
CMV Sales	1	0.49
Passenger Car Sales	1	0.57

Source: Author's calculations

From the exhaustive list of potential leading economic indicators, an optimal combination of four indicators is selected that can track NAGDP at least two quarters ahead. These indicators include IIP, M1 (money supply), cargo handled at major ports, and passenger car sales.

There are two main methods for constructing the CILI—one uses the simple average of the selected leading indicators, while the other employs statistical techniques, such as PCA.

1. Construction of CILI—Using Simple Average

Each of the potential series is first detrended. Next, to prevent more volatile components from overwhelming the index, the cyclical components are divided by the standardisation factor, as outlined in the methodology. The standardised series are then averaged with equal weights across all components in the index. This process of scaling each series to reduce the impact of more volatile series implicitly establishes a weighing scheme for the index. Finally, the raw index is adjusted for trend. Figure 11.7, given below, plots both the reference NAGDP and the CILI constructed using simple average.

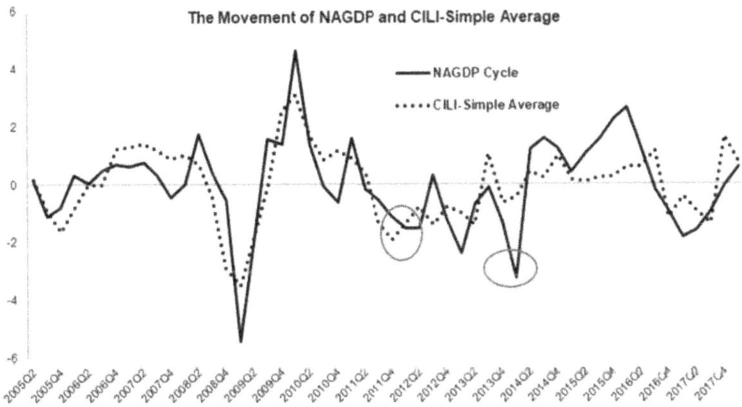

Figure 11.7: Movement of CILI—Simple Average and NAGDP (Reference Series)

Source: Author's calculations.

It is seen that the CILI leads the non-agricultural GDP cycle by one quarter and sometimes even coincides with it.

It is observed (Table 11.5) that the predictive ability of the CILI-Simple Average was poor during the recent slowdown of 2016–2017. Moreover, the CILI constructed moved more in tandem with the NAGDP during the 2009–2010 period.

Table 11.5: Lead Record of the CILI—Simple Average

NAGDP, Growth Rate Cycle		CILI—Simple Average		Lead (-)/ Lag (+) in Quarters	
Troughs	**Peaks**	**Troughs**	**Peaks**	**Troughs**	**Peaks**
	2006 Q4		2006 Q4		0
2007 Q4	2008 Q2	2007 Q4	2007 Q2	0	-4

2009 Q1	2010 Q1	2009 Q1	2010 Q1	0	0
2012 Q1	2013 Q3	2011 Q4	2013 Q3	-1	0
2014 Q1	2016 Q1	2013 Q4	2016 Q3	-1	2
2017 Q1		2017 Q3		2	
Average Duration				**0**	**-1**

Source: Author's calculations.

2. Construction of CILI—PCA Method

To improve predictability, an attempt has been made to construct the CILI using PCA. For this purpose, four potential economic indicators have been selected, as mentioned earlier—IIP, M1 (money supply), cargo handled at major ports, and passenger car sales.

It is observed that the first principal component explains the maximum variance across all the individual indicators (eigenvalue of 2.2), as shown in Table 11.6. The second principal component explains the remaining variance, with a variance of 0.8. Together, the first three principal components account for 93% of the total variation in the data.

Table 11.6: Eigenvalues of Individual TAI Indicators (PCA)

PC	Eigen Value	Difference	% Variance	Cumulative Variance
1	2.18	1.38	0.55	0.55
2	0.80	0.06	0.20	0.75
3	0.75	0.48	0.19	0.93
4	0.27	-	0.07	1.00

Source: Author's calculations.

The CILI-PCA is constructed and plotted against the reference series of NAGDP as shown in the chart below (Figure 11.8).

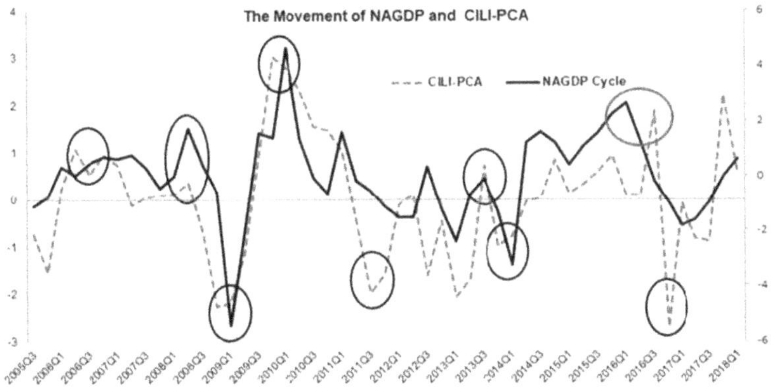

Figure 11.8: Movement of CILI-PCA and NAGDP (Reference Series)

Source: Author's calculations

The predictive ability improves when using the CILI constructed through PCA (Table 11.7). The CILI leads the NAGDP cycle peaks and troughs by one quarter. However, its predictive ability remains poor during the 2016 slowdown, as it fails to capture the downturn and lags the reference series by two quarters in 2016. Afterward, its predictive ability improves once again.

Table 11.7: Lead Record of the CILI-PCA

NAGDP, Growth Rate Cycle		**CILI-PCA**		**Lead (-)/ Lag (+) in Quarters**	
Troughs	**Peaks**	**Troughs**	**Peaks**	**Troughs**	**Peaks**
	2006 Q4		2006 Q2		-2
2007 Q4	2008 Q2	2007 Q2	2008 Q2	0	0
2009 Q1	2010 Q1	2008 Q4	2009 Q4	-1	-1
2012 Q1	2013 Q3	2011 Q3	2013 Q3	-2	0
2014 Q1	2016 Q1	2013 Q4	2016 Q3	-1	2
2017 Q1		2016 Q4		1	
Average Duration				**-1**	**-1**

Source: Author's calculations.

Next, we use a Probit model to assess the predictive ability of the CILI in forecasting the different phases of the economy, as represented by NAGDP. Three different threshold probability levels have been taken into consideration, viz., 40%, 50%, and 60%, as suggested by the literature (RBI, 2006).

Table 11.8 below shows the forecasting power of the Probit model in correctly identifying the different phases for each threshold probability level. Corresponding to a threshold level of 0.5, the estimated CILI-PCA model correctly forecasts 48% of the observations in the expansion phase and 76% of the observations in the recession phase. Overall, the model correctly forecasts 63% of the total number of observations. The predictive ability slightly deteriorates at the threshold level of 0.4.

Table 11.8: Predictive evaluation of CILI-PCA – NAGDP cycle (Probit)

Threshold Probability		0.4	0.5	0.6
Expansion	No of cases forecasted correctly	3	11	17
	Total no of cases	23	23	23
	Percentage of correctly forecasted	13.0	47.8	73.9
Recession	No of cases forecasted correctly	25	22	13
	Total no of cases	29	29	29
	Percentage of correctly forecasted	86.2	75.9	44.8
Total	No of cases forecasted correctly	28	33	30
	Total no of cases	52	52	52
	Percentage of correctly forecasted	53.9	63.5	57.7

Source: Author's calculations.

11.4.3. Slope of the Yield Curve as Lead Indicator

Figure 11.9 below traces the movement of NAGDP growth rate (the cyclical component) with that of the slope of the yield curve.

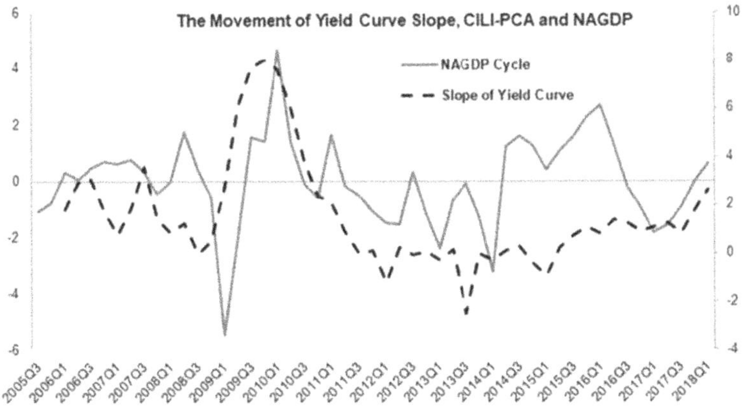

Figure 11.9: Movement of Slope of Yield Curve and NAGDP (Reference Series)

Source: Author's calculations.

It is evident that the yield curve slope leads the turning points of the NAGDP. Table 11.9 below summarises the turning points of both NAGDP and the yield curve slope. The yield curve has been able to predict the turning points of NAGDP one to two quarters ahead. An interesting point to note is that the slope of the yield curve also fails to predict the slowdown in 2016, lagging by one quarter. However, its predictive ability improves thereafter.

Table 11.9: Lead Record of the Yield Spread

NAGDP, Growth Rate Cycle		**Yield Spread**		**Lead (-)/ Lag (+) in Quarters**	
Troughs	**Peaks**	**Troughs**	**Peaks**	**Troughs**	**Peaks**
	2006 Q4		2006 Q3		-1
2007 Q4	2008 Q2	2007 Q1	2007 Q3	-1	-3
2009 Q1	2010 Q1	2008 Q3	2009 Q4	-1	-1
2012 Q1	2013 Q3	2012 Q1	2013 Q2	0	-1
2014 Q1	2016 Q1	2013 Q3	2016 Q2	-2	1
2017 Q1		2016 Q4		-1	
Average Duration				**-1**	**-1.5**

Source: Author's calculations.

Table 11.10: Predictive Evaluation of Slope—NAGDP Cycle (Probit)

Threshold Probability		0.4	0.5	0.6
Expansion	No of cases forecasted correctly	4	6	10
	Total no of cases	20	20	20
	Percentage of correctly forecasted	20.0	30.0	50.0
Recession	No of cases forecasted correctly	28	26	22
	Total no of cases	29	29	29
	Percentage of correctly forecasted	96.6	89.7	75.9
Total	No of cases forecasted correctly	32	32	32
	Total no of cases	49	49	49
	Percentage of correctly forecasted	65.3	65.3	65.3

Source: Author's calculations.

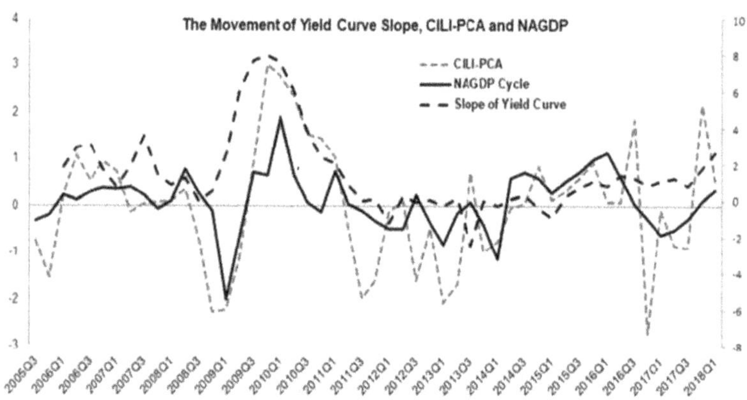

Figure 11.10: Movement of NAGDP, Slope of Yield Curve, and CILI-PCA

Source: Author's calculations.

Again, we estimate a Probit model to assess the ability of the slope of the yield curve to predict the different phases of the economy. Table 11.10 given above, summarises the forecasting power of the Probit model. Corresponding to a threshold level of 0.5, the estimated model correctly forecasts 30% of the observations in the expansion phase and 89.7% of the observations in the recession phase. Overall, the model correctly forecasts 65% of the total number of observations, which is better than the CILI constructed with four potential leading indicators.

From the above discussion, it is observed that the predictive ability of the slope of the yield curve is much better than CILI created with four indicators. This can be visualised through Figure 11.10, that plots all three series, NAGDP, CILI, and yield curve slope together.

11.5. Predictive Ability of Slope of the Yield Curve

This study explores the importance of the slope of the yield curve (or yield spread) in forecasting future non-agriculture GDP growth in India. Using data from 2005 to 2018, it is observed that the yield spread—the difference between the 10-year and 3-month government bond yields—has significant predictive power when forecasting NAGDP growth. The CILI, constructed with high-frequency potential indicators, can also predict the turning points of NAGDP. However, the slope of the yield curve is a better predictor compared to the constructed CILI. The yield curve is able to predict the turning points of NAGDP around two quarters ahead, while the CILI leads NAGDP cycle peaks and troughs by one quarter. The Probit model shows that the slope of the yield curve correctly forecasts 89.7% of the observations in the recession phase of NAGDP, whereas the CILI correctly forecasts 76% of the observations in the recession phase. This firmly confirms that the yield curve in India embodies valuable information that can help forecast future economic activity.

It may be argued that with sophisticated macro-econometric models and expert judgment, there is no need to rely on the yield spread to predict economic activity. However, the yield curve can easily supplement the results from complicated econometric models. First, prediction using the yield spread is simple and straightforward—by simply observing the difference between the 10-year government bond yield and the 3-month treasury yield, one can predict the probability of a slowdown or recession. Second, the indications of the yield curve can be used to validate the results obtained from the large econometric model. If both results are the same, confidence in the prediction increases. In the case of differences in findings, it may be advisable to double-check the assumptions and variables used in the model.

The study showed that neither the CILI nor the yield spread was able to predict the slowdown in NAGDP during 2016. This may be because the initial estimates of GDP growth for those quarters were used. As the growth data gets revised subsequently, the predictive ability of these indicators may improve as well.

CHAPTER 12

The Factors of the Yield Curve and their Dynamics

The "yield curve" or term structure of interest rates is constructed by plotting the interest rates of sovereign bonds against their respective maturities. We already know that the bond yields of all maturities change every day due to market fluctuations, which in turn alters the "shape" of the yield curve—these changes offer valuable insights into the economic outlook.

As mentioned in the previous chapter, the Fisher effect tells us that the nominal yield is the sum of two components—the expected real interest rate and expected inflation. The expected real rate is influenced by expectations of future monetary policy and reflects anticipated real growth. Furthermore, inflation is positively related to economic activity, and thus, also related to future growth. Therefore, the yield curve contains valuable information about economic activity.

In the last two decades, there have been several studies exploring the relationship between the term structure of interest rates and economic activities in an economy, examining the linkage between the real sectors of the economy and the financial sectors.

Until recently, standard macroeconomic models primarily focused on the impact of macroeconomic factors on short-term interest rates. For example, the study by Fuhrer and Moore (1995) examines the correlation between the real economy and the shortest-term interest rate of the yield curve. It was only after 2000 that studies started to explore the impact of macroeconomic factors on the entire yield curve, leading to a new segment of studies aimed at modelling the complete yield curve. The literature shows that the shape of the yield curve can be modelled using three unobservable factors—Level, Slope, and Curvature—that capture the entire information of the curve at any given time. These factors reflect market expectations about future inflation, growth, and policy rate changes in a compact form (Evans & Marshall, 1998, 2007; Ang & Piazzesi, 2003; Diebold et al., 2004, 2005). Evans and Marshall (2001) formulate several models to look at how the "level", "slope," and "curvature" factors are influenced by structural shocks identified within those models.

In India, the RBI, which follows an inflation-targeting strategy, needs to monitor the transmission of its monetary policy. This can be done by tracking the impact of policy shocks on the term structure of interest rates. Our study tries to understand the impact of macroeconomic shocks on the entire yield curve (defined by the factors of the yield curve) and thereby evaluate the influence of the RBI's policy announcements on the debt market.

The contributions of our study are two-fold. First, the yield curve factors for government bonds are computed using three different methodologies for the Indian market at high frequency—Market Proxies, Principal Components Analysis (PCA), and the Nelson-Siegel Model. These models help distill the entire yield curve into three factors—Level, Slope and Curvature. However, the factors derived from these three methods are not directly comparable, even though they exhibit some correlation. The impact of various macroeconomic shocks (such as demand, supply, policy rates, liquidity, and exchange rates) on the factors of the yield curve, derived from each of the three methods, is empirically estimated. Analysing the impact of macro shocks on these different factors helps us to demonstrate the robustness of our study. Second, the daily liquidity operations of RBI are used to derive the data on net liquidity injected into the system. If the RBI is injecting liquidity, the system is in a liquidity deficit, and vice versa. The impact of system liquidity shocks, using daily liquidity operations of the RBI, is being analysed for the first time.

Evaluating the impact of macro shocks on the factors provides a better understanding of how sudden deviations in macroeconomic variables affect the shape of the yield curve.

The study consists of two empirical sections—one for estimating the yield curve factors using three different approaches, and the other for analysing the impulse response of various macro shocks on the estimated factors.

12.1. Literature Reviews: Latent Factors of Yield Curve and Impact of Macroeconomic Parameters

There is a vast body of literature exploring the relationship between the yield curve and macroeconomic variables. A number of seminal works on latent factors of the yield curve are worth looking into. For instance, Dai and Singleton (2000), in their paper, discuss the unobserved factors that explain the yield curve. Similarly, Hördahl et al. (2002), Wu (2002) and Ang and Piazzesi (2003) incorporate macroeconomic determinants into the term structure of interest rates, capturing the dynamics of both these factors and broader macroeconomic variables. In a similar vein, Diebold and Li (2006) capture the dynamics of the factors of the yield curve—level, slope, and curvature—by using a dynamic version of the Nelson-Siegel model (1987).

Another line of research employs nonparametric methods to estimate the factors influencing the interest rate structure. Litterman and Scheinkman (1991) and Bliss (1997) use this method to identify three key factors—level, slope, and curvature—that explain the dynamics of the yield curve. Their studies find that these factors contain similar information to that derived from the Nelson-Siegel model. Together, these factors are able to explain 97% of the variations in interest rates. Moreover, Cortázar and Schwartz (1994) report similar results using PCA in the commodities market.

Several studies have examined the impact of changes in macroeconomic factors on the level, slope, and curvature of the yield curve. The study by Ang and Piazzesi (2003) finds that observable factors, including economic growth, explain most of the movement at the short end, while unobservable factors (level, slope, and curvature) explain most of the movement at the long end of the yield curve. Evans and Marshall (1998, 2007) demonstrate that macroeconomic shocks, particularly through monetary policy, have a greater impact on yields for lower maturities, thereby altering the shape of the yield curve by flattening its slope.

Diebold et al. (2004, 2005, 2006) look at the dynamic interactions between the economy and the yield curve using the Dynamic Factor Model. They investigate the potential bidirectional feedback between the yield curve and the economy, finding strong evidence of macroeconomic effects on the yield curve, with somewhat weaker evidence of yield curve effects on future macroeconomic developments. Their analysis reveals that monetary policy shocks lead to a decline in the slope of the curve, accompanied by a jump in the level, and that the expectations hypothesis of the term structure holds only during certain periods of the data. Rudebusch and Wu (2010) present strong evidence of the impact of various macroeconomic shocks, with their key finding being that inflation target shocks account for most of the variation in the level of the yield curve, while monetary policy shocks dominate the variation in slope and curvature.

Brière and Lelpo (2007) analyse the response of the Euro yield curve to macroeconomic and monetary policy announcements. Their study takes into account the sharp degree of interdependence between Euro rates and US rates, using the factors of the US yield curve to distinguish between daily variations in Euro rates driven by US influences and those resulting from European news. Acatrinei (2017) estimates a structural VECM model to explore the interaction between macroeconomic variables and the estimated factors of the yield curve in the EU. The study finds that: (1) any change in inflation leads to small increases in the level factor, leaving bond prices unchanged; (2) the slope factor decreases faster after the monetary policy shocks, primarily affecting short-term bonds; and (3) a rise in the monetary policy rate leads to a strong increase in the level factor.

The study by Kaya (2013), exploring the relationship between the yield curve and macroeconomic variables in Turkey, finds that after the adoption of the inflation targeting (IT) regime, the yield curve is mainly driven by macroeconomic variables, while prior to that, the yield curve was affected to some extent by these variables. This shift indicates that, under the IT regime, the central bank has a greater ability to affect the entire yield curve. In addition to inflation and real economic activity, the exchange rate also plays an important role in shaping the dynamics of the yield curve.

In the Indian context, Kanjilal (2011) finds strong causality from financial factors to macroeconomic factors, while the reverse causality is weaker. The causality from yield factors to macroeconomic factors is primarily driven by the fact that changes in the level of the yield curve can have an impact on inflation through changes in the monetary policy.

Shareef and Shijin (2017) use monthly macroeconomic data from India spanning eighteen years (April 1998 to May 2016) to examine the proportion of the term structure attributable to macroeconomic shocks. Their study shows that short-term rates are primarily influenced by the fiscal deficit, while long-term rates change when market participants revise their expectations on yields. Moreover, the output growth of the country is mainly depended on both long- and short-term rates, and exchange rate fluctuations play a significant role in influencing the fiscal deficit.

Sahoo and Bhattacharyya (2012) study the interactions between macroeconomic variables and latent factors of the yield curve in India over the period from 2001 to 2010 using the Structural Vector Autoregression (SVAR) model. Their findings show that monetary policy has the maximum impact on the level and curvature of the yield curve, while the exchange rate largely determines the slope. This implies that the central bank plays a crucial role in shaping market dynamics. Our study extends this study further to a longer time period and includes additional variables. Instead of using just market proxies for latent factors, we also apply PCA and the Nelson-Siegel methods.

12.2. Data and Methodology

The macroeconomic variables and yield data for this study are sourced from the CSO and RBI databases. Monthly data from January 2005 to February 2019 (m1 of 2005 to m2 of 2019) are used.

12.2.1. Yield Data

Data on benchmark Indian government bond yields have been obtained from the RBI's website. The nominal interest rates for dated government bonds are taken for maturities longer than one year, while nominal interest rates for treasury bills are taken for maturities shorter than one year. The maturities considered in the study include 3- and 6-month treasury bills, as well as 1-, 5-, and 10-year dated bonds for the period from January 2005 to February 2019.

Table 12.1 presents the descriptive statistics for the nominal interest rates of the yield curve. The average rates seem to be increasing with longer maturities over the period from January 2005 to February 2019. Moreover, yields on shorter maturities are more volatile than those on longer-term bonds, which exhibit the highest level of persistence.

Table 12.1: Descriptive Statistics of Indian Government Monthly Bond Yields

Maturity	Mean	Median	Min.	Max.	Std. Deviation
3 months	6.82	6.97	3.18	11.05	1.50
6 months	6.94	7.16	3.36	10.80	1.42
1 year	7.07	7.25	3.94	10.48	1.19
5 years	7.61	7.72	5.63	9.19	0.73
10 years	7.70	7.78	5.63	9.20	0.66

Source: Author's calculations

The correlation between interest rates is generally high. However, the correlation between the yield on the shortest maturity and those of longer maturities decreases as we move toward the longest term (the 10-year interest rate), as shown in Table 12.2.

Table 12.2: Correlation Matrix of Indian Government Monthly Bond Yields

	3 months	6 months	1 year	5 years	10 years
3 months	1.00				
6 months	0.99	1.00			
1 year	0.97	0.98	1.00		
5 years	0.81	0.85	0.87	1.00	
10 years	0.73	0.77	0.80	0.97	1.00

Source: Author's calculations

The nominal rates of government bonds and treasuries in India have exhibited several periods of substantial volatility and abrupt changes in interest rates across different maturities (Figure 12.1). Notably, the global financial crisis of 2008 and the taper tantrum along with the domestic crisis of 2013 stand out. During the height of the global financial crisis in mid-2008, the yield spread between the 1-year, 5-year, and 10-year benchmark securities turned negative. This reflected a concentration of trading around the 10-year tenor, as well as the impact of monetary policy actions at the shorter end of the curve.

From August 2008 to June 2009, interest rates across all maturities declined significantly, with the 10-year bond rate falling by more than 200 basis points. However, the slope of the yield curve (defined as the difference between long-term and short-term rates) increased to an unprecedented level, as shorter-term yields declined by about 580 basis points.

Similarly, in 2013, short-term yields spiked in comparison to long-term yields as the central bank tightened policy rates to stabilise the falling domestic currency. By August 2013, the 3-month treasury yield was almost 260 basis points higher than the 10-year benchmark. The volatility in short-term rates was significantly more pronounced than in long-term rates.

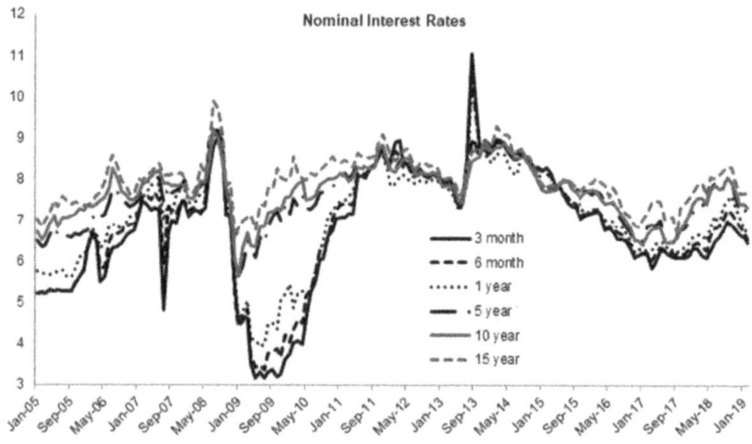

Figure 12.1: Trend of Nominal Interest Rates of Government Bonds

Source: RBI data, CMIE.

Therefore, any model used to calibrate the yield curve and its factors must be flexible enough to capture the varying shapes of the yield curve over time.

12.2.2. Other Data

For the empirical analysis of the impact of various parameters on the yield curve, monthly data on the IIP, WPI, Monetary Policy Rate, Index of 36-Currency Trade-Weighted Nominal Effective Exchange Rate (NEER), the effective Federal Funds Rate and the derived values of level, slope and curvature of the bond yield curve are considered.

Since high-frequency GDP growth data is unavailable, monthly IIP data is used as a proxy for output (Bordoloi and Rajesh, RBI, 2007). For inflation, the WPI series is used as the inflation measure in the absence of a harmonised, longer series of the CPI. The longer series for IIP, WPI and NEER is standardised through splicing.

Furthermore, we use the Repo Rate as a proxy for monetary policy. While some studies have used the call money rate (Kanjilal, 2011) or constructed a monetary policy index to represent monetary policy, we believe the Repo rate adequately reflects the policy stance. Since the Reverse Repo and MSF rates move in tandem with the Repo Rate, and the CRR has remained constant for an extended period, there is no need to construct a separate monetary policy index using the Repo, Reverse Repo, MSF, and CRR. Additionally, the call money rate in India is not an explicit policy target, unlike the US Fed's approach, though monetary operations aim to keep it within the policy corridor (between the MSF and Reverse Repo rates).

The RBI uses various instruments to manage liquidity in the system, including the CRR (Cash Reserve Ratio, which requires banks to park a portion of their deposits with the RBI), OMOs (Open Market Operations, which involve the purchase or sale of government bonds), SDF (Standing Deposit Facility, a sterilisation tool that does not require collateral for liquidity absorption), and the new Forex Swap (an instrument to inject rupee liquidity into the system through long-term foreign exchange buy/sell swaps). To measure liquidity in the system, the daily liquidity operations of the RBI are used to calculate the net liquidity injected into the system. If the RBI is injecting liquidity, the system is in a liquidity deficit mode, while if the RBI is absorbing excess liquidity, the system is in a surplus.

In the available literature in India, yield curve factors are typically estimated either by the PCA method or market proxies. In contrast, our study employs three mutually exclusive methods to estimate the yield curve factors—Level, Slope and Curvature (as outlined in the box).

Box 12.1: Yield Curve Factors Estimation

The literature highlights three distinct approaches to identify the factors of the yield curve, which are interpreted as level, slope, and curvature.

Market Proxies: The yield curve factors are usually estimated by using the standard proxies (Bekaert et al., 2010).

Level: Average of 3-month, 6-month, 1-year, 5-year, and 10-year yields.

Slope: Spread of 10-year over 3-month.

Curvature: 3-month plus 10-year minus twice of 5-year yield.

Principal Component Analysis (PCA) Approach: PCA is a non-parametric statistical technique used to convert a set of data of possibly correlated variables into a set of values of linearly uncorrelated variables. These values, known as principal components, usually have a smaller dimension than the original data. The first principal component has the largest possible variance. In the context of yield curve analysis, the PCA method is used to represent yield data across different maturities with three major components.

Nelson-Siegel (NS) Model Approach: The Nelson–Siegel framework corresponds to a parametric model that imposes structure on the factor loadings, resulting in highly precise estimation of the factors. According to the BIS (2005), many central banks around the globe use the Nelson-Siegel (1987) model to calibrate the interest rate structure because of its ease of computation and good fit to observed market interest rates.

This model can be written as:

$$y_t(\tau)\beta_{1t} + \beta_{2t}\left(\frac{1-e^{-\lambda t\tau}}{\lambda_{t\tau}}\right) + \beta_{3t}\left(\frac{1-e^{-\lambda t\tau}}{\lambda_{t\tau}} - e^{-\lambda t\tau}\right)$$

where $\lambda_t(\tau)$ corresponds to the interest rate observed at maturity τ at time t. The model is calibrated with parameters $\{\beta_1, \beta_2, \beta_3, \lambda\}$, such that the error between the observed rates and the rates obtained from the model is minimised. The parameter β_1 is associated with the level factor, β_2 with the slope factor, and β_3 with the curvature factor.

VAR and SVAR Methodology

In a multivariate autoregression, or vector autoregression of order p with N variables, or VAR(p), there are N equations, each regressed on p lags of itself and every other variable. This structure allows VAR to capture the cross-variable dynamics needed for our analysis. For example, in a two-variable VAR (1), there will be two equations, with each variable dependent on one lag of itself and one lag of the other variable.

$$y_{1't} = g_{11}y_{1't-1} + g_{12}y_{2't-1} + e_{1't} \quad (1)$$

$$y_{2't} = g_{21}y_{1't-1} + g_{22}y_{2,t-1} + e_{2't} \quad (2)$$

In matrix notation,

$$y_t = G_1\, y_{t-1} + e_t \quad (3)$$

$$\text{where,} \quad y_t \begin{bmatrix} y_{1,t} \\ y_{2,t} \end{bmatrix} \quad G_1 = \begin{bmatrix} g_{11} & g_{12} \\ g_{21} & g_{22} \end{bmatrix} \quad e_t \begin{bmatrix} e_{1,t} \\ e_{2,t} \end{bmatrix}$$

The error or shock terms are contemporaneously related such that

$$E[et\ et'] = \begin{bmatrix} \sigma^2_{e1} & \sigma_{e1,e2} \\ \sigma_{e1,e2} & \sigma^2_{e2} \end{bmatrix} = \Omega$$

But the error terms are uncorrelated through time

$$E[e_t\ e_{T'}] = \begin{bmatrix} 0 & 0 \\ 0 & 0 \end{bmatrix} \text{ for } t \neq T$$

Once the VAR model is finalised with the selected variables, the model's stability, along with the appropriate lag length, is established. However, the errors (shocks) in a VAR are usually correlated, which means impulse response functions or variance decomposition cannot be directly computed. Impulse response functions are meant to measure the change resulting from a shock, ceteris paribus. Since we are primarily interested in the transmission of individual shocks to the factors of the yield curve, rather than the coefficients of the lagged variables, we construct a SVAR model from the VAR model to investigate the response to shocks. The restrictions required in the SVAR model are derived from the literature.

The SVAR allows shocks to remain uncorrelated. In the analysis of the monetary transmission mechanism, the SVAR models have become a popular tool. According to Gottschalk (2001), the shock analysis conducted in SVAR models is the closest approximation of a controlled experiment available in empirical economics.

The SVAR model is estimated from the reduced VAR, as shown in equation (3), by multiplying by the matrix A.

$$A.y_t = A.G_1\, y_{t-1} + A.e_t$$

$$A.y_t = B_1\, y_{t-1} + u_t \qquad (4)$$

Where, $B_1 = A.G_1$ and $u_t = A.e_t$.

A is a k×k matrix whose diagonal terms (the coefficients of the ith variable in the ith equation) are scaled to 1; B_1 is a k×k matrix (for every i = 0, ..., p); and e_t is a k×1 vector of error terms. The ordering of the variables in matrix A is important in SVAR. SVAR modelling requires making assumptions about how the economy functions. Based on these assumptions, identifying restrictions are derived for the matrix A, and the corresponding empirical model is estimated. Figure 12.2 identifies the steps involved in the VAR and SVAR processes.

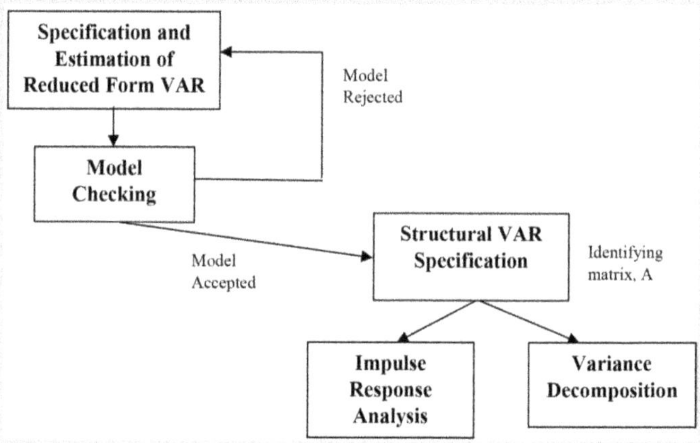

Figure 12.2: VAR and SVAR Process

12.3. Empirical Findings

The empirical study is divided into three parts: the first part identifies the three factors of the yield curve; the second part examines the correlation and causality between various macroeconomic parameters and these factors of the yield curve; and the third part uses the SVAR model to analyse the impulse response of changes in macro-variables on the factors of the bond yield curve, as estimated in the first part.

12.3.1. Yield Curve Factors Estimation

For estimating the shape of the yield curve, a large number of data points on bond yields across different maturities are necessary. We have bond yield data for the period ranging from January 2005 to February 2019, covering 3-month, 6-month, and 1-year (short-term) yields, as well as 5-year (medium-term) and 10-year (long-term) dated bond yields.

A. The Standard Market Proxies

The standard market empirical proxies representing the shape of the yield curve are as follows (Bekaert et al., 2010):

Level: Average of 3-month, 6-month, 1-year, 5-year, and 10-year yields;

Slope: Spread of 10-year over 3-month; and

Curvature: 3-month plus 10-year minus twice of 5-year yield.

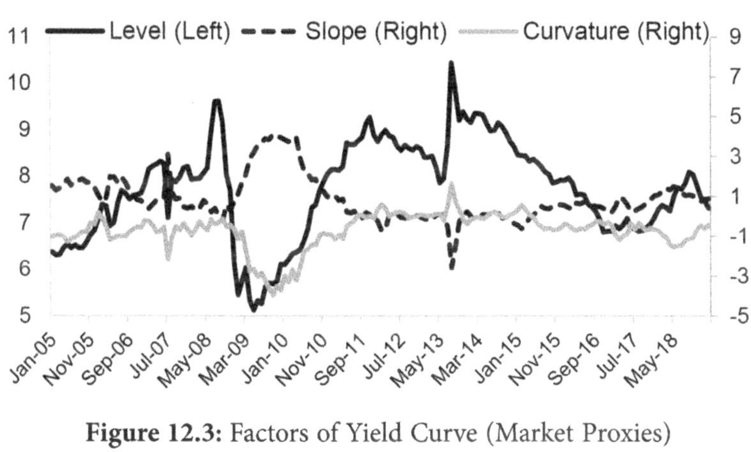

Figure 12.3: Factors of Yield Curve (Market Proxies)

Source: Author's calculations.

Ang and Piazzesi (2003) and Diebold et al. (2006) demonstrtate that the shape of the yield curve estimated using market proxies closely aligns with the shape derived from the Nelson-Siegel method. The factors estimated using this approach are shown in

Figure 12.3. Both the slope and curvature factors exhibit much higher volatility, particularly during the period from January 2009 to December 2010, when unconventional monetary policies were implemented to stimulate the economy during the financial crisis.

B. Principal Component Analysis (PCA) Approach

The PCA method seeks to maximise the variance of the data based on a set of factors of smaller dimension than the original data. Let X denotes the matrix of bond yields such that

$$X = [x_1, \ldots, x_N]^T$$

where, N = Number of observations, and T = Time period considered.

The vector X has a dimension of k (the total rates observed at each point in time, with k = 5 in our case, representing the 3-month, 6-month, 1-year, 5-year, and 10-year maturities).

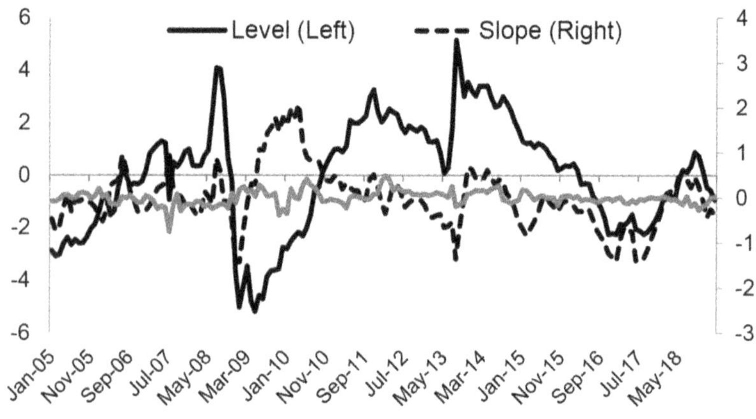

Figure 12.4: Factors Estimation under PCA Approach

Source: Author's calculations, EViews.

The Principal Component (PC) method tries to find a matrix $P = [p_1, \ldots, p_m]^T$ that maps each data point in X into a lower-dimensional space compared to the original data set ($m \leq k$, here m=3). Each vector p maximises the variance of X in orthogonal directions, with the amount of variance explained by each vector decreasing from p_1 to p_m. Each column of P corresponds to the principal component of the X matrix (Bliss, 1997). The factors derived using this methodology are shown in Figure 12.4 below.

It is observed that the first principal component explains the maximum variance across all individual indicators (with an eigenvalue of 4.5, as shown in Table 12.3). The first three principal components together account for 99% of the total variation in the data.

Table 12.3: Eigenvalues of Individual TAI Indicators (PCA Analysis)

PC	Eigenvalue	Difference	% of Variance	Cumulative Variance
1	4.5036	4.0573	0.900	0.900
2	0.4463	0.4218	0.089	0.989
3	0.0245	0.0027	0.005	0.995

Source: EViews calculations

The economic interpretation of each factor can be derived from the loadings or weights of each factor in relation to interest rates at different maturities, as shown in Figure 12.5. Since the results are dependent on the sample used, the loadings are obtained for three different samples: the first sample covers the entire period from 2005 to 2019; the second sample spans from 2005 to just prior to the financial crisis of 2008–2009; and the third sample covers the decade from 2009 to 2019. In all three samples, the results are consistent.

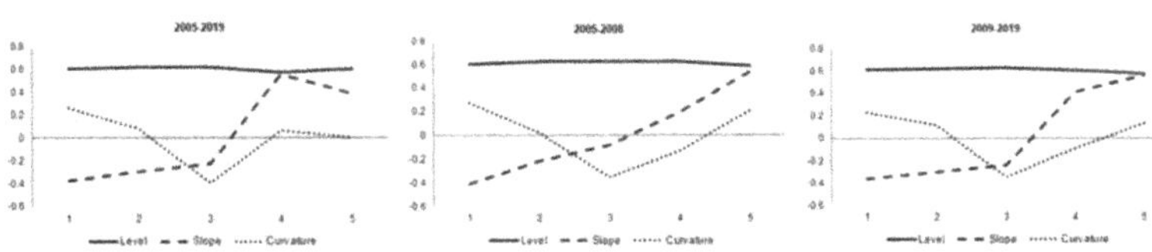

Figure 12.5: Factor Loadings of PCA Method

Source: Author's calculations.

It can be easily seen that the first factor has a loading of around 0.6 for all maturities of interest rates, indicating that it exerts a similar effect across all interest rates. Therefore, it denotes the level of the yield curve.

The second factor has negative loadings for interest rates with shorter maturities and positive loadings for longer maturities. This suggests that it represents the slope of the yield curve, as changes in this factor produce opposite effects at the short and long ends of the curve, thereby changing the slope of the yield curve.

Finally, the third factor has negative effects on the middle part of the curve and positive effects at the long end, which characterises it as the curvature. Changes in this factor affect the curvature of the yield curve.

For robustness checks, different samples were considered, all achieving similar results. The subsample from January 2005 to December 2008 was characterised by episodes of financial market turbulence, heightened risks, unconventional monetary policies, and a significant slowdown in production. The other subsample, from January 2009 to February 2019, was characterised by a gradual recovery in output growth, followed by a domestic macroeconomic crisis in 2013. These subsamples take into consideration different global and domestic financial distresses faced by the economy and their impact on interest rates.

The results are similar to those obtained by Bliss (1997) for the US yield curve, where the first factor explains about 93% of the variance, and the three factors jointly explain about 99% of the total variance. A study by Litterman and Scheinkman (1991) exhibits a similar pattern in Treasury rates, with the first factor accounting for the largest variance (90%), and the first three factors together explaining 98% of the overall variance. For the Chilean bond market, Ceballos (2014) finds that the first factor explains 93% of the variance, while the three factors cumulatively account for 99% of the variance. In all these studies, the first factor is referred to as the level, the second factor as the slope, and the third factor as the curvature.

C. Nelson-Siegel (NS) Model Approach

As discussed previously, the model used to capture the shape of the yield curve must be flexible enough to accommodate different curve shapes at different points of time (e.g., upward sloping or downward sloping curve). According to BIS (2005), many central banks around the globe use the Nelson-Siegel (1987) model to calibrate the interest rate structure due to its ease of computation and its ability to provide a good fit to observed market interest rates.

Thus, the NS model is:

$$y_t(\tau) = \beta_{1t} + \beta_{2t}\left(\frac{1-e^{-\lambda t\tau}}{\lambda_t \tau}\right) + \beta_{3t}\left(\frac{1-e^{-\lambda t\tau}}{\lambda_t \tau} - e^{-\kappa t\tau}\right) \qquad (1)$$

where, y^{τ} corresponds to the interest rate observed at time t for maturity τ. The model calibrates the parameters $\{\beta_1, \beta_2, \beta_3, \lambda\}$ in such a way that the error between the observed rates and those predicted by the model is minimised. The parameter β_1 is associated with the level factor (L), as it has a permanent effect on the overall level of the yield curve. The parameter β_2 represents the slope factor (S), as it primarily influences the short end of the curve. Finally, the parameter β_3, which has the highest impact on intermediate rates, is considered to be associated with the curvature factor (C). The movement of the factor loadings is shown in Figure 12.6 below. Moreover, the parameter λ represents the decay rate of the yield curve at longer maturities.

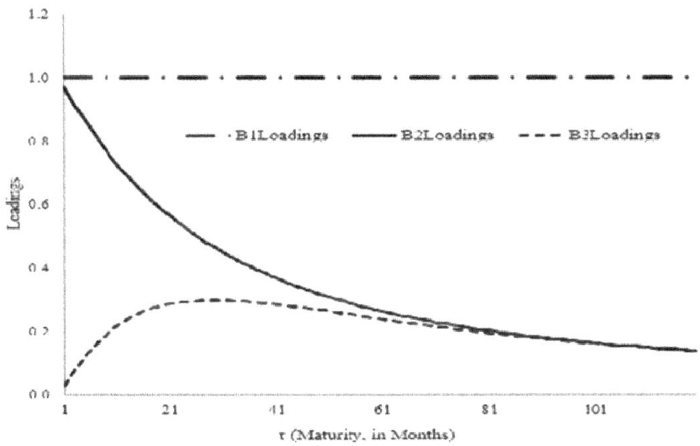

Figure 12.6: Factor Loadings of Nelson Siegel Method

Note: The factor loadings in the three-factor model is given by

$$y_t(\tau) = \beta_{1t} + \beta_{2t}\left(\frac{1-e^{-\lambda_t\tau}}{\lambda_t\tau}\right) + \beta_{3t}\left(\frac{1-e^{-\lambda_t\tau}}{\lambda_t\tau} - e^{-\lambda_t\tau}\right),$$

where the three factors are β_{1t}, β_{2t}, and β_{3t}, the associated loadings are 1, $(1-e^{-\lambda t\tau})/\lambda t\tau$ and $(1-e^{-\lambda t\tau})/\lambda t\tau - e^{-\lambda t\tau}$, and τ denotes maturity. λ is fixed at 0:0609.

Source: Author's calculations.

Diebold et al. (2006) and Ang and Piazzesi (2003) show that the shape of the yield curve estimated using the Nelson-Siegel method closely corresponds to standard market proxies.

The estimation of the model is nonlinear, as the parameter λ imposes the nonlinearity feature. In addition, the NS model imposes significant constraints on the rates, ensuring they converge to certain levels:

- As $\tau \rightarrow 0$, the estimated interest rate, as shown in equation 1, converges to $\beta_0 + \beta_1$, which is associated with the monetary policy rate.
- As $\tau \rightarrow \infty$, the estimated interest rate converges to β_0, representing the long-term rate of the economy.

The first step is to select the λ parameter of the model for two reasons: first, with a fixed λ, the model becomes linear and can be easily estimated using OLS, and second, by fixing λ, any changes in the estimated factors of the model can be interpreted as actual changes in the level, slope, and curvature of the yield curve, rather than being attributed to changes in λ.

We need to select a value of λ that minimises the root mean square error (RMSE) of adjustment to market rates observed in the daily rate during the sample period. Various studies have found that λ typically falls between 0.069 and 0.133 (Herrera and Magendzo, 1997; Morales, 2010). Diebold and Li (2006) used a value of λ = 0:0609 for US Treasuries, while Alfaro et al. (2011) concluded that λ ranges from 0.083 to 0.127. For the Chilean market, Ceballos (2014) used $\lambda = 0.11$. For our study, we have considered λ to be 0.1.

The factors of the model, β_0, β_1, and β_2, are estimated and plotted in Figure 12.7 below. It is observed that the level factor remains relatively steady, as expected from the structure of the NS model, and represents the long-term interest rate. In contrast, both the slope and curvature factors exhibit much more volatility, particularly during the periods of 2009–2010 and 2013. These periods were marked by significant macroeconomic instability and the implementation of unconventional monetary policies.

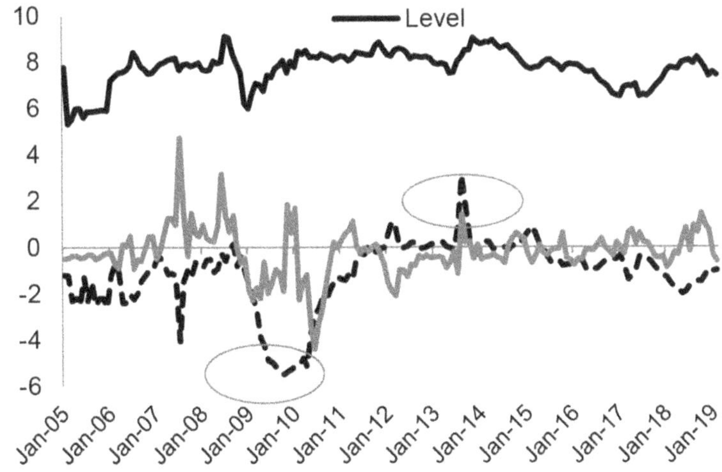

Figure 12.7: Factor Estimation under Nelson-Siegel Model

Source: Author's calculations.

Comparison of Factors

The factors obtained by the Nelson-Siegel (NS) method and PCA method are not directly comparable. The Level factor (denoted by β_0) in the NS approach is less volatile and corresponds to the long-term rate of the economy, while in the PCA method, it is a combination of all interest rates and is therefore more volatile. However, the correlation between the factors from the two methods is 0.75 for the full sample. The correlation between the Level factors obtained from the PCA method and market proxies is almost close to 1.

Meanwhile, the slope factor (S) and curvature factor (C) exhibit a high correlation in both the NS and PCA approaches, with values greater than 0.80. It is important to note that, under the PCA approach, the slope and curvature factors contribute much less in explaining the movement of interest rates, as shown by the eigenvalue table (Table 3).

The correlations of the Slope factor obtained from the market proxies with both the PCA and NS approaches are very high.

However, the correlation between the curvature factor derived from market proxies and that obtained from the other methods is low.

We can deduce that these factors, derived from various approaches, capture the information embedded in the yield curve in a compact form, even though the numbers themselves are not directly comparable. Next, we proceed to compare the effects of monetary policy, liquidity, and government borrowings on the factors, as these factors contain key information from the yield curve.

12.3.2. Correlation and Causality Analysis

The bond yields across various maturities are primarily driven by RBI's policy rate. However, some of the other potential drivers include liquidity conditions in the domestic banking system, government deficits, and market borrowings. Before estimating the SVAR model and analysing the impulse responses, we first examine the correlation between the yields of different maturities and these key drivers. Following this, we look at the causal relationships between three components of the yield curve—Level, Slope, and Curvature—and factors such as the Repo Rate, liquidity, and government borrowings. This is done by applying the Granger causality test (Granger, 1969) for the period from January 2005 to February 2019.

1. Repo and Bond Yields

The results of the correlation test between the Policy Rate and bond yields of various maturities are presented in Table 12.4 below. Three interesting facts are observed from the results:

i) The correlation with Treasury yields and dated government bond yields is notably high.

ii) The monetary policy actions have a stronger and more immediate impact on near-term rates (Estrella and Trubin, 2006).

iii) Interestingly, the highest correlation is observed with yields that have a lag of one to two months.

Table 12.4: Results of Correlation between Repo and Bond Yields

Treasuries and Bonds	Lags												
	-6	**-5**	**-4**	**-3**	**-2**	**-1**	**0**	**1**	**2**	**3**	**4**	**5**	**6**
3 Month	0.592	0.742	0.790	0.836	0.872	**0.892**	0.892	0.865	0.822	0.767	0.707	0.644	0.579
6 Month	0.707	0.759	0.809	0.857	0.892	**0.909**	0.903	0.866	0.813	0.749	0.684	0.615	0.547
1 Year	0.712	0.766	0.818	0.865	0.898	**0.911**	0.901	0.859	0.796	0.726	0.651	0.577	0.507
5 Year	0.660	0.698	0.739	0.774	**0.791**	0.787	0.753	0.686	0.594	0.500	0.417	0.340	0.280
10 Year	0.655	0.687	0.724	0.753	**0.761**	0.748	0.707	0.627	0.527	0.430	0.342	0.267	0.209

Source: Author's calculation.

This can be easily interpreted that the bond yields react to the policy rate much ahead of the actual policy announcement date. The market is forward-looking, with yields pricing in expected policy changes a couple of months ahead of the policy meeting, based on forward guidance or macroeconomic data releases. Furthermore, yields on shorter-duration bonds tend to react more strongly than those on longer-duration bonds. As a result, a policy rate cut causes the yield curve to steepen (upward sloping), as yields of shorter duration fall more than the yields of longer duration.

This is in accordance with the expectations hypothesis of the term structure, which states that long-term interest rates are the average of current and expected future short-term interest rates, along with a risk premium linked with the uncertain future short-term rates (Bernanke, 2015). As a result, changes in short-term rates have a more immediate impact. This is illustrated in Figure 12.8 below. Between December 2014 and August 2017, the RBI cut policy rates by 200 bps, causing the 10-year G-Sec yield to drop by 140 bps. However, between August 2017 and May 2018, the 10-year G-Sec Yield rose by 130 bps, despite the RBI policy rate remaining unchanged. In contrast, short-term bond yields moved in tandem with the Repo Rate during these periods.

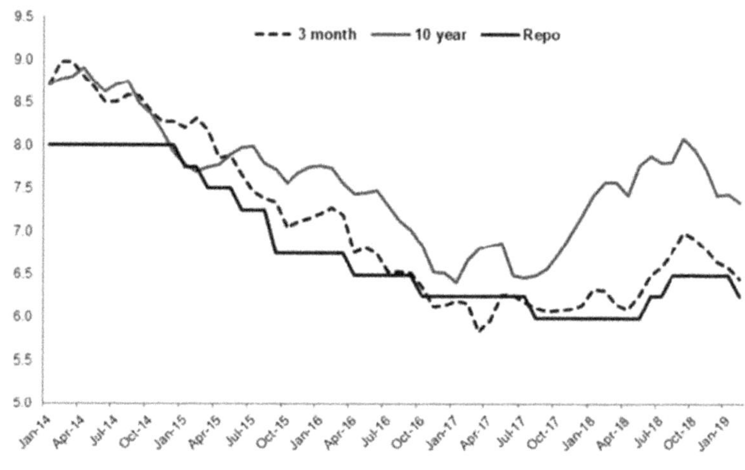

Figure 12.8: Movement of Bond Yields and Repo Rate

Source: RBI database.

Next, we look at the Granger causality between the Repo Rate and the factors of the yield curve (Level, Slope, and Curvature) in Table 12.5. The results highlight several interesting insights.

Table 12.5: Monetary Policy and Yield Curve–Granger Causality Test

Null Hypothesis	F-Statistics	Probability
LEVEL does not, Granger causes Repo.	4.80543	0.004
Repo does not, Granger causes LEVEL.	7.82705	0.0006
SLOPE does not, Granger causes Repo.	2.02706	0.1351
Repo does not, Granger cause SLOPE.	4.04368	0.0193
CURVATURE does not, Granger causes Repo.	0.09365	0.9106
Repo does not, Granger causes CURVATURE.	5.04962	0.0075

Source: Author's calculation; EViews results.

a) There exists bi-directional causality between the Repo Rate and LEVEL. This indicates that changes in monetary policy are reflected in the Levels, shifting the yield curve. Interestingly, monetary authorities also track the Levels to understand the state of the economy and incorporate these changes into their policy decisions.

b) There is unidirectional causality between the Repo Rate and SLOPE or CURVATURE. In other words, changes in the monetary policy rate affect expectations of returns across the term structure, thereby influencing both the slope and curvature of the yield curve. However, changes in the slope and curvature of the yield curve do not prompt any policy actions.

Similar conclusions were arrived at by Diebold et al. (2006) and Sahoo and Bhattacharyya (2012). The Level, rather than the shape of the yield curve (slope and curvature), is incorporated as input in the feedback mechanism for policy formulation. India's monetary policy draws insights from the market and considers the evolving expectations of market participants.

2. System Liquidity and Bond Yields

Table 12.6 below highlights the correlation between system liquidity and bond yields of various maturities.

Table 12.6: Correlation between System Liquidity and Bond Yields

Treasuries and Bonds	Lags						
	-3	-2	-1	0	1	2	3
3 Month	-0.617	-0.671	-0.729	**-0.752**	-0.738	-0.726	-0.714
6 Month	-0.614	-0.663	-0.716	**-0.732**	-0.714	-0.702	-0.686
1 Year	-0.599	-0.646	-0.685	**-0.693**	-0.680	-0.658	-0.650
5 Year	-0.608	-0.618	-0.618	**-0.602**	-0.571	-0.536	-0.514
10 Year	-0.601	-0.606	-0.591	**-0.564**	-0.526	-0.487	-0.461

Source: Author's calculation.

It is evident that the correlation between system liquidity and both treasury and dated government bond yields is high and immediate. However, the correlation decreases as we move from shorter to longer maturities, indicating that the lower end of the yield curve is more sensitive to liquidity changes than the longer end. Additionally, the correlation is highest when there is no lag. Moreover, the correlation is negative, highlighting that as liquidity increases, bond yields decrease, and vice-versa.

Next, we look at the Granger causality between system liquidity and the factors of the yield curve (Level, Slope, and Curvature) in Table 12.7.

Table 12.7: System Liquidity and Yield Curve–Granger Causality Test

Null Hypothesis	F-Statistics	Probability
LEVEL does not, Granger causes Liquidity.	6.65372	0.0017
Liquidity does not, Granger causes LEVEL.	0.42399	0.6552
SLOPE does not, Granger causes Liquidity.	0.46225	0.4975
Liquidity does not, Granger causes SLOPE.	5.22013	0.0236
CURVATURE does not, Granger cause Liquidity.	0.56685	0.4526
Liquidity does not, Granger cause Curvature.	4.53932	0.0346

Source: Author's calculation; EViews results.

There exists a causal relationship between system liquidity and the factors of the yield curve. However, surprisingly, changes in the Level lead to changes in system liquidity. At first glance, this seems to be against the popular expectation that changes in system liquidity cause changes in the levels of bond yields. This can be easily explained by the fact that monetary authorities continuously track the yield levels, and any pressure on the yield curve prompts the RBI to infuse liquidity into the system. For example, in FY 2018–19, the RBI infused durable liquidity through OMOs amounting to the tune of ₹2.9 lakh crores to prevent the bond yields from spiking up. Moreover, changes in liquidity impact both the Slope and Curvature of the yield curve, but not the reverse.

3. Government Borrowings and Bond Yields

The government uses market borrowings to finance its fiscal deficit. Increased borrowings lead to a higher supply of government bonds, which results in lower bond prices and, consequently, higher bond yields (since bond prices and yields are inversely related). However, the correlation between government borrowings and bond yields has not been empirically established. Several studies have found evidence suggesting that fiscal deficits do not determine interest rates in India, contrary to debates in policy circles (Chakraborty, 2012; Sahoo & Bhattacharyya, 2012; Akram & Das, 2014).

In the study by Geetima Das Krishna and Biswajit Nag (2018), it was concluded that fiscal deficits have no significant impact on bond yields. We tried to find a correlation between government borrowings and bond yields, using the combined central and state government borrowings (net of OMOs conducted by the RBI) as the total market supply of government bonds. The correlation between this supply and bond yields across various maturities is shown in Table 12.8 below. The correlation is very weak and even turns negative for bonds of longer maturities.

Table 12.8: Correlation between Government Debt Supply and Bond Yields

Treasuries and Bonds	**Lags**						
	-3	**-2**	**-1**	**0**	**1**	**2**	**3**
3 Month	0.161	0.152	0.112	0.118	0.138	0.125	0.119

6 Month	0.151	0.143	0.100	0.107	0.123	0.111	0.107
1 Year	0.112	0.093	0.068	0.067	0.080	0.082	0.091
5 Year	0.043	0.031	-0.004	-0.003	0.004	0.031	0.050
10 Year	-0.062	-0.077	-0.100	-0.100	-0.093	-0.061	-0.037

Source: Author's calculation

There may be several reasons for it. First, the government has undertaken a fiscal consolidation roadmap since 2003 under the FRBM Act to reduce the fiscal deficit. The deficit has been declining since then. Although the deficit increased substantially in 2009 during the financial crisis, other factors, such as demand and softer policy rates, helped keep bond yields low. The fiscal consolidation started once again from 2012.

Second, bond yields depend on supply-demand dynamics. Higher demand can absorb an increased supply of bonds. Banks are required to invest in G-secs to meet regulatory requirements like the statutory liquidity ratio (SLR), which in turn impacts bond yields. Additionally, a sizable portion (>50%) of SLR holdings is classified as "Held to Maturity", affecting market liquidity and yields. Akram and Das (2019) argue in their recent paper that this aligns with Keynesian views and modern money theory, which holds that increased government expenditures result in rising central bank reserves and banking deposits, as the central bank credits the banks to facilitate the government's borrowing and expenditures.

Third, a fast-growing economy like India, with high consumption, generates a greater demand for investments. These investment opportunities in the domestic market also attract foreign funds. As a result, the net impact on bond yields is determined by the interplay of supply and demand dynamics.

Fourth, whenever adverse supply-demand dynamics put upward pressure on bond yields, the RBI typically responds by infusing liquidity into the system through OMOs. So, there is a reverse causality from the Level to Supply, as discussed in the technical section. Interestingly, changes in supply affect both the slope and curvature of the yield curve.

Box 12.2: Technical Section—Structural VAR Analysis

Robustness of VAR Model

The estimated VAR model is tested for stability and lag-length criteria.

1. The lag-length criteria, tested with a maximum of 12 lags, indicate that the optimum lag length is 2. This is in line with our assumption that financial market participants quickly incorporate and process all available information.
2. The inverse roots of the AR characteristic polynomial are found to be inside the unit circle. If the roots were outside, it would suggest that the model is unstable, with variables integrated to order 1 and cointegration between them. In that case, the impulse response would not be valid.
3. Residual diagnostics show that the values lie within the dotted lines, and the residuals exhibit no sinusoidal patterns, indicating that they are completely random with no correlation or seasonality.

Structural VAR

Three separate six-variable SVAR models are considered, each for Level, Slope, and Curvature. The US Fed funds rate is considered as an exogenous variable, as it serves as a global interest rate indicator. Additionally, two dummy variables (dum1 and dum2) are used as exogenous variables to take care of unusual volatility during the 2008 global financial crisis and the 2013 domestic macro instability.

The model is estimated in levels, without taking into account the issue of "unit roots," as suggested by the literature. Sims et al. (1990) argue that the objective of estimating a VAR model in levels is to examine the underlying relationships among variables. Differencing the series does not improve asymptotic efficiency and discards valuable information, as in a VAR framework, the estimation and interpretation of individual coefficients are of little relevance. The endogenous variables included in the model are:

Output (IIP): Y_t
Inflation (WPI): Π_t
Monetary Policy (Repo): M_t
Liquidity: Q_t
Exchange Rate (NEER): E_t
Level/ Slope/ Curvature of Yield Curve: L_t, S_t, C_t
Exogenous Variable (Fed Fund Rate): F_t
α: coefficients

The following theoretical restrictions are put on the matrix A (equation 4) to identify the structural relationship:

$$\begin{pmatrix} 1 & 0 & 0 & 0 & 0 & 0 \\ \alpha_{21} & 1 & 0 & 0 & 0 & 0 \\ 0 & \alpha_{32} & 1 & 0 & 0 & \alpha_{36} \\ 0 & 0 & \alpha_{43} & 1 & 0 & 0 \\ \alpha_{51} & \alpha_{52} & \alpha_{53} & \alpha_{54} & 1 & 0 \\ \alpha_{61} & \alpha_{62} & \alpha_{63} & \alpha_{64} & \alpha_{65} & 1 \end{pmatrix} \begin{pmatrix} Y_t \\ \Pi_t \\ M_t \\ Q_t \\ L_t / S_t / C_t \\ E_t \end{pmatrix} \begin{pmatrix} \varepsilon_{Yt} \\ \varepsilon_{\Lambda t} \\ \varepsilon_{Mt} \\ \varepsilon_{Qt} \\ \varepsilon_{L_t/S_t/C_t} \\ \varepsilon_{Et} \end{pmatrix} \quad (5)$$

The restrictions on matrix A are formulated based on existing literature and the analysis done in the previous section. It is a standard assumption that aggregate demand shocks (represented by IIP) are not contemporaneously affected by other macroeconomic factors in the model. Therefore, all other coefficients in the matrix are set to zero. An aggregate supply shock (represented by WPI) is contemporaneously related only to the overall demand shock. Monetary policy reacts contemporaneously to price changes and exchange rate movements, as the RBI reacts to volatility in the exchange market. Output is not included in the monetary policy shock, as changes in real output do not immediately prompt a reaction from the central bank. Liquidity in the system reacts to monetary policy shocks. The shape of the yield curve (Level, Slope, and Curvature) is contemporaneously affected by price, output, and monetary policy shocks in the model, through the Fisher effect, the Taylor principle, and the expectation channel, respectively. The exchange rate has been placed last in the ordering, as it reacts simultaneously to all shocks, which is a standard practice in VAR literature. In a managed floating exchange rate regime like India's, the exchange rate reacts immediately to all macroeconomic shocks.

In Sections 4.2.1 and 4.2.2, we have observed that both monetary policy and liquidity react contemporaneously to Level. So, the matrix A for Level is redefined as below:

$$\begin{pmatrix} 1 & 0 & 0 & 0 & 0 & 0 \\ \alpha_{21} & 1 & 0 & 0 & 0 & 0 \\ 0 & \alpha_{32} & 1 & 0 & \alpha_{35} & \alpha_{36} \\ 0 & 0 & \alpha_{43} & 1 & 0 & 0 \\ \alpha_{51} & \alpha_{52} & \alpha_{53} & \alpha_{54} & 1 & 0 \\ \alpha_{61} & \alpha_{62} & \alpha_{63} & \alpha_{64} & \alpha_{65} & 1 \end{pmatrix} \begin{pmatrix} Y_t \\ \Pi_t \\ M_t \\ Q_t \\ L_t \\ E_t \end{pmatrix} \begin{pmatrix} \varepsilon_{Yt} \\ \varepsilon_{\grave{A}t} \\ \varepsilon_{Mt} \\ \varepsilon_{Qt} \\ \varepsilon_{L} \\ \varepsilon \end{pmatrix} \quad (6)$$

Impulse Response Analysis

The impulse responses of shocks from various endogenous variables to the level, slope, and curvature of the yield curve are estimated. Figure 12.9 illustrates the impulse response of monetary policy tightening on the various factors of the yield curve. As expected, an increase in monetary policy rates leads to an increase in the level of the yield curve up to the third month, after which it begins to decrease. A contractionary monetary policy is typically implemented in response to higher inflation in the short term, which shifts the yield curve upward temporarily. In the long run, as inflation softens, the level moves down. Next, the slope declines for about six months following monetary policy tightening, as short-term yields rise more than long-term yields, leading to a flattening of the yield curve. After that, the slope increases. This suggests that, in the short term, the expectation hypothesis dominates, while in the long run, term-premia[3] considerations dominate, as investors need to be compensated with higher returns for holding longer maturity bonds. Furthermore, tighter monetary policy is expected to ease inflation and improve the economic outlook, leading to higher yields in the future. Third, policy rate hikes immediately lead to a decline in curvature, as short-term yields increase relatively more than long-term yields. As the literature suggests, investors expectation of returns from medium-term as indicated by "preferred habitat" theory[4] of term structure dominate here. These results are in line with the findings of Diebold et al. (2006) and Sahoo and Bhattacharyya (2012).

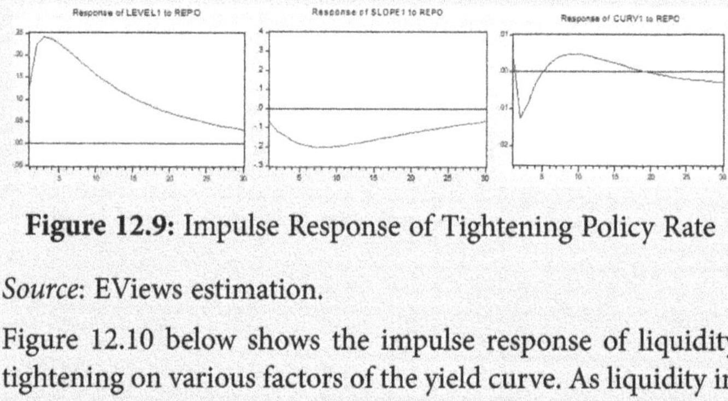

Figure 12.9: Impulse Response of Tightening Policy Rate

Source: EViews estimation.

Figure 12.10 below shows the impulse response of liquidity tightening on various factors of the yield curve. As liquidity in the system tightens, the level of bond yields rises immediately. Short-term yields always react more than long-term yields,

3. Term-premia: Investors may require compensation for holding a security for longer period. The "term premium" refers to such compensation and any other sources of deviation from the expectation hypothesis.
4. Preferred Habitat theory: Different bond investors prefer different maturity length (e.g., pension funds' preference for long-term bonds) over another and are only willing to buy bonds outside of their maturity preference if a risk premium for the maturity range is available. This theory is consistent with both the persistence of the normal yield curve shape and the tendency of the yield curve to shift up and down while retaining its shape. The Preferred Habitat Theory is another form of the Market Segmentation theory.

which causes the slope to decrease in tandem. But the level of yields begins to fall after about two months. This happens as the central bank reacts to tightening liquidity by infusing liquidity through various tools—frictional liquidity via the daily Repo window and durable liquidity through OMOs and forex interventions. The impact of liquidity tightening is more immediate compared to monetary policy shocks.

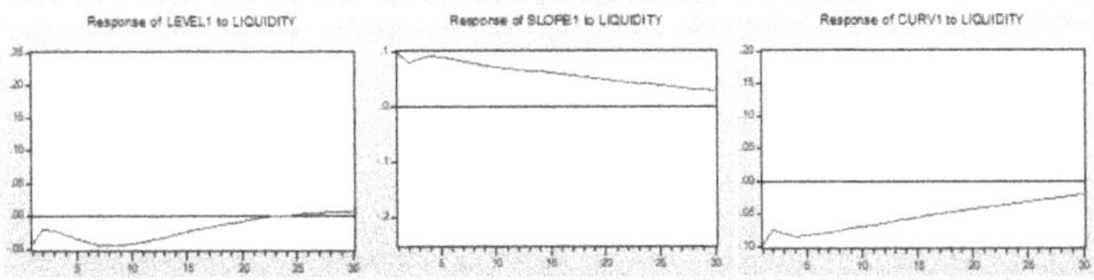

Figure 12.10: Impulse Response of Liquidity Shocks

Source: EViews estimation

After analysing the impact of policy rates and liquidity on the factors of the yield curve, we now briefly look at the effects of demand, supply, and exchange rate shocks (represented by IIP, WPI, and NEER in our model) on the three factors of the yield curve. This analysis indicates how the yield curve absorbs various macroeconomic data announcements (Figure 12.11).

The overall demand shock, represented by IIP, results in an immediate softening of the level of yields for a couple of months, after which it stabilises and increases slightly. Simultaneously, it leads to an increase in the slope and a decline in curvature for about two months, before they move in the opposite direction. The impact of the demand shock is relatively small. The immediate increase in output generates positive sentiment about the economy, causing the level of yields to decline slightly. However, over time, concerns about overheating or rising inflation expectations emerge, which leads to an increase in the slope and a decline in curvature initially. Ultimately, long-term positive expectations contribute to the steepening of the yield curve.

The impact of the supply shock, represented by WPI, is more pronounced. As expected, an increase in inflationary pressure increases the level of the yield curve. Simultaneously, the slope declines as short-term rates increase more than long-term rates. However, over time, the level comes down, and the slope increases as higher nominal interest rates attract capital inflows due to the interest rate differential. As capital flows put pressure on the exchange rate, the RBI intervenes to manage the volatility of the exchange rate. This intervention increases liquidity, leading to higher demand for government securities. The liquidity effect dominates, causing short-term rates to decline more relative to long-term rates. The impact of hardening inflation on slope and curvature is along expected lines. In the short term, the expectation hypothesis dominates, while in the long-term, term-premia considerations dominate.

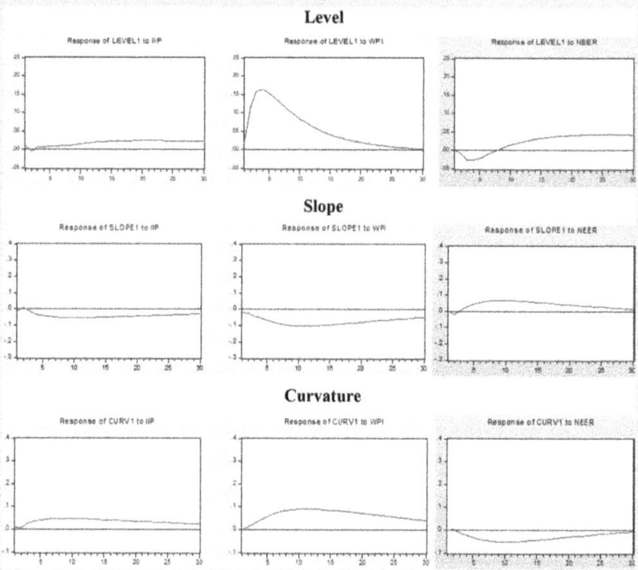

Figure 12.11: Impulse Response of Demand, Supply, and Exchange Rate Shocks

Source: EViews Estimate

(The SVAR output is shown in Appendix II)

The impact of an exchange rate shock, represented by NEER, is found to be small on the level but quite comparable on the slope, in relation to other shock responses. An appreciation of the exchange rate reduces inflationary pressure as imported goods, including oil (which India imports over 70% of its demands), become cheaper. This, in turn, eases the level of yields through the Fisher Effect. Moreover, as mentioned earlier, the RBI would intervene to prevent excessive appreciation of the exchange rate to avoid negatively impacting domestic exports. This intervention in the forex market increases liquidity, helping to soften the level of yields. The movement of the slope and curvature aligns with the expectation hypothesis in the short-term and term-premia considerations in the long-term.

Decomposition of Shocks

The variance decomposition of shocks is generated in EViews, as shown in Table 12.9. This gives insights into the relative dominance of various shocks on the Level, Slope, and Curvature of the yield curve. The key findings can be summarised as follows:

Level: For the level, the monetary policy shock is the dominant factor among the various shocks, and its influence remains significant over an extended period, peaking at six months. The inflation and liquidity shocks are felt immediately, with the inflation shock increasing over time and peaking at six months, while the liquidity shock fades out. In contrast, output and exchange rate shocks have negligible effects.

Slope: For the slope, the liquidity shock has dominance immediately in influencing the slope of the yield curve, with the monetary policy shock gradually gaining importance over time. Supply shocks also gain relevance, and notably, the exchange rate shock appears to be an important factor for the slope of the yield curve, second only to monetary policy shocks over time.

Curvature: For the curvature, the liquidity shock is dominant immediately. However, over time, the output shock becomes more influential in determining the curvature of the yield curve.

Table 12.9: Variance Decomposition of Various Shocks

LEVEL

Month	Shocks					
	IIP	WPI	Repo	Liquidity	Level/Slope /Curvature	NEER
	Demand	Supply	Monetary Policy	Liquidity	Level	Exchange Rate
1	0.010	0.775	23.548	1.392	74.276	0.000
6	0.079	17.610	41.000	0.569	40.401	0.341
12	0.065	16.172	41.933	1.262	40.152	0.416
24	0.334	14.468	42.035	1.286	39.524	2.353
30	0.521	14.131	41.610	1.302	39.018	3.419

SLOPE

Month	Shocks					
	IIP	WPI	Repo	Liquidity	Level/Slope /Curvature	NEER
	Demand	Supply	Monetary Policy	Liquidity	Slope	Exchange Rate
1	0.863	0.307	0.590	2.591	95.650	0.000
6	1.349	7.341	4.089	3.350	82.807	1.065
12	1.599	7.838	7.628	3.695	74.964	4.275
24	1.306	9.555	16.079	5.286	57.850	9.924
30	1.276	9.900	17.508	5.686	54.893	10.737

CURVATURE

Month	Shocks					
	IIP	WPI	Repo	Liquidity	Level/Slope /Curvature	NEER
	Demand	Supply	Monetary Policy	Liquidity	Curvature	Exchange Rate
1	1.927	1.916	0.062	3.480	92.614	0.000
6	5.193	2.047	1.244	3.034	88.432	0.050

12	5.276	4.373	1.728	3.291	85.256	0.075
24	6.015	5.726	1.840	3.422	82.529	0.468
30	6.108	5.709	1.984	3.405	82.013	0.782

Source: Author's calculations.

These results are consistent with the findings of Bekaert et al. (2010) and Sahoo and Bhattacharyya (2012), which highlight that monetary policy and inflation are dominant factors influencing the level and slope of the yield curve. Just like in the study by Sahoo and Bhattacharyya (2012), but in contrast to Bekaert et al. (2010), we find an impact of output shocks on curvature and exchange rate shocks on the slope of the yield curve over time. The literature attributes this difference to (i) the imperfect and less mature financial markets, and (ii) a managed float exchange rate regime in India vis-a-vis flexible exchange rate system in the US.

However, there is one important additional observation from our study. By incorporating the impact of liquidity, we find that the liquidity shock has a more significant immediate effect on both the slope and curvature of the yield curve.

12.4. Interpreting the Empirical Results

The empirical results obtained above lead us to the following conclusions:

- The monetary policy has significant influence over the level and shape of the yield curve. Its influence on yields is the maximum at the shorter end of the curve and weakens as maturity increases. Moreover, the central bank appears to be highly sensitive to financial market dynamics, operating within a market-oriented policy framework that incorporates feedback from market developments into its decision-making process.
- Among the other variables, system liquidity shocks have an immediate impact on yields, while the effects of aggregate demand shocks build up over time. Supply shocks exert a much stronger influence on levels of the bond yields

compared to other variables (excluding the Repo rate). Additionally, the exchange rate plays a role in shaping the yield curve, primarily through the liquidity channel, as the RBI proactively manages volatility in the forex market.

- The Indian bond market can be explained by standard market theories. The expectation theory dominates at the shorter end, while the preferred habitat theory (market segmentation theory that reflects preferred maturity segments of investors) and term premia considerations (liquidity risk premium that investors demand for longer maturities) influence the medium to long end of the curve.
- Despite consistent large government borrowing programs and the RBI's dual role as both debt manager and monetary policy authority, the shape of the yield curve is primarily influenced by policy rates. Thus, the RBI plays a central role in the debt market and is key to its further development.

12.5. Conclusion

In this study, the structural factors of nominal rates for the Indian bond market are estimated for the period 2005–2019, using monthly data and three mutually exclusive approaches—Market Proxies, the Nelson-Siegel (NS) method, and the Principal Components Approach (PCA). These three methodologies are used to estimate and compact the information contained in the yield curve into three factors: level (L), slope (S), and curvature (C). The response of these derived factors to a wide range of macroeconomic shocks is then analysed. Even though the factors derived from the different methodologies are not directly comparable, the effects of various shocks on the estimated factors are consistent across both approaches, thereby confirming the robustness of our analysis.

This study contributes to the available research on the overlapping areas of the macroeconomic and financial sectors in India. While a significant body of research has focused on the term structure of the Indian bond market from either a macroeconomic or financial theory perspective, there has been a growing interest in understanding the macroeconomic impact on the term structure of interest rates. This study explores the dynamic interaction of macroeconomic shocks on the term structure, as defined by the latent factors (level, slope, and curvature) of the yield curve.

Additionally, the study also looks at the impact of system liquidity on the yield curve using a VAR model, noting that tight liquidity significantly affects bond yield levels and that the central bank is highly sensitive to system liquidity conditions.

The empirical results show that the monetary policy shocks have the greatest impact on the yield curve, with the effect being more pronounced at the shorter end of the curve. In addition, monetary policy has a stronger impact on the level of yields compared to the slope and curvature. Notably, the level of yields—rather than the slope or curvature—is closely monitored by the RBI and serves as a key input for its policy decisions. India's monetary policy extracts information from the market and takes into consideration the evolving expectations of market participants within a market-oriented policy framework.

Among the other macroeconomic factors, liquidity shocks have an immediate impact. Similarly, inflation and supply shocks also have a larger, more immediate effect, while output shocks are smaller and have a longer-term impact. Exchange rate shocks are instantaneous and notably influence the slope of the yield curve. These impacts also act through the liquidity channel, as the RBI tries to manage volatility in the forex market.

The Indian bond market can be explained by standard market theories. The expectation theory of the term structure dominates in the short run, while the preferred habitat theory and term premia considerations become more influential in the medium to long run.

In conclusion, RBI policy actions have a significant impact on the yield curve, particularly at the shorter end. Any policy change is reflected across bond yields of all maturities. The RBI also closely monitors and incorporates the level of yields as a key input in its policy decisions. This is understandable given that the RBI, with its dual mandate as both the monetary authority and debt manager, is responsible for ensuring that the government borrowing costs remain low while maintaining financial stability. The RBI faces a tough balancing act, but despite these conflicting priorities, its policy announcements significantly influence the Indian debt market. Therefore, we can conclude that the sovereign bond yields can act as an effective conduit of transmission of policy actions to the real economy, as other financial instruments are calibrated in reference to the sovereign yield curve.

We also find that liquidity has an immediate and dominant impact on the slope and curvature of the yield curve. Our study empirically proves that liquidity can be used to help expedite the monetary policy transmission. A policy easing cycle needs to be supplemented with ample liquidity in the banking system to facilitate faster transmission of rate changes, and vice versa.

Recently, the transmission of policy rate reductions has been hampered by balance sheet stress in the banking sector, increased risk aversion in the financial sector, and high public sector borrowing.

Like other empirical studies in this field, our study could not establish a significant direct correlation between government debt supply and bond yields, as this relationship is influenced by more nuanced demand-supply dynamics in the market. It is well-known that a sustained high fiscal deficit leads to increased government borrowings from the domestic market, which puts upward pressure on bond yields. The Indian government has been on a fiscal consolidation path since 2003 (with some deviation during the financial crisis of 2008). Moreover, banks are mandated to invest in government securities through regulations, and the RBI intervenes in the market whenever supply increases. As a result, it has been difficult to arrive at any meaningful conclusions regarding the interaction between the market supply of sovereign debt and bond yields.

B. CORPORATE BOND MARKET

CHAPTER 13

Determinants for Development of Corporate Bond Market

The Indian economy has been facing several headwinds in recent years, including an uncertain global growth outlook, the longer-than-expected deleveraging process of banks and corporates, hampered monetary policy transmission, tight credit conditions, and weak investments. With GDP growth already below potential even pre-pandemic, authorities have been trying to revive growth through coordinated monetary and fiscal policies. Credit is the lifeblood of an economy, and in India, it is evident that bank lending alone cannot effectively meet domestic demand. It is imperative to remove any financing constraints by developing alternative financing channels to supplement bank credit. A deep, large, and liquid corporate bond market can play a crucial role in bridging the funding gap, especially in infrastructure financing. In the absence of such a market, the burden of financing such infrastructure projects falls on banks and the government. This has already led to challenges, as Indian banks, trying to finance long-term infrastructure projects with short-term liabilities, are now struggling with piles of bad loans.

Despite the relatively long history of the corporate bond market in India, the size of the public issue segment has remained quite insignificant, even though the equity market is quite active. Even today, most large corporate debt issuers are "quasi government" entities, such as public sector banks, oil companies, and government-sponsored FIs.

During his visit to India in October 2019, World Bank President David Malpass suggested a three-pronged approach to boost economic growth, one of which focused on the development of the corporate bond market. He said, "Encourage progress in three primary areas—One is to allow the growth of the banking sector itself including the private sector. Second is the deepening of the corporate bond market and mortgage market, and the third is regulation of non-bank financial companies, which have grown with the Indian financial system but entails some risks."

Although the amount of domestic corporate bonds outstanding has been expanding for years, the NBFC crisis of 2018, coupled with corporate debt defaults, has hindered market progress. The growth rate of local currency corporate debt has slowed since 2017, reaching its lowest rate of 9.7% in over a decade by May 2019, according to a Bloomberg Economics index.

This chapter examines the determinants of corporate bond market development. Given the small size of India's corporate debt market, it is difficult to establish causality through empirical analysis based solely on the factors of the Indian economy. A larger data set is needed. Therefore, this study tries to bridge the gap by considering nine Asian economies—India, China, Indonesia, Japan, Malaysia, Philippines, Singapore, Thailand and South Korea—each with a large corporate bond market, for a comparative study.

13.1. Literature Review: Factors Determining Development of Corporate Bond Market

Studies have identified several factors essential for the develop-ment of the corporate bond market. A stable political environment, along with predictable policy expectations, plays a crucial role in boosting business and investors' confidence (Kviback, 2000; Hove, 2008). A stable macroeconomic environment attracts capital flows, improves market liquidity, and encourages investment in corporate bonds. Moreover, a conducive taxation framework gives the corporate bond market a more level playing field with the government bond market and the loan segments within the banking sector.

Fabella and Madhur (2003) point out that factors like the size of the economy, its natural openness, the size of the banking system, and exchange rate variability impact the corporate bond market. A minimum size of the economy is necessary for bond market development, as small issuances in minor economies may not be attractive enough to multinational corporations and potential foreign investors (Demirguc-Kunt, 2005). In an open economy, capital financing through the bond market faces fewer constraints. The more open an economy is, the less suppressed its securities markets tend to be (Rajan & Zingales, 2001).

Although banks compete with bond markets as sources of financing, the existence of a large and well-developed banking system is vital for the development of the corporate bond market, as banks serve as dealers and market makers, facilitating the smooth operation of this market (Hawkins, 2002; Baharuddin et al., 2011). Several studies have explored whether debt securities and bank loans are substitutes (Bolton & Freixas, 2000) or complements (Holmstrom & Tirole, 1997). Based on data for the United States over 1979–1999, Davis and Ioannidis (2002) provide an empirical study that establishes a positive relation between debt security financing and bank financing, contrasting with Davis (2001). Their findings also show that corporate debt securities issuance, compared to bank loans, is more sensitive to cost factors and less sensitive to the business cycle (Davis, 2001; Davis & Ioannidis, 2002). As a result, an economy highly dependent on bank financing would show more cyclically volatile funding for firms compared to one with both a corporate bond market and a banking system. Sharma (2000) also noted that in environments where investor rights are weak, savers may prefer to invest through banks rather than bonds, as politically well-connected banks are better positioned to enforce their claims.

A stable exchange rate reduces investment risk, and a less volatile exchange rate can foster the development of the bond market (Bhattacharya, 2011).

Investors' confidence in a country's regulatory framework is essential to create a deep corporate bond market with wider investor base. Studies have shown that factors such as a robust regulatory and supervisory framework, professional accounting practices, trading and price transparency, credible rating agencies, and strong bankruptcy laws are essential for the growth of the corporate bond market (Kviback, 2000; Fabella & Madhur, 2003; Plummer, 2003).

Without proper market infrastructure, it is not possible to enhance trading efficiency and develop the secondary market. Robust and efficient trading, clearing, settlement, and depository systems help reduce trading costs and price volatility, minimise market fragmentation, facilitate order flow, improve price discovery, and ensure wide dissemination (IOSCO, 2011). In the Sub-Saharan market, where the bond market remains underdeveloped, Banimadhu (2003) shows that the clearing and settlement systems for bond trading are generally inefficient, with substantial delays in the process.

Various intermediaries, including banks, bond insurers, rating agencies, PDs, credit analysts, and brokers, play a crucial role in the development of the corporate bond market (Leigland, 1997).

Long-term corporate debt and equity can be substitutes for each other, although the substitution elasticity can be very small (Friedman, 1979, 1985; Roley, 1982). On the order hand, no empirical conclusions have been drawn regarding the substitutability of short-term debt and equity.

Several studies on Asian economies following the crisis of 1997–98 underscore the importance of a strong corporate bond market to avoid future systemic risks. It is recommended that these countries should focus more on providing an enabling environment, enhancing corporate governance and legal processes, increasing the role and reliability of credit ratings, developing a government bond market with a benchmark yield curve, improving market infrastructure, widening private placements, providing real-time delivery systems, and strengthening regulatory frameworks to develop their bond markets (Sharma, 2001; Batten & Kim, 2001). Fabella and Madhur (2003), in their study on East Asia bond markets, suggests that establishing a stable macro-environment and a healthy government bond market, alongside completing the post-crisis agenda for restructuring the banking sector, improving corporate governance, enhancing regulatory frameworks, rationalising tax policy, and broadening the investor base, are necessary for building a sustainable bond market in these countries. While primary markets in Asia depend on quasi-government issuers, secondary markets suffer from narrow investor bases, insufficient microstructures, and information asymmetry (Gyntelberg et al., 2005). Bhattacharya (2013) analysed the development of government and corporate bond markets in 10 Asian countries over the period of 1998 to 2008. His findings suggest that factors such as the size and economic development of a country, its openness, and the variability in interest rates are strong predictors of the development of the corporate bond market.

Eichengreen and Luengnaruemitchai (2004) use panel data from 41 countries covering the period from 1990 to 2001 to provide a comprehensive analysis of the factors influencing corporate financing through bond markets. They identify 15 determinants of bond market development, including economic size, natural openness, the legal system, geographical and disease endowments, the riskiness of the investment environment, law and order, weak corporate governance and transparency, the development stage of the economy, the size and concentration of the banking system, the absence of public sector funding needs, poor regulatory enforcement, interest rate variability, interest rate levels, and exchange rate regimes. Burger and Warnock (2006) analyse the development of bond markets in 49 countries and find that countries with stable inflation rates and stronger creditor rights tend to have more developed bond markets. Bae (2012) investigates the determinants of government, financial, and corporate bond market development using data from 43 countries over the period of 1990 to 2009. His findings indicate that the degree of economic development is the most important variable in explaining cross-country variations in all three types of bond markets. Fink et al. (2003) use panel data from 13 highly developed economies over the period 1950 to 2000 to examine the relationship between the development of aggregate bond markets and real GDP. The external corporate financing pattern is also influenced by macroeconomic factors like the phase of business cycle, inflation rate, interest rate structure, etc (Choe, Masulis, & Nanda, 1993; Park & Shenoy, 2002; Korajczyk & Levy, 2003; Bondt, 2005).

Ringui (2012) examines the factors influencing Kenya's corporate bond market. He carries out a structured survey on 60 listed firms on the Nairobi Securities Exchange and finds that the political environment, investor base, regulatory framework, size of the banking sector, the cumbersome nature of issuance process, and macroeconomic factors are important to the development of corporate bond markets in Kenya.

In summary, a well-developed corporate bond market fosters an efficient corporate financial structure, facilitates the presence of rating agencies, promotes the proliferation of financial derivatives, and helps reduce systemic risk, thereby preventing financial crises (Hakkanson, 1999).

The World Bank (2000) identifies seven key components necessary for the effective functioning of vibrant corporate bond markets: (i) a disclosure and information system, (ii) a credit rating system, (iii) effective bankruptcy laws, (iv) market intermediaries, (v) institutional investors, (vi) a trading system and clearing platform, and (vii) a depository system. In addition, diversified investment instruments and a conducive taxation framework are also suggested by the IOSCO (2011) report, based on surveys of 36 emerging markets.

As the importance of corporate bond markets became more obvious, many global institutions, including the International Monetary Fund (IMF), the European Bank for Reconstruction and Development (EBRD), and the Organization for Economic Co-Operation and Development (OECD), developed a joint "diagnostic framework" to promote and guide the development of these markets (IMF, EBRD and OECD, 2013).

However, such studies are scanty in the context of India. Bose and Coondoo (2003) try to understand the nature and extent of imperfections in the Indian corporate bond market using available data on the secondary market. They feel that much needs to be done to address issues such as information asymmetry, low liquidity, and the consequent distortions in the corporate debt segment of the Indian capital market. Raghavan and Sarwono (2012) conduct a study on the determinants of the corporate bond market in India and conclude that the growth of the government bond market has a major positive influence on the development of the corporate bond markets, whereas bank lending has a negative impact. Other factors, including the size of the economy, market openness, the size of the stock market, and institutional factors like corruption, show little to no impact. Maurya and Mishra (2016) present evidence that corporate bond issuance is significantly correlated with the foreign exchange reserves. Using multiple regression analysis, they conclude that GDP and trade openness do not significantly explain the volume of corporate bond issuances in India.

13.2. Corporate Bond Market: Pre-conditions, Advantages and Risks

The literature identifies several preconditions necessary for the establishment, benefits, and management of a well-functioning corporate bond market. These preconditions include:

- A stable macroeconomic and political environment, along with conducive tax policies.
- A developed government securities market, which provides the necessary market infrastructure, a skilled dealer community, and a benchmark yield curve for default-free securities.
- A well-established equity market culture.
- Minimal government interference in the corporate bond market.
- A high savings rate with limited crowding out of private sector investment.
- Efficient infrastructure, including cost-effective trading, clearing, and settlement systems.
- A diverse and substantial base of issuers, along with a wide investor base.
- Timely, reliable, and accurate financial reporting by firms that is publicly available.
- A strong community of professional financial analysts to help make an informed decision.

- Reliable rating agencies to ensure proper risk assessment.
- An efficient bankruptcy law and a supportive legal environment.

The development of an efficient corporate bond market offers several benefits for issuers, investors, and the overall economy:

- Diffusing stress on the banking sector by diversifying credit risks.
- Diffusing foreign exchange, interest rate, and refunding risks.
- Supplying long-term funds for long-term investment needs.
- Supplying long-term investment products tailored for long-term investors.
- Lowering funding costs by avoiding liquidity premiums.
- Providing products with flexibility to meet the specific needs of both investors and borrowers.
- Promoting more efficient capital allocation.
- Reducing reliance on volatile foreign funds.
- Enhancing transparency and disclosure of companies.

However, there are also risks associated with investment in corporate bonds:

1. **Interest rate risk**: The risk that rising interest rates will lower a bond's price, potentially resulting in capital loss for the investor.
2. **Reinvestment risk**: It refers to the probability of a fall in market interest rates in future, which would, in turn, reduce the additional income from reinvesting the cash flows from a bond (at a lower rate).
3. **Inflation risk:** The risk that inflation will erode the purchasing power of the income derived from the bond investment.
4. **Liquidity risk:** The risk related to the ease of accessing cash before the bond's maturity.
5. **Default risk (or credit risk):** The risk that the issuer of the bond may fail to make timely payments of principal or

interest. Default risk is gauged by quality ratings assigned by credit rating agencies.

13.3. Data and Methodology Used in the Study

1. Data

Time-series data for eleven variables (Table 13.1) covering nine Asian economies from 2005 to 2018 have been collected from the Asian Development Bank, World Development Indicators of the World Bank, IMF International Financial Statistics, and the RBI database (see Appendix III for sources).

Table 13.1: Determinants for Development of Corporate Bond Market

Category	Factors	Relationship	Description
Economy			
	Stage of Development (GDP per Capita)	Positive	The development stage of an economy may influence bond market development positively. (Bhattacharya, 2011; Eichengreen and Luengnaruemitchai, 2004).
	Openness of Economy (Trade of Goods and Services as % of GDP)	Positive	In an open economy, the tendency of banks being reluctant to allow bond markets to encroach on their market share will be less effective. There would be healthy competition for corporate financing from all available sources. (Fabella and Madhur, 2003; Rajan and Zingales, 2001; Bhattacharya, 2011; Eichengreen and Luengnaruemitchai, 2004).
	Total Savings (Gross Domestic Savings as % of GDP)	Positive	Higher domestic savings may provide higher resources for the bond market to tap into.
	Total Investments (Gross Capital Formation as % of GDP)	Positive	A higher gross capital formation in the economy may be related to increase in corporate bond market size. The investments by private firms may happen as firms borrow through the bond market.
	Exchange Rate Volatility (Annual Standard Deviation of NEER)	Negative	A stable exchange rate reduces risks for the investors, particularly for the foreign investors and thereby encourages the development of the corporate bond market. (Fabella and Madhur, 2003; Bhattacharya, 2011)

Financial System			
	Equity Market (Market Capitalization of Listed Domestic Companies)	Positive	Stock market size is a measure of the overall capital market development. Empirically the substitution elasticity between the long-term corporate debt and equity is found to be small. A mature equity market can have a positive relationship. (Raghavan and Sarwono, 2012; Rajan and Zingales, 2001).
	Govt. Bond Market (Government Bond Outstanding as % of GDP)	Positive	A well-developed government bond market puts in place the required infrastructure for trading, maker makers, regulations. It provides the benchmark yield curve. Keynesian theory argues that an increase in government expenditure encourages economic activity and enhances consumption and, hence, crowds in private investment. (Raghavan and Sarwono, 2012; Sharma, 2001; Batten and Kim, 2001; Fabella and Madhur, 2003).
	Banking Sector (Domestic Credit to Private Sector by Banks as % of GDP)	Positive	Robust banking system is essential as banks act as dealers and market makers for smooth operation of the market. (Fabella and Madhur, 2003; Baharuddin et al. 2011; Hawkins, 2002; Eichengreen and Luengnaruemitchai, 2004).
	Interest Rate Differential (Corporate minus Govt Bond Yield)	Negative	Higher interest rate spread denotes increasing cost of borrowing due to higher perceived risk. (Davis, 2001; Davis & Ioannidis, 2002; Bhattacharya, 2011).
Institutional Framework			
	Corruption Index (Annual Corruption Index)	Negative	Perceived corruption in public sector can act as a deterrent for investors. (Fabella and Madhur, 2003; Plummer, 2003; Kviback, 2000; Eichengreen and Luengnaruemitchai, 2004).
	Regulation Quality (Annual Regulatory Quality)	Positive	Strong bankruptcy law and supportive legal framework increase investors' confidence in the regulatory and supervisory framework of the country. (Sharma, 2000; Fabella and Madhur, 2003; Plummer, 2003; Kviback, 2000; Eichengreen and Luengnaruemitchai, 2004; Burger and Warnock, 2006).

Note: Regulatory Quality captures the perceptions of the ability of the government to formulate and implement sound policies and regulations that permit and promote private sector development. Higher the number, better is regulatory quality.

The Corruption Perceptions Index (CPI) ranks countries based on their perceived levels of corruption in the public sector. The CPI defines corruption as "the misuse of public power for private benefit". It currently ranks 176 countries on a scale from 100 (very clean) to 0 (highly corrupt).

Table 13.2 lists the Asian economies considered in this study and captures the trend of government and corporate bond outstanding as a percentage of GDP over the period from 2005 to 2018.

From Table 13.2, we can conclude that:

- There are considerable variances among the Asian countries used in the study.
- South Korea has the biggest corporate bond market in the region, accounting for 73% of GDP, while Indonesia has the smallest, at just 2.8% of GDP.
- On the other hand, Japan has a large government bond market, at 212% of GDP, but its corporate bond market is relatively small, comprising only 14.5% of GDP.
- Most Asian economies exhibit a rising trend in the corporate bond outstanding-to-GDP ratios over the period. However, Japan displays a decreasing trend.
- Government bonds represent a significant part of the overall bond market in most of the Asian economies under consideration. Corporate bond financing remains less prevalent, though Malaysia and Singapore show a declining trend in government bond outstanding.

2. Methodology

The determinants highlighted in the Table 13.1 have been tested using the Fixed Effect (FE), Random Effect (RE), and Two-Stage Instrumental Variable (IV) Method, based on cross-sectional panel data for nine selected Asian economies from 2005 to 2018, with annual frequency.

A multiple regression model is used to examine the relationship between Corporate Bond Outstanding and the independent variables (determinants). Equation 1 is used to model the determinants of bonds market size.

Table 13.2: Total Bond Outstanding as % GDP of Selected Asian Economies

Country		2005	2006	2007	2008	2009	2010	2011	2012	2013	2014	2015	2016	2017	2018
India	G	30.9	29.2	29.1	32.0	35.8	35.2	37.4	38.9	40.1	41.4	42.2	42.4	42.5	42.6
	C	1.0	2.0	4.0	3.0	6.0	11.7	12.0	13.0	13.1	14.0	14.7	15.7	16.0	16.1
China	G	25.8	25.1	28.9	27.6	29.9	29.2	28.8	29.9	30.9	32.0	38.7	47.8	51.2	53.2
	C	2.1	3.0	3.4	4.4	8.0	9.9	11.1	14.0	18.0	20.9	24.1	27.3	27.3	28.8
Indonesia	G	14.4	12.5	12.1	9.7	9.7	9.3	9.2	9.5	10.4	11.5	12.7	14.3	15.5	16.0
	C	2.1	1.8	2.0	1.4	1.5	1.7	1.9	2.2	2.3	2.1	2.2	2.5	2.9	2.8
Japan	G	123.9	129.7	134.7	144.8	164.8	173.8	185.4	192.4	198.6	202.4	196.6	198.8	209.7	212.4
	C	16.7	16.0	16.3	16.8	18.3	18.0	18.0	17.3	16.5	15.8	14.8	14.1	14.3	14.5
Philippines	G	39.5	38.0	36.8	35.1	44.5	42.4	43.0	45.8	48.2	48.8	49.9	50.8	51.2	52.9
	C	31.7	31.7	34.7	34.2	40.5	37.7	36.7	41.3	41.7	41.3	43.1	43.4	47.2	48.6
Malaysia	G	38.5	35.2	32.6	32.2	31.9	31.3	30.4	33.5	33.1	30.8	29.6	27.5	28.2	27.5
	C	0.9	1.7	2.1	2.7	4.4	4.3	4.5	5.0	5.2	6.1	6.1	6.2	6.5	7.5
Singapore	G	36.7	36.3	36.0	38.2	43.8	40.5	39.4	38.7	32.4	24.6	25.0	25.0	24.8	25.4
	C	28.3	28.2	28.3	28.4	26.2	25.9	26.7	29.6	30.9	32.3	33.1	32.5	30.2	32.2
S. Korea	G	20.9	23.7	24.6	25.4	27.5	27.4	28.6	29.4	31.6	36.4	38.7	39.8	40.4	41.1
	C	31.5	33.7	38.5	42.6	49.9	51.9	56.1	63.2	68.2	67.8	72.3	71.4	72.3	73.3
Thailand	G	26.6	26.0	25.7	25.0	29.9	28.6	27.4	29.5	32.1	31.8	34.0	33.0	33.4	33.8
	C	7.6	10.4	10.3	10.3	12.3	11.6	12.1	14.2	15.6	17.5	18.3	20.1	20.0	21.2

Note: G = Government; C = Corporate; *Source*: AsiaBondsOnline.

$$\mathbf{CorD\_GDP_{it}} = A_o + A_{1t}GDP\_Capita_{it} + A_{2t}GovD\_GDP_{it} + A_{3t}GDS\_GDP_{it} + A_{4t}GFCF\_GDP_{it} + A_{5t}Int\_Diff_{it} + A_{6t}MktCap\_GDP_{it} + A_{7t}BankCred\_GDP_{it} + A_{8t}Trade\_GDP_{it} + A_{9t}ExRateVol_{it} + A_{10t}Corrup\_I_{it} + A_{11t}Reg\_Qua_{it} + U_{it} \quad (1)$$

Where, i = country, 1 to 9, (India, China, Indonesia, Japan, Philippines, Malaysia, Singapore, South Korea, Thailand); and t = years, 2005 to 2018.

Dependent variable:

$CorD\_GDP_{it}$ = Total corporate bond outstanding as a % to GDP of ith country in year t.

Independent variables:

GDP_Capita_{it} = Per capita GDP terms of ith country in year t;

$GovD\_GDP$ = Total government bond outstanding as a % to GDP of ith country in year t;

GDS_GDP_{it} = Gross domestic savings as % of GDP of ith country in year t;

$GFCF\_GDP_{it}$ = Gross capital formation as % of GDP of ith country in year t;

Int_Diff_{it} = Difference between corporate and govt. bond yield for ith country in year t;

$MktCap\_GDP_{it}$ = Market capitalization of listed domestic companies as % of GDP for ith country in year t;

$BankCred\_GDP_{it}$ = Domestic credit by the banking sector to the private sector as % of GDP for ith country in year t;

$Trade\_GDP_{it}$ = Trade as % of GDP for ith country in year t;

$ExRateVol_{it}$ = Exchange rate volatility for ith country in year t;

$Corrup\_I_{it}$ = Annual corruption index for ith country in year t;

Reg_Qua_{it} = Annual regulatory quality for ith country in year t;

A_o = Constant or intercept;

A_{it} = Coefficients of the independent variables; and

U_{it} = Independent normal distribution error terms with mean zero.

The number of variables considered exceeds the number of countries. In the Random Effect model for panel data, the number of independent variables cannot exceed the number of cross-sections (or countries, in this case). So, it is essential to first evaluate the independent variables for their significance in the model. The correlation between the variables is looked at so that the highly correlated variables can be removed. Using highly correlated variables together in a model can lead to spurious results.

13.4. Empirical Results

13.4.1. Correlation Estimation

The correlation coefficients between the variables are given in Table 13.3. It is observed that both the Corruption Index and Regulatory Quality are highly correlated with each other, as well as with GDP per capita and market capitalisation.

In the working paper by ADB (Kee-Hong Bae, 2012), it is stated that institutional variables are less significant in the context of the local currency bond market compared to their role in international bond issuance. In our study, we have considered the Corruption Perception Index and Regulatory Quality as proxies for institutional variables. Correlation plots are shown in Appendix III.

Table 13.3: Correlation Coefficient

	BANKCRED_GDP	CORRUP_I	EXRATEVOL	GDP_CAPITA	GFCF_GDP	GOVD_GDP	INT_DIFF	MKTCAP_GDP	REG_QUA	TRADE_GDP
BANKCRED_GDP	1.00	0.46	-0.11	0.46	0.28	0.19	-0.59	0.32	0.53	0.25
CORRUP_I	0.46	1.00	-0.06	0.93	-0.23	0.50	-0.27	0.72	0.93	0.63
EXRATEVOL	-0.11	-0.06	1.00	-0.08	0.01	-0.01	0.05	-0.20	-0.08	-0.15
GDP_CAPITA	0.46	0.93	-0.08	1.00	-0.23	0.50	-0.28	0.62	0.93	0.53
GFCF_GDP	0.28	-0.23	0.01	-0.23	1.00	-0.27	0.16	-0.27	-0.34	-0.27
GOVD_GDP	0.19	0.50	-0.01	0.50	-0.27	1.00	-0.49	0.02	0.38	-0.22
INT_DIFF	-0.59	-0.27	0.05	-0.28	0.16	-0.49	1.00	0.07	-0.34	0.15
MKTCAP_GDP	0.32	0.72	-0.20	0.62	-0.27	0.02	0.07	1.00	0.75	0.85
REG_QUA	0.53	0.93	-0.08	0.93	-0.34	0.38	-0.34	0.75	1.00	0.68
TRADE_GDP	0.25	0.63	-0.15	0.53	-0.27	-0.22	0.15	0.85	0.68	1.00

Source: Author's calculations.

13.4.2. Panel Regression

First, a pooled panel regression is done, neglecting the cross-sectional and time-series nature of the data. The simple OLS regression allows us to observe the effect of independent variables on the dependent variables, without accounting for the fact that the data is both cross-sectional and time series. By pooling the data, we deny the heterogeneity or individuality that may exist among different countries.

From the original equation (Equation 1) considered earlier, two different models are used. It is found that the variable Gross Domestic Savings (GDS_GDP) is statistically insignificant, it is removed from the first equation. In this model, we also exclude institutional variables such as the Corruption Index and Regulation Quality.

Model 1:

$$CorD\_GDP_{it} = A_{12} + A_{13t}GovD\_GDP_{it} + A_{14t}GDP\_Capita_{it} + A_{15t}GFCF\_GDP_{it} + A_{16t}Int\_Diff_{it} + A_{17t}MktCap\_GDP_{it} + A_{18t}BankCred\_GDP_{it} + A_{19t}Trade\_GDP_{it} + A_{20t}ExRateVol_{it} + U_{it} \quad (2)$$

Moreover, institutional variables such as the Corruption Index and Regulatory Quality are highly correlated to each other, as well as with GDP per capita and market capitalisation. As a result, only the Corruption Index is considered in the second model, while GDP per capita and market capitalization are excluded. Using all three variables together (MktCap_GDP, GDP_Capita, and Corrup_I) would lead to misleading results.

Model 2:

$$CorD\_GDP_{it} = A_{21} + A_{22t}GovD\_GDP_{it} + A_{23t}GFCF\_GDP_{it} + A_{24t}Int\_Diff_{it} + A_{25t}BankCred\_GDP_{it} + A_{26t}Trade\_GDP_{it} + A_{27t}ExRateVol_{it} + A_{28t}Corrup\_I_{it} + U_{it} \quad (3)$$

Since the Corruption Index used in the study ranges from high values for very clean economies to 0 for highly corrupt ones, a positive correlation indicates that cleaner economies contribute positively to the development of the corporate bond market.

Columns 1 and 2 in Table 13.4 present the results of the pooled simple regression for the dependent variable, Corporate Bond Outstanding, in relation to the other independent variables.

Next, the Fixed and Random Effects methods are used to eliminate time-invariant unobserved effects before estimation. The FE model accounts for heterogeneity or individuality among countries by allowing each country to have its own intercept term. While the intercept may differ across countries, it remains constant over time, that is, it is time-invariant. In contrast, the Random Effects (RE) model assumes a common mean value for the intercept across all countries. The RE model eliminates unobserved effects in the error term, which are assumed to be uncorrelated with all the explanatory variables.

Table 13.4: Regression Results for Panel Regression Dependent Variable: Corporate Bonds Outstanding as % of GDP (CorD_GDP)

Independent Variables	Pooled Panel Regression		Fixed Effects	Random Effects	Panel EGLS with Cross-section SUR	
	Col 1	Col 2	Col 3	Col 4	Col 5	Col 6
	Model 1	Model 2	Model 1	Model 1	Model 1	Model 2
GovD_GDP	-0.209***	-0.308***	-0.120***	-0.206***	0.0238***	0.0178***
GDP_Capita	0.0003***		0.0001	0.0003***	0.0002***	
GFCF_GDP	-1.107***	-1.549***	-0.753***	-1.128***	-0.5675***	-0.762***
Trade_GDP	-0.097***	-0.130***	0.139***	-0.099***	0.0598***	0.021***
MktCap_ GDP	0.108***		-0.025	0.117***	0.0122***	
BankCred_ GDP	0.377***	0.429***	0.205***	0.379***	0.4080***	0.4157***
ExRateVol	1.244***	0.693**	-0.201	1.392***	0.1924***	-0.240***
Int_Diff	-0.255	0.993	0.226	-0.101	-0.8591***	-0.415***
Corrup_I		0.683***				0.2544***
Panel Observations	126	126	126	126		
R-Square	0.741283	0.766896	0.950102	0.751163		

Notes: *** means significance at a 1% level, ** means significance at a 5% level, and * significance at a 10% level.

After estimating the results using both the Fixed and RE models, as shown in columns 3 and 4 of Table 13.4, the Hausman Test is used to check the suitability of the models. The null hypothesis is that the "Random Effects model is appropriate." A significant p-value would indicate that the null hypothesis is rejected, leading us to accept the RE model. The Hausman test shows that the null hypothesis is rejected at the 1% significance level. Thus, it is concluded that the

FE model is more appropriate for estimating the factors influencing corporate bond issuance. The R-square value is also quite high for the FE model.

Panel data models may exhibit heteroscedasticity and correlation between errors, both contemporaneously and over time. In our study, there are large variations in corporate and government bond outstanding (as a % of GDP) among the Asian economies. This issue can be addressed in EViews using the Generalized Least Squares (GLS) specification. The cross-section SUR (Seemingly Unrelated Regressions) method allows a reasonable GLS output, correcting for heteroskedasticity and contemporaneous correlation. Columns 5 and 6 in Table 13.4 present the results of the Panel Estimated Generalized Least Squares (EGLS) with cross-section SUR for Models 1 and 2.

The results obtained from the Panel EGLS with cross-section SUR show that all the independent variables are statistically significant and exhibit the correct signs in relation to the development of the corporate bond market. However, the results from the simple FE model present some contradictions, with certain determinants found to be statistically insignificant.

The findings from the Panel EGLS with cross-section SUR in Table 13.4 can be interpreted as follows:

- This model explains almost all the variations in total corporate bonds outstanding.
- The stage of development has a positive influence on the corporate bond market; it is statistically significant, though the effect is very small in magnitude.
- Both the openness of the economy and market capitalisation are statistically significant and positively influence the corporate bond market.
- Further, we find that the size of the banking system and market capitalisation have positive and statistically significant relationships with corporate bond market development.

- There is a negative relationship between corporate bonds and the interest rate spread, defined as the difference between the corporate and government bond yields. The negative coefficient suggests that higher borrowing costs are related to a smaller bond outstanding size.
- Similarly, there is a negative and statistically significant relationship with exchange rate volatility (column 6). However, there are also a few results indicating that exchange rate volatility is either not significant or positively related to corporate bond outstanding. As exchange rates of most Asian economies are either pegged to the US dollar or managed by central banks through market intervention, it is possible that volatility was low during the period considered. Moreover, domestic corporate bonds are issued in local currencies.
- The Corruption Index is statistically significant, meaning that the perception of a less corrupt or well-regulated economy is favourable for corporate bond market development.
- Most importantly, government debt outstanding is statistically significant with a positive sign, indicating that a developed government securities market provides the necessary market infrastructure, an experienced dealer community, and a benchmark yield curve for the corporate bond market. However, the Pooled Panel regression and FE model indicate a negative relationship with corporate bond outstanding, meaning that government bonds can crowd out corporate bonds.

The study is repeated using the instrumental variable method to reduce the dependence between the error term and explanatory variables, thereby validating the results already obtained (refer to the box).

13.1: Technical Section: Instrumental Variable Model

The IV method uses an appropriate exogenous variable as an instrument to reduce the dependence between the error term and the explanatory variables. Identifying the appropriate IV is crucial. In this case, we consider a model to explain government bond outstanding, with the fiscal deficit as a percentage of GDP (FD_GDP) being selected as the IV.

$$GovD\_GDP_{it} = F\ (FD\_GDP_{it}, GFCF\_GDP_{it}, GDP\_Capita_{it})\ (4)$$

where, FD_GDP = Fiscal deficit as a percentage of GDP.

Table 13.5: Regression Results for Government Bond Outstanding

Dependent Variable: Government Bond Outstanding as % of GDP (GovD_GDP).

Independent Variables	**Model 1**
FD_GDP	-1.0237***
GFCF_GDP	-0.6010***
GDP_Capita	0.0002***
Panel Observations	126
R-Square	0.988294

Notes: *** means significance at a 1% level, ** means significance at a 5% level, and * significance at a 10% level.

The regression results in Table 13.5 show that as the fiscal deficit becomes more negative, government bond outstanding increases, as expected from theory. The value of GovD_GDPit is estimated using the above equation, and the estimated or forecasted value is referred to as GovD_GDPFit. Figure 13.1 plots both the actual and forecasted values of government bond outstanding.

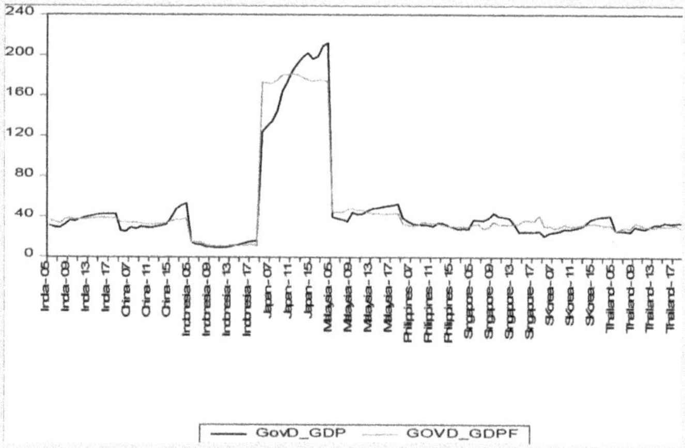

Figure 13.1: Actual and Estimated Values of Government Bond Outstanding

Source: EViews Estimates.

Next, we use the estimated value of GovD_GDPit in Model 1 and Model 2 for corporate debt outstanding, while removing the variables already used in equation (4). These new models are referred to as Model 3 and Model 4.

Model 3:

$$CorD\_GDPit = F\ (GovD\_GDPF_{it},\ Int\_Diff_{it},\ MktCap\_GDP_{it},\ BankCred\_GDP_{it},\ Trade\_GDP_{it},\ ExRateVol_{it}) \quad (5)$$

Model 4: (including the variables for institutional quality like Corruption Index)

$$CorD\_GDP_{it} = F\ (GovD\_GDPF_{it},\ Int\_Diff_{it},\ BankCred\_GDP_{it},\ Trade\_GDP_{it},\ ExRateVol_{it},\ Corrup\_I_{it}) \quad (6)$$

The results are summarised in Table 13.6.

Table 13.6: Regression Results for Panel EGLS with Cross-section SUR

Dependent Variable: Corporate Bond Outstanding as % of GDP (CorD_GDP).

Independent Variables	GLS	
	Model 3	Model 4
GovD_GDPF	0.5949***	0.6107***
Trade_GDP	0.0687***	0.0507***
MktCap_GDP	0.0214***	
BankCred_GDP	0.3977***	0.3707***
ExRateVol	-0.175***	-0.2574***
Int_Diff	-1.0125***	-0.6910***
Corrup_I		0.2296***
No of Observations	126	126
R-Square	0.987464	0.988808

Notes: *** means significance at a 1% level, ** means significance at a 5% level, and * significance at a 10% level.

All the determinants are statistically significant at the 1% level. The openness of the economy (measured as trade as a % of GDP) has a positive sign and is statistically significant at the 1% level, consistent with our hypothesis. The size of the banking system and the capital market both show a positive and significant relationship with corporate debt outstanding. The exchange rate volatility and interest rate differences are also significant with negative signs, which is consistent with our expectations. A higher cost of borrowing for corporates (as indicated by a high-interest rate difference) adversely impacts the corporate debt market. Similarly, higher exchange rate volatility has a detrimental impact. The size of the government bond market shows a positive and significant relationship, as observed in the previous results. Thus, a well-developed government bond market supports the development of the corporate bond market.

13.5. Summarising: Variables for the Development of Corporate Bond Market

The corporate bond market in Asia has witnessed considerable growth in recent years, yet it remains relatively small compared to the overall bond market. This study attempts to identify the primary determinants of corporate bond financing in nine major Asian economies: India, China, Indonesia, Japan, Malaysia, the Philippines, Singapore, Thailand and South Korea.

The results obtained through the econometric models indicate that government debt outstanding has a positive relationship with corporate bond outstanding, as seen in the literature. In other words, a well-functioning and deep government bond market is a prerequisite for the development of the corporate bond market, as it provides market infrastructure and a benchmark yield curve for corporate bonds. However, the FE model results, which do not account for heteroscedasticity in the data, suggest a negative correlation, implying that higher government debt could potentially crowd out the corporate sector. Therefore, while a robust government bond market is essential for the development of the corporate bond market, further exploration of the relationship is needed.

The stage of economic development (GDP per Capita) and the banking system (measured by domestic credit to the private sector) both show positive relationships with corporate bonds, which aligns with our expectations. Similarly, trade openness has a significant positive influence on the corporate bond market. Therefore, further opening up trade in these economies will help develop the corporate bond market.

On the other hand, exchange rate volatility and interest rate differences show a significant negative relationship with the corporate bond market. Higher interest rates for corporate bonds hinder the development of the corporate bond market.

To strengthen the corporate bond market, these key determinants need to be enhanced. The Indian corporate bond market has been developing slowly but still has a long way to go. Recent defaults in large NBFCs have increased risk aversion. However, such episodes of defaults and corporate failures occurred in the early stages, even in economies with well-established corporate bond markets. The institutional quality has a significant positive impact on the corporate bond market. Therefore, developing robust financial market institutions, strong regulators, reliable credit rating agencies, better investor protection rights, and improved corporate governance and transparency will improve investors' trust and help in the growth of the market.

Well-developed corporate bond markets in Asia will provide alternate sources of financing, reducing the heavy reliance on the banking sector. This will also help channel large household savings into financial instruments, addressing the significant infrastructure financing needs.

CHAPTER 14

Implication for Financial Sector: An Empirical Analysis

The results of the empirical analysis in the previous chapter show that the stage of economic development, the size of the banking system, trade openness, and strong institutional quality have a positive impact on the development of the corporate bond market, while exchange rate volatility and interest rate differences have a significant negative impact. Most importantly, a deep and liquid government bond market is absolutely essential for the development of the corporate bond market, as it provides market infrastructure and a risk-free bond yield curve that serves as a benchmark for other financial instruments. Proper market infrastructure enhances efficiency in trading, clearing, and settlement, leading to lower trading costs and reduced price volatility. It also facilitates order flow and improves price discovery. Well-functioning intermediaries, such as banks, PDs, and brokers, are important for the development of the corporate bond market (Leigland, 1997; IOSCO, 2011). However, a contradicting negative correlation suggests the possibility of higher government debt crowding out the corporate sector.

Thus, there is a need to understand whether high government borrowing can crowd out private investment. This empirical analysis tries to explore and understand the influence of the government bond market on the corporate bond market. Using panel regression with data from Asian economies, we attempt to draw general insights into whether government spending crowds out or crowds in private investment, and, based on this, derive conclusions relevant to the Indian economy. Developing economies usually experience variations in government spending due to various economic or natural shocks, which is why we employ Vector Autoregression (VAR) to analyse the dynamic relationship between government spending and private investment in India. We also look at the impulse response to unexpected shocks in government spending.

We interpret the results from the Indian policy perspective. Our findings suggest that government consumption expenditure negatively impacts private investment, effectively crowding it out. Thus, a robust government bond market is an essential but not sufficient condition for the development of the corporate bond market. The quality of government expenditure plays a critical role—direct productive expenditure in infrastructure or improvement in the "ease of doing business" helps crowd in private investment. In contrast, social expenditure such as salaries and consumption subsidies tend to crowd out private investment, increasing the cost of financing for the private sector.

14.1. Theoretical Framework

Keynes argued that government borrowing (through bonds) can be beneficial in creating economic stimulus. However, on the other hand, monetarists believe that expansionary fiscal policies may result in higher interest rates, which could negatively affect the private sector. This crowding-out effect is a prominent economic theory suggesting that increased public sector borrowing can reduce private sector spending and hurt the development of the corporate bond market.

As shown in Figure 14.1, in the financial market, an increase in government borrowing can shift the demand curve for financial capital to the right, from D0 to D1, thereby raising the equilibrium interest rate from E0 to E1. This rise in borrowing costs can crowd out private investment.

On the other hand, if the government borrows and spends on infrastructure, it can lead to an increase in public physical capital, which benefits the economy in the long run. Over time, this may shift the supply curve to S1, ultimately lowering the interest rate.

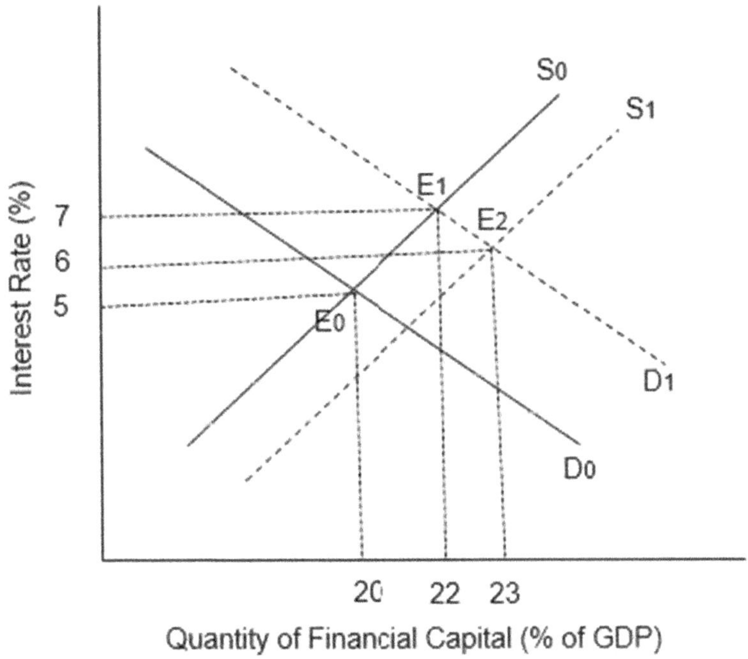

Figure 14.1: Budget Deficit and Interest Rate

The literature does not specify a threshold size for the government bond market that can facilitate the development of the corporate bond market, as this varies from country to country. For example, in Japan, the outstanding government bonds account for 212% of GDP, yet bond yields remain low due to strong domestic demand for government bonds.

Thus, market dynamics and demand-supply nuances decide the size of the government bond market that can help develop the corporate bond market.

14.2. Literature Review: Government Expenditure and Corporate Borrowings

The literature shows that a well-functioning government bond market is essential for the development of the corporate bond market. The government bond market is the source for the government to raise funds to finance its fiscal deficit, while the corporate bond market provides a source of private investment. Both the government and corporates compete for the same pool of resources available in the economy, leading to ongoing debate over the size of the government bond market and the type of government expenditure that can help develop the corporate bond market. This raises several questions:

- Do government borrowings through the bond market crowd out private investments?
- If the government borrows to fund certain types of expenditure, does it attract private investment? In other words, does the quality of government expenditure matter?
- Is there an optimal level of government borrowing that crowds in private investment?

There is a body of research examining the relationship between the quality of government borrowings and their impact on private investment. A significant debate exists regarding the size of the government bond market and the type of government expenditure that can either facilitate corporate borrowing through debt instruments or help develop the corporate bond market.

The literature talks about the crowding-out effect between public and private investment (Sunderrajan & Thakur, 1980; Kulkarni & Balders, 1998; Alsenia et al., 2002). Studies have found that government spending on infrastructure such as roads, highways, sewage systems, ports, airports, skill development and research can enhance productivity and improve the ease of doing business, giving the private sector a level playing field which crowds in private investment, particularly in developing economies (Fernald, 1999; Ahmed & Miller, 1999; Muhammad et al., 2012; Fujii et al., 2013).

On the other hand, public spending—whether tax- or debt-financed—on social security and welfare tends to crowd out private investment in both developed and developing economies. Ahmed and Ammad (2020) show that physical public investment has stronger crowding-in effects than social public investment in Pakistan. In India, it has been found that during periods of macroeconomic uncertainty, high government expenditures hurt private investment (Muthu, 2010; Singh, 2012). Moreover, in China, government investment in private goods through state-owned enterprises significantly crowds out private investment (Xu & Yan, 2014). Thus, higher government borrowing to fund consumption expenditure can crowd out private investment and hinder the development of the corporate bond market.

14.3. Data and Methodology

The annual time-series data for eleven variables, as highlighted in the previous chapter (Table 13.1 and Table 13.2), along with data on private investment, government consumption expenditure, and lending rates for nine Asian economies for the period 2005–2018, have been collected from the Asian Development Bank, World Development Indicators (World Bank), the IMF International Financial Statistics, and the RBI database.

As the literature suggests that a robust government bond market is essential for the development of the corporate bond market, is there a relationship between government expenditure and private investment?

It is already established that the government bond market is essential for the development of the corporate bond market. We now explore whether the development of the corporate bond market may be affected by the quality of government expenditure.

We use the GLS panel regression method to analyse the relationship between the quality of government expenditure and private investment in Asian economies. The aim is to understand whether government consumption expenditure negatively impacts or crowds out private investment. In other words, we aim to explore whether the development of the corporate bond market is influenced by the quality of government expenditure. The model we use is:

Private Investment = F (Government consumption expenditure, Lending rate) (1)

Next, to extend the analysis to the Indian context, we use the VAR method to understand the relationship between disaggregated government expenditure (including consumption and public investment) and private investment in India. We use VAR model because it is well-suited for analysing multivariate time series, making it especially useful for describing the dynamic behaviour of economic and financial time series. VAR also allows us to look at the causal impacts of unexpected shocks or innovations to the specified variables in our model.

Private investment = F (GDP, Government consumption expenditure, Public investment) (2)

14.4. Empirical Results

1. Private Investment and Government Consumption Expenditure in Asian Economies

A robust government bond market is necessary for the development of the corporate bond market. The literature says that increased government borrowings for consumption expenditure can raise the prices of goods and services, leading to higher capital costs, which in turn crowds out private investment.

We use equation (1) to find the relationship between private investment as a percentage of GDP (part of Fixed Capital Investment, PvtInv_GDP), government consumption expenditure as a percentage of GDP (GCE_GDP), and the lending rate. Table 14.1 shows the results of the panel regression for select Asian economies.

PvtInv_GDP = F (GFCE_GDP, Lending_Rate) (3)

Table 14.1: Regression Results for Private Investments

Dependent Variable: Private Investment as % of GDP (PvtInv_GDP).

Independent Variables	Results
GFCE_GDP	-0.2679***
Lending_Rate	-0.1784***
Panel Observations	96

Notes: *** means significance at a 1% level, ** means significance at a 5% level, and * significance at a 10% level.

The results show that both government consumption expenditure and high lending rates negatively impact private investment. The coefficients are negative, large, and statistically significant. In other words, as the government increases spending on various consumption expenditures—such as salaries, subsidies, interest expenses, etc.—through borrowing, it crowds out private investment.

Box 14.1: Technical Section

Does Government Expenditure Crowd in or Crowds Out Private Investment in India?

Through our panel regression, we conclude that government consumption expenditure negatively impacts private investment. We now aim to delve deeper into the impact of a disaggregated measure of government expenditure (government consumption and public investment) on private investment in India, using equation (2).

Gross Capital Formation in India is divided into three broad sectors—public, private corporate, and household sectors. The household sector is conceived as the "residual" sector and may not provide reliable data, so it is kept out of our study. We consider the annual data on Real GDP by expenditure from FY 1995 to FY 2018. All variables—Real GDP (GDP), Government Final Consumption Expenditure (GFCE), Public Gross Capital Formation (PuGCF), and Private Gross Capital Formation (PvGCF)—are converted to natural logarithms to make them stationary.

We use a VAR model for several reasons. First, it is a straightforward model for analysing multivariate time series. Second, it is especially useful for describing the dynamic behaviour of economic and financial time series. Third, it helps to look at the causal impacts of unexpected shocks or innovations to the specified variables in the model.

The model is first tested for lag-length criteria, and it is found that a lag of one is sufficient, which is appropriate given that we are using annual data. Next, we check the robustness of the model. The inverse roots of the AR characteristic polynomial are found to be inside the unit circle, indicating that the model is stable (see Appendix IV). The residual diagnostics show that the values fall within the dotted line, and the residuals are completely random with no sinusoidal movement, suggesting that there is no correlation or seasonality.

The normalised parameter estimate of the cointegration vector is:

LPVGCF =

0.656*LPVGCF(-1) + 1.73*LGDP(-1) - 1.14*LGFCE(-1) - 0.044*LPUGCF(-1) - 7.136
(1.88327) (-1.47908) (-0.09442)

The figures in parentheses are the t-values. The EViews result for this VAR model is given in the Appendix IV.

The signs of the variables confirm the theory in the literature. The overall GDP has a positive relationship with private investment, as the coefficient is large, positive, and statistically significant. On the other hand, there exists a negative relationship between government consumption and private investment, with the coefficient being large, negative, and statistically significant.

The Impulse Response functions also show the dynamic effects of disaggregated measures of GDP, government consumption, and public investment on private investment (Figure 14.2).

Figure 14.2 clearly shows that one standard deviation shock to overall GDP positively impacts private investment. Similarly, one standard deviation shock to Government Final Consumption Expenditure (LGFCE) has a negative effect on private investment (LPvGCF). In other words, government consumption negatively impacts or crowds out private investment. This impact or shock persists for a long time, and it takes time for private investment to return to equilibrium.

Public investment (LPuGCF) shows a small negative impact in the short term. This may be due to some public investment being undertaken by heavily subsidised and inefficient public sector enterprises in various sectors, which reduces opportunities for private investment.

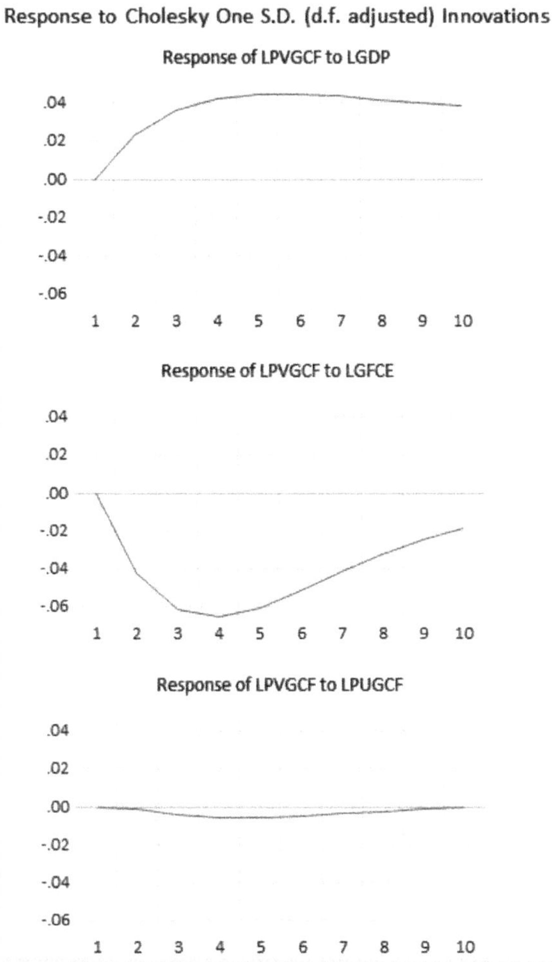

Figure 14.2: Impulse Response of Shocks

Source: EViews Results.

The variance decomposition of shocks gives insight into the dominance of various shocks (Table 14.2). We find that

Government Consumption Expenditure becomes increasingly dominant over time compared to other shocks.

Table 14.2: Variance Decomposition of Shocks

Period	S.E.	LPVGCF	LGDP	LGFCE	LPUGCF
1	0.188772	100.0000	0.000000	0.000000	0.000000
2	0.235227	95.75180	0.979975	3.264619	0.003602
3	0.261642	89.08112	2.714472	8.179137	0.025275
4	0.279103	82.51012	4.725326	12.70475	0.059802
5	0.291178	77.15060	6.728019	16.02868	0.092708
6	0.299669	73.17177	8.591830	18.12124	0.115159
7	0.305760	70.33322	10.27480	19.26592	0.126058
8	0.310279	68.30019	11.78040	19.79073	0.128683
9	0.313795	66.78274	13.13294	19.95708	0.127237
10	0.316690	65.57450	14.36383	19.93674	0.124932

Cholesky Ordering: LPVGCF LGDP LGFCE LPUGCF

Source: EViews Results.

14.5. Implication of Large Government Bond Market on Financial Market

To boost the corporate bond market, the RBI mandated in 2016 that large corporations raise 25 percent of their incremental or fresh long-term borrowings from the bond market. In 2018, SEBI came out with the proposal to implement the same from 1st April 2019. Successive budgets have announced measures to develop the corporate bond market. In the Budget of 2020, the Finance Minister announced several initiatives, including tax concessions and increased investment limits for foreign investors.

It has been found that a well-developed government debt market is a prerequisite for a strong corporate bond market, as it develops the market infrastructure and benchmark yield curve. The corporate bond market is significant in economies that have a robust government bond market. However, our analysis shows that high government borrowings for social expenditures, such as salaries and subsidies, can crowd out the corporate sector. Therefore, while a government bond market is necessary, it is not a sufficient condition for the development of the corporate bond market. The quality of government expenditure matters. We can conclude that government consumption expenditure crowds out private investment. Besides, increased government expenditure or large government borrowings also increase the cost of financing for the private sector, as both compete for the same pool of resources.

In India, although the fiscal deficit trend of the central government shows credible consolidation since FY 2011–12, the actual government debt is significantly understated. The latest Comptroller and Auditor General's (CAG's) report details how various government expenses, such as subsidies and project finances, have been kept off the books, funded through public sector companies, or simply rolled over to the next year. This practice has been going on for several years irrespective of the political party in power at the centre.

High public borrowings put pressure on risk-free bond yields. As shown in Figure 14.3 below, the government has been borrowing at an average interest rate of 7% to 8% since 2009. While the average interest rate has come down in recent years, it is still considerably high.

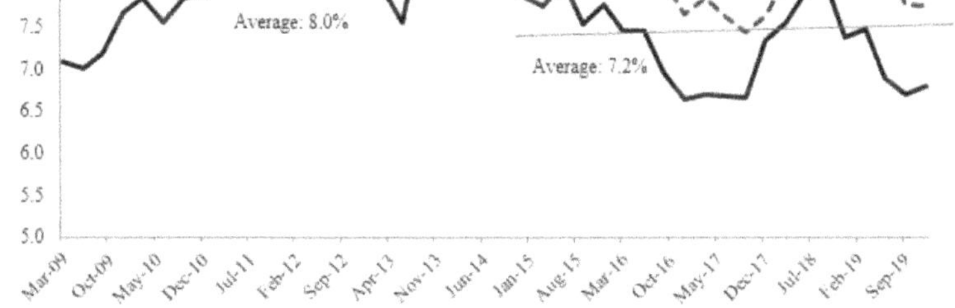

Figure 14.3: Trend of Interest Rates of 10-year G-Sec and 10-year AAA Corporate Bonds in India

For example, in most developed economies, the government has been borrowing at nearly zero percent interest rates since the global financial crisis. A comparison of lending rates across a few Asian economies also shows that the lending rate in India is relatively high (Table 14.3).

Table 14.3: Lending Rate in 2015 (%)

Country	Lending Rate
India	10.0
Japan	1.1
Korea	3.5
Malaysia	4.6
Philippines	5.6
Thailand	4.7

Source: World Bank.

Corporates are required to pay a risk premium on top of the risk-free rates, forcing private players to bear high interest costs in the domestic market. As seen in Table 14.4, the interest rates paid by issuers of bonds rated below A are exorbitant in India. This results in the crowding out of private investment.

Table 14.4: Historical Spread Analysis (Average, in Basis Points) of Corporate Bonds

Year	Ratings									
	AAA	AA	A1	A2	A	BBB	BB	B	C	D
2011-12	119	189	248	-	202	185	227	-	-	-
2014-15	46	123	179	141	149	351	83	138	566	-
2016-17	73	221	240	-	343	720	1,042	1,699	-	-
2017-18	74	171	177	825	352	500	957	1,052	-	-
2018-19	105	183	199	-	232	460	602	885	687	656
Apr-2019	114	241	-	-	369	678	838	1,529	781	807

Source: Rakshitra, CCIL.

The corporate bond market is directly related to government investment in economic assets. According to IFS-IMF data, the "Net investment in government nonfinancial assets as a percentage of GDP" for South Korea was 1.8%, while that for India was 0.05% in 2013. The corporate bond market in South Korea is large, accounting for 73% of GDP, whereas in India, it stands at only 16%.

In India, the FRBM Act mandates that the revenue deficit should be zero, or the government should borrow only for capital expenditure. However, in FY 2020, the fiscal and revenue deficits of India were at 4.6% and 3.3% of GDP, respectively. This indicates that the government borrowed to fund its revenue expenditure, with only1% allocated to capital expenditure.

High government borrowing pushed interest rates up and prevented the transmission of significant policy rate cuts by the RBI (Reserve Bank of India) to the real economy in FY 2020. In June 2019, former RBI Deputy Governor Viral Acharya warned, "Not only does government borrowing crowd out the private sector, but it can also induce the private sector to borrow more short-term, which increases financial fragility."

It is seen that economies with large corporate bond markets tend to have fiscal surpluses, such as South Korea (+1.6), Singapore (+2.5), and Thailand (+1.2) in 2018. Thus, higher government borrowing to fund revenue expenditure can hurt the development of the corporate bond market.

The study primarily contributes to the debate among policymakers on the importance of distinguishing between different areas of government spending to facilitate the growth of the corporate bond market. Moreover, government borrowing should be managed in a way that maintains a balanced demand-supply dynamic to prevent an increase in the cost of capital. While it may be challenging to empirically prove that higher government borrowing leads to a higher interest rate, as it is a complex function of savings and investments within the economy. We observe that during crises, as government borrowing increases, the RBI often infuses liquidity, and households increase their savings. This, in turn, increases loanable funds, which may prevent borrowing costs from rising.

It has been found that government spending on infrastructure such as roads, highways, sewage systems, ports, airports, skill development, and research improves productivity and the ease of doing business, providing the private sector with a level playing field which crowds in private investment—particularly for developing economies (Fernald, 1999; Ahmed & Miller, 1999; Mohammad et al., 2012; Fujii et al., 2013). On the other hand, public spending (both tax- and debt financed) on social security and welfare tends to crowd out private investment in both developed and developing economies. Moreover, we found that increased government borrowing raises the prices of goods and services, which, in turn, increases the cost of capital and crowds out private investment.

Therefore, we can conclude that a deep and liquid government bond market is essential for the development of the corporate bond market. However, it is important to differentiate between the areas of government spending to effectively facilitate the corporate bond market and manage government borrowing to prevent the cost of capital from rising.

A well-developed corporate bond market in India is necessary to provide alternative sources of financing, reduce the heavy reliance on the banking sector, and help meet the country's large infrastructure investment needs.

CHAPTER 15

Conclusion and Recommendations

The sovereign bond market in India has grown significantly over the last two decades. Reforms initiated since the 1990s have led to increased trading volumes, a longer maturity profile, and greater diversification in both market participants and instruments. The outstanding stock of government securities (both central and state) as a proportion of GDP has jumped up from 14.7% in 1992 to 54% in 2021.

In India, the government bond market dominates the debt market, with the corporate bond market remaining relatively small in comparison. Sovereign bonds outweigh corporate bonds in terms of both outstanding securities and trading volumes. More than 66% of the total outstanding debt instruments are government securities, and the dominance of government securities in the secondary market is even more pronounced, accounting for a whopping 90% of transactions in recent years.

A comparison with Asian peers indicates that the Indian government bond market is reasonably large within the region. However, the corporate bond market, although smaller, still plays a significant role in satisfying the financing needs of the economy. Foreign investments in Indian government securities are notably lower than those in smaller Asian economies like Indonesia and Malaysia, where foreign participation is relatively higher. A vibrant bond market, with a well-functioning corporate debt market, is essential for fostering economic growth and ensuring stability in the financial sector.

15.1. Sovereign/Government Bond Market

In our study of the government bond market, we first examine the drivers of government bond yields in India to understand the impact of fiscal and monetary policies. Our findings indicate that interest rates on longer-maturity government bonds in India are positively correlated with short-term interest rates on Treasury bills, even after controlling for various macroeconomic variables, such as inflation, industrial production growth, and the debt ratio. Higher (or lower) long-term government bond yields are influenced by higher (or lower) short-term interest rates and inflation rates. This suggests that the central bank's policy can strongly influence long-term government bond yields through short-term interest rates. This relationship holds true across periods of globalisation, unconventional monetary policies in developed economies, and divergent monetary policies across various economies.

Our study also finds that the slope of the yield curve—the difference between the yields of 10-year and 3-month government bonds—can have significant predictive power for forecasting the economic cycle. It is an even more reliable predictor compared to a lead indicator constructed with high-frequency economic data. The yield spread can predict turning points in the growth rate cycle up to two quarters in advance.

Our study explores the dynamic interaction of macroeconomic shocks on the entire term structure, or yield curve. The empirical results show that monetary policy shocks have the greatest impact on the yield curve, with the effect being most pronounced at the shorter end of the curve. In addition, monetary policy has a stronger impact on the level of the yield curve than on its slope or curvature. Among other macroeconomic factors, liquidity shocks have an immediate effect. Similarly, inflation or supply-side shocks also have a large and instantaneous impact, while output shocks are smaller and have more long-term effects. Exchange rate shocks are both instantaneous and relatively pronounced on the slope of the yield curve. These impacts often operate through the liquidity channel, as the RBI tries to manage volatility in the forex market.

In summary, we can conclude the following:

1. **Impact of RBI's Monetary Policy:** The RBI's monetary policy has a significant impact on the yield curve, with its impact being more pronounced at the shorter end.
2. **Short-Term Interest Rates and Long-Term Yields:** Interest rates on longer-maturity government bonds in India are influenced by short-term treasury bill rates. The central bank's credibility and its ability to effectively communicate its policy intentions are crucial in maintaining short-term interest rates within its policy band, which in turn facilitates the transmission of monetary policy across the yield curve.
3. **RBI's Focus on Yield Levels:** The RBI continuously monitors the level of yields (rather than the slope or curvature) and incorporates this as a key input in its policy decisions. In other words, India's monetary policy extracts information from the market, taking into account the evolving expectations of market participants. The RBI operates within a market-oriented policy framework.
4. **RBI's Dual Mandate:** Acting as both the monetary authority and the government's debt manager, the RBI has the responsibility to ensure that government borrowing costs remain low while maintaining financial stability. This dual mandate requires a careful balancing act. Despite these potentially conflicting interests, RBI's policy announcements have a significant influence on the Indian debt market. Thus, sovereign bond yields serve as an effective conduit for transmitting policy actions to the real economy, as other financial instruments are calibrated against the sovereign yield curve.
5. **Liquidity and Policy Transmission:** Liquidity plays a crucial role in expediting monetary policy transmission. A policy easing cycle needs to be supplemented with easy liquidity in the banking system to ensure faster transmission of rate changes, and vice versa.

6. **Yield Spread and Economic Cycle:** The yield spread, defined as the difference between the 10-year and 3-month government bond yields, can predict turning points in the economic cycle up to two quarters in advance. This supports the conclusion that the yield curve in India embodies valuable information that can help forecast future economic activity.
7. **Market Theories and the Indian Bond Market:** The Indian bond market is well-explained by standard market theories. The expectation theory of the term structure is dominant in the short run, while preferred habitat theory and term premia considerations are dominant in the medium to long run.

15.2. Corporate Bond Market

The corporate bond market in India has remained relatively underdeveloped, accounting for only 16% of GDP in 2017. Furthermore, only large companies dominate the corporate bond market. The problems are manifolds, including weak market infrastructure, low liquidity in secondary market, a narrow investor base, inadequate credit assessment skills, high cost of issuance, a limited set of issuers, and a lack of diverse instruments.

The Indian corporate debt market is riddled with several problems. Access to domestic bond issuance has largely been confined to large and highly rated corporates, primarily attributed to the risk aversion of investors, investment restrictions on institutional investors like pension funds and insurance companies, and the lack of reliable tools for credit pricing and risk assessment in these markets.

It is found that the level of economic development (GDP per Capita) and the strength of the banking system (domestic credit to the private sector) have a positive relationship with the development of the corporate bond market. Similarly, trade openness has a significant positive influence. Therefore, further opening up trade in these economies can contribute to the growth of the corporate bond market. On the other hand, exchange rate volatility and interest rate difference have a significant negative relationship with the market.

Higher interest rates for corporate bonds hurt the development of the corporate bond market. To strengthen this market, it is essential to improve these key determinants.

The results obtained from the econometric models show that while a robust government bond market is necessary for the development of the corporate bond market, it is not a sufficient condition on its own. The quality of government expenditure plays a crucial role. It is important to distinguish between public expenditure that crowds in private investment and the level of government borrowing, which can drive up the cost of capital. In India, the government has been primarily borrowing to fund its consumption expenditure, with only a small percentage allocated to capital expenditure. The high level of government borrowing for consumption has pushed interest rates high, which, in turn, have crowded out private investment. Moreover, it has also prevented the transmission of significant policy rate cuts by the RBI to the broader economy.

Recommendations for Developing a Liquid Corporate Bond Market:

1. **Public Debt Issuance and Monetary Policy:** A large public debt issuance for revenue spending can render monetary policy actions ineffective by interfering with transmission mechanisms and crowding out private investment. Much of the problems in the corporate debt market will be solved if the government reduces borrowings for non-productive expenditure. A part of the fiscal deficit can be met by divesting shares in public sector enterprises, monetizing non-core public assets (such as golf courses), and cutting back on wasteful subsidies and programs that do not contribute to economic growth. Increasing the share of capital expenditures will also help crowd in private investment, making more resources available to the corporate sector and reducing the cost of funds, thereby addressing some supply-side issues.
2. **Development of A-Rated Bond Market:** There is a need to deepen the market for A-rated bonds, as this would allow smaller corporates to tap funding at lower interest

rates, while enabling investors to diversify their portfolios without taking on significant additional risks. This could resolve both supply and demand-side challenges. Key steps in this process include the development of a CDS market and the establishment of a credit guarantee enhancement corporation.

3. **Tri-Party Repo Market in Corporate Debt Securities:** The development of a tri-party repo market for corporate debt securities would provide participants the opportunity to borrow against securities, offering short-term liquidity. This would, in turn, boost demand and liquidity for lower-rated corporate bonds.
4. **Coordination Among Regulatory Authorities:** There should be better coordination among regulatory authorities such as the RBI, SEBI, IRDAI, and PFRDA. These institutions must increase their consultations and ensure they are not working at cross-purposes, leading to a more streamlined and effective regulatory framework.
5. **Strengthening Corporate Governance:** A deep corporate bond market cannot be expected if investors have little confidence in corporate management. Creditors' confidence is built on strong corporate governance, robust accounting and auditing standards, transparent financial reporting systems, and effective legal protection of their rights. As the Insolvency and Bankruptcy Code (IBC) becomes more effective, it will instil higher confidence in investors by facilitating timely resolution and recovery, further driving demand for A-rated bonds.
6. **Enhancing the Credibility of Credit Ratings:** The credibility of the rating process can be strengthened by complementing ratings from domestic rating agencies with those from internationally recognised agencies. In emerging markets, the lack of sophisticated credit risk assessments has been a major limitation to the growth of corporate bond markets.

7. **Improving Disclosure Requirements:** Regulators should look at the disclosure requirements for public debt issuances to reduce the cost, time, and complexity of compliances. On the other hand, the disclosure requirements for private placements should be increased to address information asymmetry in the market.
8. **Encouraging Retail Investment in Corporate Bonds:** Retail investors mostly invest in the corporate bond market through mutual funds. Given the low level of financial literacy in the country, the government can incentivise individuals to invest more in financial instruments rather than traditional assets like gold and real estate through favourable taxation policies. The recent problems in the NBFC space, including debt defaults, have dented confidence in the corporate bond market. Strengthening regulatory oversight, improving governance, and ensuring greater transparency in the market will help restore investor trust and attract more retail participation.

15.3. Implication for Financial Market and Economic Growth

With India's GDP growth falling below its potential, authorities are trying to revive growth through coordinated monetary and fiscal policies. India's GDP growth has plunged to a 26-quarter low of 4.5% in September 2019, continuing a downward trend that started from a high of 8.1% in March 2018.

While global headwinds contribute to this slowdown, domestic issues have exacerbated the problem. The root cause of this problem can be traced back to 2010, when corporations borrowed heavily from banks during the economic boom to invest in various infrastructure projects. However, many of these projects failed to materialise for various reasons. As a result, highly leveraged corporate balance sheets morphed into bad loans on bank books. This created the "twin balance sheet" (TBS) problem, where stressed balance sheets of both corporates and banks slowed down investment. Banks, burdened with double digit NPAs, became increasingly risk-averse and scaled back lending. However, the ample liquidity available after the demonetisation in 2016 allowed Non-Banking Financial Companies (NBFCs), or shadow banks, to step in and fill the gap left by traditional banks. These NBFCs, in turn, were funded by banks and mutual funds, helping to sustain some level of credit flow in the economy.

By mid-2018, the loan book of NBFCs had grown to a substantial 25% of total outstanding credit in India, doubling over the past decade. However, a sudden default by a large NBFC in September 2018 created panic and raised concerns about the asset quality of other NBFCs. Banks, already struggling with NPAs, stopped financing NBFCs, leading to a severe liquidity crunch in the shadow banking sector. As a result, NBFCs pulled back from lending. Meanwhile, banks, which were just beginning to recover from their NPA issues, did not step in to meet the demand, exacerbating the situation. This has since been referred to as the Triple Balance Sheet problem by Nomura, involving the balance sheets of banks, NBFCs, and corporates.

The over-leveraged real estate sector, already facing difficulties in recent years, saw its challenges worsen as the liquidity squeeze in the NBFC sector intensified. The dependence of real estate developers on NBFC funding had sharply increased, rising from 35% in FY 2012 to 60% in FY 2019, further aggravating the problem.

In the 2019 paper "India's Great Slowdown: What happened? What's the way out?", Arvind Subramanian, along with IMF's former India head Josh Felman, highlights that India is grappling with a "Four Balance Sheet" challenge—comprising banks, infrastructure companies, NBFCs and real estate companies. This issue is creating a detrimental interest-growth dynamic. Subramanian makes a distinction between the first and second waves of the Twin Balance Sheet (TBS) problem. TBS-1 refers to bank loans made to infrastructure sector companies during the investment boom of 2004-11 that later turned bad, while TBS-2 is primarily a post-demonetisation phenomenon, involving NBFCs and real estate firms. These financial sector issues are significantly slowing down economic growth.

Arvind Subramanian states, "In this situation, the standard remedies are no longer available. Monetary policy cannot revive the economy because the transmission mechanism is broken. Fiscal policy cannot be used because the financial system would have difficulty absorbing the large bond issues that a stimulus would entail. The traditional structural reform agenda—land and labour market measures—will not address the current problems."

According to an RBI report, business financing shrank by 87% in FY 2020 up to mid-September. Credit to the real sector acts as the lubricant that drives economic activities and growth. With bank credit growth plummeting, it is no surprise that India's GDP growth rate has slowed significantly. With nominal GDP growth at around 6% and the cost of capital at around 10%, corporates will find it harder to service their debt. Therefore, an alternative source of financing, other than the banks, is necessary to make funding less sensitive to the business cycle.

The literature suggests that an under-developed corporate bond market often results in an over-dependence on bank funding. In the presence of imperfect banking regulatory supervision and high government interference in credit allocation through government-directed preferences, there may be inadequate risk assessment. This can eventually lead to an increase in NPAs and contribute to undesirable systemic risk.

India must look beyond banks to meet its growing infrastructure financing needs. It is imperative to remove any financing constraints for corporates by developing alternative financing channels that supplement bank credit. A well-functioning corporate bond market can play a critical role in bridging the funding gap in the country. Through this market, the private sector can access long-term capital at a reasonable cost without depending on the already stressed banking sector burdened by NPAs. Additionally, it can help channel large household savings into financial instruments, thereby addressing the large infrastructure financing needs. The new bankruptcy code initiated in India is expected to strengthen creditors' rights and contribute to the deepening of the bond market.

Tight fiscal space and concerns over a potential credit rating downgrade have prevented the central government from announcing the demand stimulus badly needed to kick start growth amid the sharp slowdown caused by COVID-19. The bulk of the stimulus measures announced were in the form of loan guarantees, which were expected to increase the government's contingent liabilities rather than its fiscal deficit, with banks playing a central role in mitigating the COVID-related economic slowdown. However, weak financial sector balance sheets and heightened risk aversion may reduce the effectiveness of these stimulus measures. The current macro-environment is conducive to bring about tough reforms needed in the corporate bond market.

15.4. State Government Debt and Fiscal Prudence

The debt levels of several Indian states have reached unsustainable levels due to a variety of factors, including a slowdown in their own tax revenues, a high share of committed expenditures, the ballooning liabilities of state-owned DISCOMs, and rising subsidy burdens, particularly from non-merit freebies. The situation was further exacerbated by the impact of COVID-19.

A bulletin published by the RBI's Department of Economic and Policy Research in June 2022, under the guidance of Deputy Governor, Dr Michael Patra, warned that the debt stock of the five most indebted states—Bihar, Kerala, Punjab, Rajasthan and West Bengal—has become unsustainable., Over the last five years, their debt growth has outpaced the growth of their Gross State Domestic Product (GSDP). The debt-to-GSDP ratio of these states has crossed 30%, pushing them to the brink of a fiscal cliff. These states are now forced to borrow just to meet the repayment obligations on existing debt. Following the Sri Lankan crisis, the RBI's risk analysis has sharply shifted focus to these highly indebted states, earning them the sobriquet "mini-Lankas."

The situation has also brought attention to the various freebies announced by states ahead of elections. It has become a common practice for political parties to promise freebies to win elections.

What began as promises of basic or essential goods has evolved into the provision of luxury items, such as laptops and mobile phones.

With the Supreme Court stepping into the "freebies" debate, the issue has moved beyond plain politics. Several questions have been raised: Does promising freebies amount to bribing voters? Are all freebies wasteful, or can some be considered legitimate social welfare schemes? What kind of election promises result in inefficient utilisation of public funds?

Experts believe that there is no clear correlation between election win and the announcement of freebies.

There are instances where parties have failed to win assembly elections despite offering significant sops. In some states, it is widely accepted that the government changes every five years, regardless of the promise of freebies. Both general and state elections have witnessed promises ranging from monthly allowances for women over 18, guaranteed job for all youth, and free electricity up to a certain limit, to monthly unemployment doles.

Higher spending on education and healthcare for the poor should not be classified as freebies. However, promising luxury goods for free using public money can breed inefficiencies within the system. Most states can hardly afford such expenditures.

States will need incentives and hand-holdings to bring them to the path of fiscal prudence. Economic development depends on better debt management by the states. The RBI is already working with the states to build a robust State Development Loan (SDL) market and has begun publishing SDL-related and other state-specific fiscal data on regular basis. The investors need to actively utilise these data to make informed investment decisions. It is, also, necessary for states to get their state SDLs rated by reputed credit rating agencies just like urban municipalities. The fiscally prudent states need to be rewarded with lower borrowing costs.

15.5. Limitations and Future Research Directions

There are a few limitations in this study that can be explored in future studies:

1. It is commonly observed in the bond market that sovereign bond yields react to government borrowings, with bond yields rising (prices falling) in expectation of a higher government fiscal deficit or increased borrowing. However, our study could not empirically establish this correlation between government borrowings and bond yields, contrary to the expectations in policy circles. Moreover, there exists several studies that have found no evidence of a fiscal deficit influencing interest rates in India (Chakraborty, 2012; Sahoo & Bhattacharyya, 2012; Akram & Das, 2014). We tried to find the correlation between bond yields and both the fiscal deficit (as a percentage of GDP) and total government borrowings net of OMOs but found no significant relationship.

   As discussed before, there may be several reasons for this lack of correlation. First, since 2003, the government has undertaken a fiscal consolidation roadmap (FRBM Act) to reduce the deficit. Second, bond yields depend on nuanced supply-demand dynamics, with banks mandated through the Statutory Liquidity Ratio (SLR) to invest in government securities, thus influencing demand. Third, when adverse supply-demand dynamics force bond yields to rise, the RBI typically responds by infusing liquidity into the system through OMOs (buying bonds), which softens bond yields. Finally, the actual government debt is often understated. The total government borrowings, which include both central and state borrowings, along with borrowings through special bonds, NSSF loans, and government-serviced bonds issued by public sector entities, are much higher than the reported figures. The actual picture of government debt can be obtained by considering the total PSBR.

   While historical data for PSBR is not available, it can be roughly estimated, and we believe there might be a correlation between PSBR and bond yields that needs to be explored. On the other hand, the correlation between bond yields and government borrowings might be captured through high-frequency data on the government's monthly net borrowings.

2. The RBI has been easing policy rates since February 2019. However, the transmission channel to the real economy has been significantly impacted. Despite a cumulative Repo rate cut of 135 basis points, the deposit rate has only fallen by 25 basis points, and the base rate (lending) has dropped by just 2 basis points. The weighted average lending rate on outstanding rupee loans has seen little change. Several factors contribute to the stickiness in lending rates, with the impaired balance sheets of banks being the primary reason for the non-transmission of policy rate cuts. Even though NPAs in banks are coming down, it is still elevated. The current growth slowdown and banks' exposure to the NBFC and real estate sectors suggest that NPAs could rise again. As a result, the expected transmission of rate cuts to the real economy through the yield curve has not materialised. The yield curve has steepened, with short-term bond interest rates falling in line with rate cuts, while longer-term rates have remained relatively unchanged. In December 2019, the RBI adopted a version of "operation twist," selling short-term bonds while buying long-term bonds in order to flatten the yield curve and facilitate the transmission of the policy easing cycle. This aspect was not covered in our study but warrants further analysis in future research.

3. Our study showed some interesting relationships between the government bond market and the corporate bond market. While a government bond market is essential for the development of the corporate bond market, it is not the sufficient condition. A deep and liquid government bond market provides the necessary market infrastructure and a benchmark yield curve. However, a very large government bond market can, in all possibilities, crowd out the corporate bond market. It has been found that when the government spends on infrastructure, it improves productivity and creates an

enabling environment for private sector investment—particularly in developing economies. Thus, there is a distinction to be made between the types of government expenditure funded by borrowing. In addition to that, we also found that higher government borrowing increases the cost of capital, which in turn crowds out private investment. Therefore, it is important to distinguish between the areas of government spending that facilitate the development of the corporate bond market and the overall level of government borrowing to avoid pushing the cost of capital too high.

Further exploration is needed on the types of government spending across various sectors. The study could be extended to find the relationship between sector-specific capital expenditure by the government and the development of the corporate bond market.

Appendices

APPENDIX I

Chapter 11

Dynamic Cross Correlation of the indicators with Non-Agriculture GDP (Quarterly Date) - Growth Rate Cycle

Lead (-)/ Lag (+)	-8	-7	-6	-5	-4	-3	-2	-1	0	1	2	3	4	5	6	7	8
IIP	0.10	0.05	0.14	0.09	0.03	0.12	**0.22**	**0.47**	0.63	0.53	0.34	0.07	-0.10	-0.33	-0.08	-0.09	-0.03
IIP Manufacturing	0.13	0.05	0.11	0.05	0.01	0.33	0.17	**0.42**	0.59	0.51	0.32	0.06	-0.14	-0.35	-0.08	-0.09	-0.02
IIP Electrical	-0.20	-0.12	0.08	0.08	0.13	0.15	0.04	0.08	0.10	-0.14	-0.35	-0.28	-0.29	-0.15	-0.14	-0.17	-0.31
M3	0.12	0.17	0.15	0.22	0.23	0.23	0.33	**0.34**	0.26	0.23	0.30	0.33	0.36	0.41	0.28	0.24	0.28
M1	0.29	0.31	0.29	0.26	0.20	0.25	**0.39**	**0.68**	0.64	0.55	0.44	0.12	-0.03	-0.35	-0.15	0.04	0.15
Currency with Public	-0.17	0.08	0.22	[illegible]	0.05	0.36	0.18	0.30	0.45	0.57	0.53	0.04	-0.01	-0.35	-0.04	0.14	0.14
Repo	0.09	0.12	0.08	-0.09	-0.24	-0.33	-0.44	[illegible]	-0.19	-0.15	-0.20	-0.25	-0.22	-0.22	-0.28	-0.29	-0.29
Bank Credit	0.28	0.32	0.27	0.26	0.15	0.31	-0.05	0.04	0.16	0.23	0.41	[illegible]	0.32	0.29	0.25	0.11	0.22
Non Food Credit	0.30	0.33	0.29	0.28	0.18	0.34	-0.02	0.07	0.18	0.30	0.43	0.42	0.32	0.29	0.25	0.12	0.23
Exports	0.00	0.08	0.00	[illegible]	-0.26	-0.39	-0.24	[illegible]	0.37	0.43	0.32	0.18	0.20	0.23	0.27	0.15	0.11
Imports	-0.03	0.02	0.12	[illegible]	-0.16	-0.33	-0.28	0.09	0.44	0.53	0.39	0.15	0.13	0.25	0.30	0.37	0.30
Non-Crude Imports	-0.10	-0.07	0.08	0.08	-0.01	-0.23	-0.20	[illegible]	0.47	0.57	0.50	0.23	0.17	0.25	0.23	0.27	0.17
Rupees per US dollar	-0.01	0.01	0.01	0.04	0.04	-0.32	-0.15	-0.27	-0.30	-0.30	-0.31	-0.30	-0.31	-0.33	-0.35	-0.36	-0.38
Central Government Expenditure	-0.08	-0.30	0.05	0.20	0.35	0.23	-0.01	[illegible]	0.21	0.15	0.16	0.24	0.23	0.32	0.30	0.31	0.05
Foreign Tourist Arrival	-0.04	0.10	0.09	[illegible]	-0.07	-0.13	-0.03	0.28	0.44	0.23	0.07	[illegible]	-0.08	-0.33	-0.17	0.00	-0.01
Cargo at Major Ports	0.29	0.30	0.27	0.32	0.31	0.32	**0.41**	**0.68**	0.72	0.43	0.22	0.00	0.04	0.07	0.00	[illegible]	-0.29
Revenue from Railway Freight	0.39	0.40	0.31	[illegible]	-0.04	0.34	0.19	**0.43**	0.27	0.35	-0.21	-0.16	0.16	0.22	0.16	0.14	0.24
WPI	-0.39	-0.20	-0.11	[illegible]	-0.37	-0.47	-0.50	-0.34	-0.07	0.13	0.13	0.08	0.10	0.14	0.27	0.34	0.35
WPI Primary	-0.52	-0.43	-0.32	[illegible]	-0.21	-0.23	-0.28	[illegible]	0.10	0.23	0.16	0.06	0.04	0.33	0.19	[illegible]	0.26
WPI Manufactured	-0.31	-0.13	-0.05	[illegible]	-0.35	-0.42	-0.46	-0.30	-0.08	0.33	0.13	0.07	0.08	0.15	0.30	0.36	0.33
Brent Oil Price ($/bl)	-0.11	-0.06	-0.18	-0.45	-0.66	-0.75	-0.65	-0.39	-0.28	-0.32	-0.39	[illegible]	-0.13	-0.12	-0.11	-0.01	0.09
CMV Sales	-0.31	-0.20	-0.17	[illegible]	-0.14	-0.11	0.13	**0.49**	0.54	0.45	0.21	-0.07	-0.06	0.34	0.18	0.29	0.32
Passenger Car Sales	-0.26	-0.13	0.00	0.08	0.15	0.25	**0.42**	**0.57**	0.58	0.43	0.27	[illegible]	0.36	0.24	0.17	0.18	0.23
2- and 3-Wheeler sales	-0.35	-0.15	-0.07	[illegible]	-0.11	-0.13	-0.08	[illegible]	0.18	0.23	0.07	0.00	0.04	0.13	0.13	0.28	0.35
Sensex (Index)	-0.26	-0.25	-0.31	-0.36	-0.22	-0.35	0.06	[illegible]	0.05	-0.36	-0.15	-0.23	-0.24	-0.23	-0.35	-0.34	-0.29
Rural Wages	-0.55	-0.59	-0.61	-0.60	-0.56	-0.53	-0.51	-0.45	-0.33	-0.25	-0.15	-0.05	0.05	0.19	0.29	0.30	0.29
US GDP	-0.07	-0.03	-0.10	[illegible]	-0.23	-0.22	-0.05	[illegible]	0.11	[illegible]	-0.30	-0.30	-0.23	-0.33	-0.36	-0.04	0.23

APPENDIX II

Chapter 12

SVAR results for Level

Structural VAR Estimates:					
Sample (adjusted): 2005M03 2019M01					
Included observations: 167 after adjustments					
Estimation method: method of scoring (analytic derivatives)					
Structural VAR is just-identified.					
Restriction Type: short-run pattern matrix.					
A =					
1	0	0	0	0	0
C(1)	1	0	0	0	0
0	C(4)	1	0	C(12)	C(15)
0	0	C(7)	1	C(13)	0
C(2)	C(5)	C(8)	C(10)	1	0
C(3)	C(6)	C(9)	C(11)	C(14)	1
B =					
C(16)	0	0	0	0	0
0	C(17)	0	0	0	0
0	0	C(18)	0	0	0
0	0	0	C(19)	0	0
0	0	0	0	C(20)	0
0	0	0	0	0	C(21)
	Coefficient	Std. Error	z-Statistic	Prob.	
C(1)	1.266856	0.137818	9.192218	0	
C(2)	-0.41752	0.131524	-3.17449	0.0015	
C(3)	1.086843	7.800604	0.139328	0.8892	
C(4)	-0.58615	1.814105	-0.32311	0.7466	
C(5)	0.058574	0.04364	1.342203	0.1795	
C(6)	0.579561	2.151742	0.269345	0.7877	
C(7)	0.61813	0.643228	0.960981	0.3366	
C(8)	-0.57918	0.223797	-2.58796	0.0097	

C(9)	-0.53822	12.81359	-0.042	0.9665	
C(10)	0.564378	0.08586	6.57321	0	
C(11)	-0.03768	0.932463	-0.04041	0.9678	
C(12)	2.143754	16.79293	0.127658	0.8984	
C(13)	-0.68599	2.33687	-0.29355	0.7691	
C(14)	-0.71939	3.080762	-0.23351	0.8154	
C(15)	-0.57389	1.270846	-0.45158	0.6516	
C(16)	0.246971	0.013514	18.27567	0	
C(17)	-0.43986	0.024068	-18.2757	0	
C(18)	0.907062	4.88266	0.185772	0.8526	
C(19)	-0.40034	0.237116	-1.68837	0.0913	
C(20)	-0.14065	0.018163	-7.74329	0	
C(21)	1.665674	6.013425	0.276992	0.7818	
Log likelihood	-3.83E+10				
Estimated A matrix:					
1	0	0	0	0	0
1.266856	1	0	0	0	0
0	-0.58615	1	0	2.143754	-0.57389
0	0	0.61813	1	-0.68599	0
-0.41752	0.058574	-0.57918	0.564378	1	0
1.086843	0.579561	-0.53822	-0.03768	-0.71939	1
Estimated B matrix:					
0.246971	0	0	0	0	0
0	0.439856	0	0	0	0
0	0	0.907062	0	0	0
0	0	0	0.400341	0	0
0	0	0	0	0.140645	0
0	0	0	0	0	1.665674

SVAR results for Slope

Structural VAR Estimates:					
Sample (adjusted): 2005M03 2019M01					
Included observations: 167 after adjustments.					
Estimation method: method of scoring (analytic derivatives).					
Structural VAR is over-identified (2 degrees of freedom).					
Restriction Type: short-run pattern matrix.					
A =					
1	0	0	0	0	0
C(1)	1	0	0	0	0
0	C(4)	1	0	0	C(13)
0	0	C(7)	1	0	0
C(2)	C(5)	C(8)	C(10)	1	0
C(3)	C(6)	C(9)	C(11)	C(12)	1
B =					
C(14)	0	0	0	0	0
0	C(15)	0	0	0	0
0	0	C(16)	0	0	0
0	0	0	C(17)	0	0
0	0	0	0	C(18)	0
0	0	0	0	0	C(19)
	Coefficient	Std. Error	z-Statistic	Prob.	
C(1)	1.237712	0.186425	6.639197	0	
C(2)	-0.06556	1.007466	-0.06508	0.9481	
C(3)	0.458934	0.739014	0.621009	0.5346	
C(4)	-0.43004	0.067598	-6.36177	0	
C(5)	-0.51841	0.331477	-1.56393	0.1178	
C(6)	-0.61414	2.087219	-0.29424	0.7686	
C(7)	0.372111	0.12121	3.069962	0.0021	
C(8)	0.644905	1.060396	0.608174	0.5431	
C(9)	-0.00026	2.713301	-9.45E-05	0.9999	

C(10)	-0.78447	8.020735	-0.09781	0.9221	
C(11)	2.215864	4.464131	0.496371	0.6196	
C(12)	1.276379	3.54321	0.360232	0.7187	
C(13)	-1.95568	0.163687	-11.9477	0	
C(14)	0.469683	0.0257	18.27567	0	
C(15)	1.131533	0.061915	18.27567	0	
C(16)	0.736327	0.091821	8.019122	0	
C(17)	0.425253	0.112314	3.786268	0.0002	
C(18)	-2.48098	5.233987	-0.47401	0.6355	
C(19)	-2.59225	3.751028	-0.69108	0.4895	
Log likelihood	-1.08E+10				
LR test for over-identification:					
Chi-square(2)	2.15E+10		Probability	0	
Estimated A matrix:					
1	0	0	0	0	0
1.237712	1	0	0	0	0
0	-0.43004	1	0	0	-1.95568
0	0	0.372111	1	0	0
-0.06556	-0.51841	0.644905	-0.78447	1	0
0.458934	-0.61414	-0.00026	2.215864	1.276379	1
Estimated B matrix:					
0.469683	0	0	0	0	0
0	1.131533	0	0	0	0
0	0	0.736327	0	0	0
0	0	0	0.425253	0	0
0	0	0	0	2.480979	0
0	0	0	0	0	2.592253

SVAR results for Curvature

Structural VAR Estimates:					
Sample (adjusted): 2005M03 2019M01					
Included observations: 167 after adjustments.					
Estimation method: method of scoring (analytic derivatives).					
Failure to improve after 1 iteration.					
Structural VAR Estimates:					
Sample (adjusted): 2005M03 2019M01					
Included observations: 167 after adjustments.					
Estimation method: method of scoring (analytic derivatives).					
Structural VAR is over-identified (2 degrees of freedom).					
Model: Ae = Bu where E[uu']=I					
Restriction Type: short-run pattern matrix.					
A =					
1	0	0	0	0	0
C(1)	1	0	0	0	0
0	C(4)	1	0	0	C(13)
0	0	C(7)	1	0	0
C(2)	C(5)	C(8)	C(10)	1	0
C(3)	C(6)	C(9)	C(11)	C(12)	1
B =					
C(14)	0	0	0	0	0
0	C(15)	0	0	0	0
0	0	C(16)	0	0	0
0	0	0	C(17)	0	0
0	0	0	0	C(18)	0
0	0	0	0	0	C(19)
	Coefficient	Std. Error	z-Statistic	Prob.	
C(1)	0.660478	0.275805	2.394725	0.0166	
C(2)	-1.74627	0.158553	-11.0138	0	

C(3)	-0.63633	0.222149	-2.86444	0.0042	
C(4)	-0.11197	0.00938	-11.937	0	
C(5)	0.245378	0.128163	1.914585	0.0555	
C(6)	-0.42789	0.149331	-2.86539	0.0042	
C(7)	-1.29859	0.169259	-7.67222	0	
C(8)	-0.26423	1.125509	-0.23477	0.8144	
C(9)	0.732786	1.288315	0.568794	0.5695	
C(10)	-0.67754	0.175878	-3.85232	0.0001	
C(11)	-2.39229	0.196068	-12.2013	0	
C(12)	0.939446	0.083136	11.30005	0	
C(13)	0.005118	0.009699	0.527682	0.5977	
C(14)	0.573974	0.031406	18.27567	0	
C(15)	-2.05E+00	0.111939	-18.2757	0	
C(16)	-0.12091	0.006787	-17.8155	0	
C(17)	5.10E-01	0.027895	18.2687	0	
C(18)	1.155615	0.063532	18.18944	0	
C(19)	-1.23029	0.067792	-18.1479	0	
Log likelihood	-1.39E+10				
LR test for over-identification:					
Chi-square(2)	2.77E+10		Probability	0	
Estimated A matrix:					
1	0	0	0	0	0
0.660478	1	0	0	0	0
0	-0.11197	1	0	0	0.005118
0	0	-1.29859	1	0	0
-1.74627	0.245378	-0.26423	-0.67754	1	0
-0.63633	-0.42789	0.732786	-2.39229	0.939446	1
Estimated B matrix:					

0.573974	0	0	0	0	0
0	2.045754	0	0	0	0
0	0	0.120911	0	0	0
0	0	0	0.50961	0	0
0	0	0	0	1.155615	0
0	0	0	0	0	1.230288

APPENDIX III

Chapter 13

Simple Regression Analysis—Correlation Plots

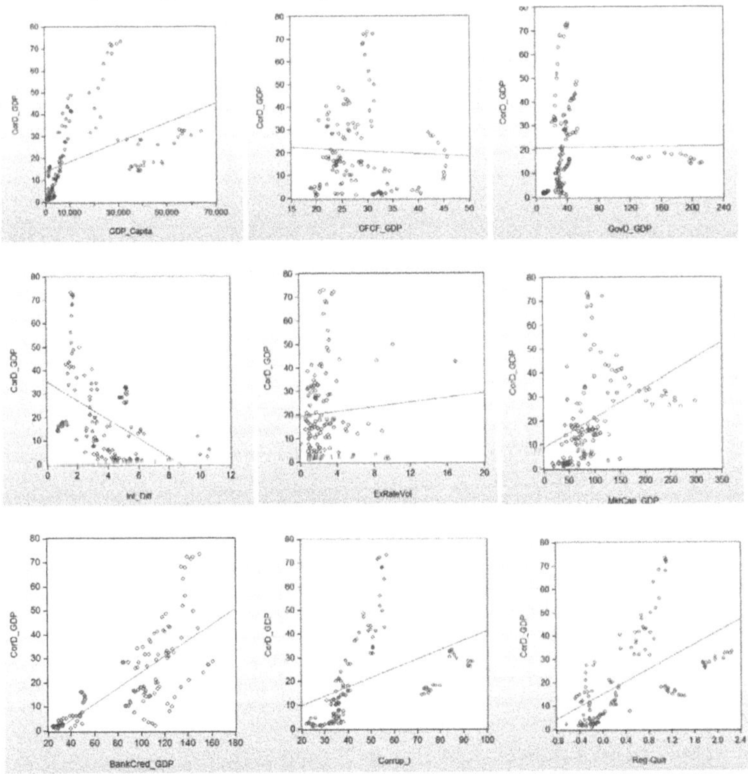

Data and Sources

Category	Factors	Definition	Source
Economy			
	Size of Economy	Log of Current GDP (lnGDP)	IMF, World Economic Outlook Database
	Stage of Development	GDP per capita (GDP_Capita)	IMF, World Economic Outlook Database
	Openness of Economy	Trade of Goods & Services as a % of GDP (Trade_GDP)	World Bank Word Development Indicators
	Total Savings	Gross Domestic Savings as % of GDP (GDS_GDP)	World Bank Word Development Indicators
	Total Investments	Gross Capital Formation as % of GDP (GFCF_GDPit)	World Bank Word Development Indicators
	Exchange Rate Volatility	Annual standard deviation of NEER (ExRateVol)	Asia Regional Integration Center, ADB, aric.adb.org
	Fiscal Deficit	Government Fiscal Deficit as % of GDP (FD_GDP)	Asian Development Bank (ADB), RBI data
Financial System			
	Equity Market	Market capitalization of listed domestic companies (% of GDP)	World Bank Word Development Indicators
	Govt Bond Market	Government Bond Outstanding as % of GDP (GovD_GDP)	Asia Bond Monitor, Asian Development Bank (ADB)
	Banking Sector	Domestic credit to private sector by banks as % of GDP (BankCred_GDP)	IMF, International Financial Statistics
	Interest rate differential	Interest rate (Corporate minus Govt Bond Yield) (Int_Diff)	World Bank-Word Development Indicators, RBI data
	Corporate Bond Market	Corporate Bond Outstanding as % of GDP (CorD_GDP)	Asia Bond Monitor, Asian Development Bank (ADB)
Institutional Framework			
	Corruption Index	Annual Corruption Index (Corrup_I)	Corruption Perceptions Index 2018
	Regulation Quality	Annual Regulatory Quality (Reg_Qua)	World Bank Worldwide Governance Indicators

APPENDIX IV

Chapter 14

Lag Length Criteria

VAR Lag Order Selection Criteria

Endogenous variables: LPVGCF LGDP LGFCE LPUGCF

[Log of Private Gross Capital Formation (PvGCF), Real GDP (GDP), Government Final Consumption Expenditure (GFCE), and Public Gross Capital Formation (PuGCF)]

Sample from 1995 to 2018

Total Observations: 21

Lag	LogL	LR	FPE	AIC	SC	HQ
0	57.98316	NA	6.88e-08	-5.141253	-4.942297	-5.098074
1	163.3428	160.5480*	1.44e-11*	-13.65170	-12.65691*	-13.43580
2	174.3026	12.52544	2.83e-11	-13.17167	-11.38106	-12.78306
3	200.9811	20.32648	1.87e-11	-14.18867*	-11.60224	-13.62735*

* indicates lag order selected by the criterion
LR: sequential modified LR test statistic (each test at 5% level)
FPE: Final prediction error
AIC: Akaike information criterion
SC: Schwarz information criterion
HQ: Hannan-Quinn information criterion

We can see that lag 1 has the maximum number of stars (significant), Thus, lag 1 is sufficient for the model.

Stability of the Model

The inverse roots of AR characteristics polynomial are found to be inside the unit circle which indicates that the model is stable.

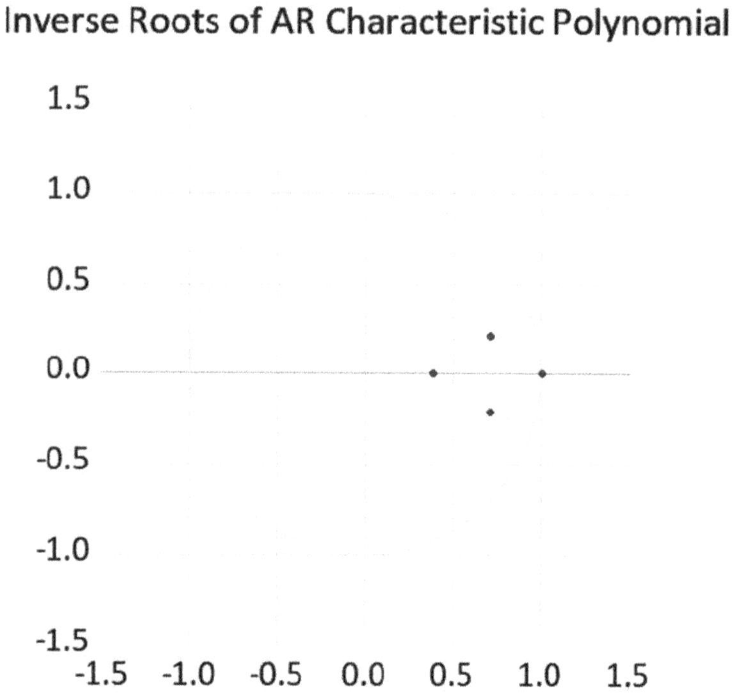

VAR Output

Vector Autoregression Estimates

Sample from 1996 to 2018

Includes 23 observations after adjustments

Standard errors in () and t-statistics in []

	LPVGCF	LGDP	LGFCE	LPUGCF
LPVGCF(-1)	0.655584	-0.014344	-0.009540	0.145107
	(0.22814)	(0.02074)	(0.04488)	(0.05120)
	[2.87355]	[-0.69170]	[-0.21256]	[2.83395]
LGDP(-1)	1.733562	1.065385	0.190503	0.852526
	(0.92050)	(0.08367)	(0.18109)	(0.20659)
	[1.88327]	[12.7332]	[1.05197]	[4.12660]
LGFCE(-1)	-1.135437	-0.069527	0.684094	-0.430428
	(0.76766)	(0.06978)	(0.15102)	(0.17229)
	[-1.47908]	[-0.99641]	[4.52971]	[-2.49827]
LPUGCF(-1)	-0.043920	0.029173	0.110041	0.422510
	(0.46514)	(0.04228)	(0.09151)	(0.10439)
	[-0.09442]	[0.69001]	[1.20254]	[4.04730]
C	-7.135699	-0.239641	0.068026	-1.908816
	(3.84602)	(0.34959)	(0.75663)	(0.86318)
	[-1.85535]	[-0.68550]	[0.08991]	[-2.21138]
R-squared	0.956670	0.998716	0.993194	0.994583
Adj. R-squared	0.947041	0.998431	0.991681	0.993380
Sum sq. resids	0.641427	0.005300	0.024825	0.032309
S.E. equation	0.188772	0.017159	0.037137	0.042367
F-statistic	99.35352	3500.558	656.6495	826.2906
Log likelihood	8.529294	63.68422	45.92536	42.89527
Akaike AIC	-0.306895	-5.102976	-3.558727	-3.295241
Schwarz SC	-0.060049	-4.856129	-3.311881	-3.048395
Mean dependent	15.64714	17.96732	15.72042	15.31817
S.D. dependent	0.820288	0.433160	0.407173	0.520704

Determinant resid covariance (dof adj.)	1.20E-11
Determinant resid covariance	4.51E-12
Log likelihood	169.8889
Akaike information criterion	-13.03381
Schwarz criterion	-12.04643
Number of coefficients	20

Bibliography

Acatrinei, M. (2017). *Macroeconomic Fundamentals and Latent Factor of the EU Yield Curve.* Financial Stability Report.

Acharya, V. (2018). *Understanding and Managing Interest Rate Risk at Banks.* Reserve Bank of India Bulletin, 7–17.

Acharya, V., Kulkarni, N., Nanawati, B., & Saggar, S. *Why less can be more: Crowding out effects of government financing.* IIMA-World Bank Research Conference on Financial Distress, Bankruptcy, and Corporate Finance, August 9–10, 2019, at IIMA.

Aguiar, M., & Gopinath, G. (2007). Emerging Market Business Cycles: The Cycle is the Trend. *Journal of Political Economy, 115*(1).

Ahmed, H., & Miller, S. M. (2000). Crowding-out and crowding-in effects of government expenditure. *Contemporary Economic Policy, 18*(1), 124–133.

Ahmed, Q. M., & Ammad, S. (2020). Public investment efficiency and sectoral economic growth in Pakistan. *Development Policy Review,* 9(3), 450–470. https://doi.org/10.1111/dpr.12493

Akram, T. (2014). The economics of Japan's stagnation. *Business Economics, 49*(3), 156–75. http://dx.doi.org/10.1057/be.2014.19

Akram, T., & Das, A. (2014a). Understanding the low yields of the long-term Japanese sovereign debt. *Journal of Economic Issues, 48*(2), 331–340. https://dx.doi.org/10.2753/JEI0021-3624480206

Akram, T., & Das, A. (2014b). *The determinants of long-term Japanese Government bonds' low nominal yields.* Levy Economics Institute Working Paper No. 818. Annandale-on-Hudson, NY: Levy Economics Institute of Bard College.

Akram, T., & Das, A. (2015a). *Does Keynesian theory explain Indian government bond yields?* Levy Economics Institute, Working Paper

No. 834. Annandale-on-Hudson, NY: Levy Economics Institute of Bard College.

Akram, T., & Das, A. (2015b). A Keynesian explanation of Indian government bond yields. *Journal of Post Keynesian Economics, 38*(4), 565–587. https://dx.doi.org/10.1080/01603477.2015.1090294

Akram, T., & Das, A. (2017). *The Long-run determinants of Indian government bond yields.* Working paper, Levy Economics Institute of Bard College.

Akram, T., & Li, H. (2016). *The empirics of long-term U.S. interest rates.* Levy Economics Institute, Working Paper No. 863. Annandale-on-Hudson, NY: Levy Economics Institute of Bard College.

Akram, T., & Li, H. (2017). What keeps long-term U.S. interest rates so low? *Economic Modelling, 60,* 380–390. https://dx.doi.org/10.1016/j.econmod.2016.09.017

Ang, A., & Piazzesi, M. (2001). *A no-arbitrage vector autoregression of term structure dynamics with macroeconomic and latent variables.* NBER Working Paper No. 8363, Issued in July 2001.

Alesina, A., Ardagna, S., Perotti, R., & Schiantarelli, F. (2002). Fiscal Policy, Profits, and Investment. *The American Economic Review, 92*(3), 571–589.

Asian Development Bank. (n.d.). *Asian Bonds Online: Asian Bond Markets Initiative.* https://asianbondsonline.adb.org

Asian Development Bank. (n.d.). *Asia Bond Monitor Series.* https://www.adb.org/publications/series/asia-bond-monitor

Australian Government Department of the Treasury. (2002). *Review of the Commonwealth Government Securities Market.* Commonwealth of Australia. https://treasury.gov.au/sites/default/files/2019-03/CCSMReview.pdf

Bae, K.-H. (2012). *Determinants of local currency bonds and foreign holdings: Implications for bond market development in the People's Republic of China.* ADB Working Paper Series on Regional Economic Integration (No. 97), pp. viii & 1–56.

Baharuddin, N.S., Khamis, Z., Mahmood, W. M. W., & Dollah, H. (2011). Determinants of capital structure for listed construction companies in Malaysia. *Journal of Applied Finance and Banking, 1*(2),115–132.

Bank for International Settlements. (n.d.). *Quarterly reports.*

Barrios, S., Iversen, P., Lewandowska, M., & Setzer, R. (2009). *Determinants of Intra-Euro area government bond spreads during the financial crisis (No. 388).* Directorate General Economic and Monetary Affairs (DG ECFIN), European Commission.

Batten, J., & Kim, Y.H. (2001). Expanding long-term financing through bond market development: A post-crisis policy task. *Government Bond Markets in Asia*, 290–360.

Berk, J., & Van Bergeijk, P. (2001). On the information content of the yield curve: Lessons for the Eurosystem? *Kredit und Kapital, 34*(1), 28–47.

Bernard, H., & Gerlach, S. (1996). *Does the term structure predict recessions? The international evidence* (BIS Working Papers, No. 37). Bank for International Settlements.

Bernoth, K., von Hagen, J., & Schuknecht, L. (2004). *Sovereign risk premia in the European government bonds market* (ECB Working Paper No. 369). European Central Bank, University of Mannheim.

Bhattacharya, B.N. (2011). *Bond Market Development in Asia: An Empirical Analysis of Major Determinants.* ADBI Working Paper Series.

Bhattacharya, R., & Patnaik, I. (2015). Financial inclusion, productivity shocks, and consumption volatility in emerging economies. *World Bank Economic Review, 30*(1), 171–201.

Bhattacharya, I., & Sahoo, S. (2012). Yield Curve Dynamics of the Indian G-Sec Market: A Macro-Finance Approach. *Indian Economic Review, 47*(2).

Bhaumik, S.K., Bose, S., & Coondoo, D. (2003). The emerging Indian bond market: Evolution, problems, and prospects. *Journal of Global Financial Markets, Spring*, 33–43.

Bank for International Settlements (BIS). (1999). *How should we design deep and liquid markets? The case for government securities.*

Bolton, P., & Freixas, X. (2000). Equity, bonds, and bank debt: Capital structure and financial market equilibrium under asymmetric information. *Journal of Political Economy, 108*(2), 324–351.

Bondt, G.D. (2002). *Euro Area Corporate Debt Securities Market: First Empirical Evidence* (Working Paper Series No.164). European Central Bank.

Bordoloi, S., & Rajesh, R. (2007). *Forecasting the turning points of the business cycles with leading indicators in India: A probit approach.* Singapore Economic Review Conference 2007, August 2–4, 2007, Singapore.

Boschan, C., & Banerji, A. (1990). A reassessment of composite indexes. In P.A. Klein (ed.), *Analyzing Modern Business Cycles: Essays Honouring Geoffrey H. Moore* (pp. 123–145). Armonk, NY: M.E. Sharpe.

Bose, S., & Coondoo, D. (2003). A study of the Indian corporate bond market. *Money and Finance.*

Brière, M., & Ielpo, F. (2007). *Yield curve reaction to macroeconomic news in Europe: Disentangling the US influence.* SSRN.

Bry, G., & Boschan, C. (1971). *Cyclical analysis of time series: Selected procedures and computer programs* (Technical Paper No. 20). National Bureau of Economic Research.

Budget Division, Department of Economic Affairs, Ministry of Finance, Government of India. (2024). *Quarterly report on public debt management, Q1 2024.* Ministry of Finance, Government of India. https://dea.gov.in/reports-public-debt-management

Burger, J.D., & Warnock, F.E. (2004). *Foreign participation in local-currency bond markets* (International Finance Discussion Papers No. 794). Board of Governors of the Federal Reserve System.

Burger, J.D., & Warnock, F.E. (2006). Local Currency Bond Markets. *IMF Staff Papers*, 53 (Special Issue), 115–132.

Burns, A.F., & Mitchell, W.C. (1946). *Measuring business cycles.* National Bureau of Economic Research.

Butler, L. (1978). *Recession? A market view.* Federal Reserve Bank of San Francisco.

Care Ratings Report. (2014). *Indian Bond Market: Striking a Chord with Asian Peers.*

CCIL. (n.d.). *Rakshitra: Financial stability reports.* https://www.ccilindia.com/Research/CCILPublications/Pages/Rakshitra.aspx

Centre for Monitoring Indian Economy Pvt. Ltd. (n.d.). *CMIE Database.* https://www.cmie.com/

Chakraborty, L. (2012). *Interest rate determination in India: Empirical evidence on fiscal deficit—Interest rate linkages and financial crowding out* (Economics Working Paper Archive). The Levy Economics Institute, New York.

Chandrasekhar, C.P. (2016). Revving up the bond market. *Economic and Political Weekly, LI*(10), 37.

Chaudhari, K., Raje, M., & Singh, C. (2014). *Corporate bond markets in India: A study and policy recommendations.* Indian Institute of Management.

Chen, N.F. (1991). Financial Investment Opportunities and the Macroeconomy. *Journal of Finance, 46*(2), 529–554.

Chimm, M., & Kucko, K. (2010). *The predictive power of the yield curve across countries and time* (NBER Working Paper Series 2010-16398). Cambridge: National Bureau of Economic Research.

Chitre, V.S. (1982). Growth cycles in the Indian economy. *Artha Vijnana, 24*, 293–450.

Chitre, V.S. (1986). *Indicators of business recessions and revivals in India.* Gokhale Institute of Politics and Economics Working Paper.

Chitre, V.S. (2001). Indicators of business recessions and revivals in India: 1951–82. *Indian Economic Review, 36*(1).

Choe, H., Masulis, R., & Nanda, V. (1993). Common stock offerings across the business cycle: Theory and evidence. *Journal of Empirical Finance, 1*(1), 3–31.

Codogno, L., Favero, C., & Missale, A. (2003). Yield Spreads on EMU Government Bonds. *Economic Policy, 18*(37), 503–532.

CRISIL Limited. (2018). *CRISIL Yearbook on the Indian debt market 2018.* https://www.crisil.com/content/crisilcom/en/home/our-analysis/reports/2018/10/crisil-yearbook-on-the-indian-debt-market-2018.html

Cullity, J.P., & Banerji, A. (1996). *Composite indexes: A reassessment.* Meeting on OECD Leading Indicators, Paris.

Das Krishna, G., & Nag, B. (2018). Long-run determinants of sovereign bond yields. *Economic and Political Weekly, 53*(13).

Das Krishna, G., & Nag, B. (2020). Indian corporate bond market: A perspective. *Economic and Political Weekly, 56*(20).

Das Krishna, G., & Nag, B. (2020). *Predictive power of yield curve: An evidence from India.* IIMB Management Review.

Das Krishna, G., & Nag, B. (2020). Does government bond market influence corporate bond market? *Empirical Economic Letters, 19*(9).

Davis, E.P. (2001). *Multiple avenues of intermediation, corporate finance, and financial stability.* IMF Working Paper, 01/115.

Davis, E.P., & Ioannidis, C. (2002). *Does the availability of bank borrowing and bond issuance smooth overall corporate financing?* Brunel University Working Paper.

De Ketelaere, B., Hubert, M., & Schmitt, E. (2015). *Overview of PCA-based Statistical Process Monitoring Methods for Time-Dependent, High-Dimensional Data.* Journal of Quality Technology, *47*(4), 1–17.

De Leeuw, F. (1991). Towards a theory of leading indicators. In Lahiri and Moore (eds.), *Leading Economic Indicators: New Approaches and Forecasting Records*, Cambridge University Press, Cambridge.

Demirguc-Kunt, A., & Levine, R. (1996). Stock market development and financial intermediaries: Stylized facts. *The World Bank Economic Review, 10*(2), 341–369.

Demirguc-Kunt, A. (2005). *Cross-Country Empirical Studies of Systemic Bank Distress.*

De Pace, P. (2011). *GDP growth predictions through the yield spread: Time variation and structural breaks* (Working Paper 2011-38). Euro Area Business Cycle Network.

Diebold, F. X. (2019), *Econometric data science: A predictive modelling approach.* University of Pennsylvania.

Diebold, F. X., Piazzesi, M., & Rudebusch, G.D. (2005). Modelling Bond Yields in Finance and Macroeconomics. *American Economic Review, 95*(2), 415–420.

Diebold, F. X., Rudebusch, G. D., & Aruoba, S.B. (2006). The macroeconomy and the yield curve: A dynamic latent factor approach. *Journal of Econometrics, 131*(1–2), 309–338.

Dua, P., & Banerji, A. (1999). An Index of Coincident Economic Indicators for the Indian Economy. *Journal of Quantitative Economics*, 15, 177–201.

Dung, L. P., & Quang, N. T. (2015). *The development of corporate bond markets: A cross-country analysis.* Proceedings of the Second Asia-Pacific Conference on Global Business, Economics, Finance and Social Sciences.

Eichengreen, B., & Luengnaruemitchai, P. (2004). *Why doesn't Asia have Bigger Bond markets?* National Bureau of Economic Research. https://dx.doi.org/10.3386/w10576.

Engen, E., & Hubbard, G. (2004). *Federal Government debt and interest rates* (Working Paper No. 1068). National Bureau of Economic Research.

Engle, R., & Granger, C. (1987). Co-integration and error correction: Representation, estimation, and testing. *Econometrica*, *55*(2), 251–276.

Estrella, A., & Hardouvelis, G. A. (1991). The term structure as a predictor of real economic activity. *Journal of Finance*, *46*(2), 555–576.

Estrella, A., & Mishkin, F. S. (1996). The yield curve as a predictor of U.S. recessions. *Current Issues in Economics and Finance–Federal Reserve Bank of New York*, *2*(7), 1–6.

Estrella, A., & Mishkin, F. (1997). The predictive power of the term structure of interest rates in Europe and the United States: Implications for the European Central Bank. *European Economic Review*, *41*(7), 1375–1402.

Estrella, A., & Trubin, M. (2006). The yield curve as a leading indicator: Some practical issues. *Current Issues in Economics and Finance*, *12*(5).

Evans, C. L., & Marshall, D. A. (1998). Monetary policy and the term structure of nominal interest rates: Evidence and theory. *Carnegie-Rochester Conference Series on Public Policy*, *49*, 53–111.

Evans, C. L., & Marshall, D. A. (2007). Economic determinants of the nominal treasury yield curve. *Journal of Monetary Economics*, *54*(7), 1986–2003.

Fabella, R., & Madhur, S. (2003). *Bond market development in East Asia: Issues and challenges.* Asian Development Bank.

Fernald, J. G. (1999). Roads to prosperity: Assessing the link between public capital and productivity. *American Economic Review, 89*(3), 619–638.

Ferris, J. S., & Voia, M. C. (2015). The effect of federal government size on private economic performance in Canada: 1870–2011. *Economic Modelling, 49*,172–185. https://doi.org/10.1016/j.econmod.2015.04.006

Fink, G., Haiss, P., & Hristoforova, S. (2003). *Bond markets and economic growth.* IEF Working Paper No.49.

Friedman, B. M. (1985). Crowding out or crowding in? Evidence on debt-equity substitutability. *Brookings Papers on Economic Activity, 9*(3), 593–641.

Friedman, B. M. (1978). Crowding out or crowding in? The economic consequences of financing government deficits. *Brookings Papers on Economic Activity*, 3, 593–654.

Fujii, T., Hiraga, K., & Kozuka, M. (2013). Effects of public investment on sectoral private investment: A factor-augmented VAR approach. *Journal of the Japanese and International Economies, 27*, 35–47. https://doi.org/10.1016/j.jjie.2012.11.003.

Geyer, A., Kossmeier, S., & Pichler, S. (2004). Measuring systematic risk in EMU government yield spreads. *Review of Finance, 8*(2), 171–197.

Giacomini, R., & Rossi, B. (2006). How stable is the forecasting performance of the yield curve for output growth? *Oxford Bulletin of Economics and Statistics, 68*(1), 783–795.

Gottschalk, J. (2001). *An introduction to the SVAR Methodology: Identification, interpretation, and limitations of SVAR models.* IMF Working Paper.

Government of India. (2025). *Economic survey 2024–2025.* Ministry of Finance, Government of India. https://www.indiabudget.gov.in/economicsurvey/

Government of India. (2018). *Union budget 2018–19.* Ministry of Finance, Government of India. https://www.indiabudget.gov.in/budget2018-2019/budget.asp

Government of India. (2019). *Union budget 2019–20*. Ministry of Finance, Government of India. https://www.indiabudget.gov.in/budget2019-20/index.php

Greenwald, D. (Ed.). (1994). *The McGraw-Hill encyclopedia of economics*. McGraw-Hill.

Gyntelberg, J., Ma, G., & Remolona, E.M. (2005). *Corporate bond markets in Asia*. BIS Quarterly Review.

Hakansson, N. H. (1999). *The role of a corporate bond market in an economy and in avoiding crises*. IBER RPF-287.

Harris, L. E. (1990). Statistical Properties of the Roll Serial Covariance Bid-Ask Spread Estimator. *Journal of Finance, 45*(2), 579–590.

Harvey, C. R. (1988). The Real Term Structure and Consumption Growth. *Journal of Financial Economics, 22*, 305–333.

Hatekar, N. (1994). Historical behaviour of the business cycles in India: Some stylized facts for 1951–85. *Journal of Indian School of Political Economy, 6*(4).

Hauner, D., & Kumar, M. (2009). *Fiscal policy and interest rates: How sustainable is the new economy?* (Working Paper 06/112). International Monetary Fund.

Hautsch, N., & Ou, Y. (2008). *Yield curve factors, term structure volatility, and bond risk premia*. SFB 649 Discussion Paper 2008-053.

Hawkins, J. (2002). *Bond markets and banks in emerging economies*. Bank for International Settlements.

Himachalapathy, R., & Rakshitha, V. (2016). A study on the impact of selected monetary, fiscal, economic variables on the Indian bond market. Working Paper, St. Joseph's College of Commerce.

Holstrom, B., & Tirole, J. (1997). Financial intermediation, loanable funds, and the real sector. *Quarterly Journal of Economics, 112*(3), 663–691.

Hove, T. (2008). *Bond market development in emerging economics: A case study of bond exchange of South Africa (BESA)*. Bank for International Settlements.

Hvozdenska J. (2015). The yield curve as a predictor of gross domestic product growth in Nordic countries. *Procedia, Economics, and*

Finance, 26, 438–445. https://www.sciencedirect.com/science/article/pii/S2212567115008710/pdf?md5=5cbdd15051b646e993d45ec580801781&pid=1-s2.0-S2212567115008710-main.pdf

International Monetary Fund. (2002). *Emerging local bond markets.* Global Financial Stability Report.

International Monetary Fund. (2003). *Local securities and derivatives markets in emerging markets: Selected policy issues.* Global Financial Stability Report.

International Monetary Fund (2005). *Global financial market developments.* Global Financial Stability Report.

International Monetary Fund (2006). *Structural changes in emerging sovereign debt and implications for financial stability.* Global Financial Stability Report.

Jagidar, B. (2001). Bonding with Bonds. *Economic and Political Weekly, 36*(13).

Kanagasabapathy, K., & Goyal, R. (2002). Yield spread as a leading indicator of real economic activity: An empirical exercise on the Indian economy. IMF Working Paper.

Kanjilal, K. (2011). Macroeconomic factors and yield curve for the emerging Indian economy. *Macroeconomics and Finance in Emerging Market Economies, 4*(1), p. 57–83. https://doi.org/10.1080/17520843.2011.548612

Kanjilal, K. (2014). Rational Expectation Hypothesis: Empirical Evidence from Government Debt Market in India. *International Journal of Indian Culture and Business Management, 9*(3), 353–370.

Kessel, R. A. (1965). *The cyclical behaviour of the term structure of interest rates.* National Bureau of Economic Research.

Keynes, J. M. (1930). *A treatise on money, Vol. II: The applied theory of money.* London: Macmillan.

Keynes, J. M. (1936). *The general theory of employment, interest, and money.* New York: Palgrave Macmillan.

Khan, H. R. (2016). *Indian debt market 2020—The underpinnings & the path ahead.* 17th Annual Conference of FIMMDA (Fixed Income Money Market and Derivatives Association of India). London: PDAI (Primary Dealers' Association of India).

Khan, H. R. (2012). *Developing Indian capital markets: The way forward.* FICCI's 9th Annual Conference on Capital Markets: CAPAM.

Khandwala, H. (2015). Yield curve as a leading indicator in predicting economic slowdowns: An evidence from India. *Journal of Stock & Forex Trading, 4*(2), 1–5.

Kinoshita, N. (2006). *Government debt and long-term interest rate* (Working Paper 06/63). International Monetary Fund.

Klein, P. A. (1998). *Swedish business cycles: Assessing the recent record* (Working Paper 21). Federation of Swedish Industries, Stockholm.

Klein, P. A., & Moore, G. H. (1985). *Monitoring growth cycles in market-oriented countries: Developing and using international economic indicators.* NBER Studies in Business Cycles, No. 26. Cambridge, MA: Ballinger.

Kolluria, B., Wahabb, S., & Wahabc, M. (2015). An examination of co-movements of India's stock and government bond markets. *Journal of Asian Economics, 41*, 39–56.

Korajczyk, R., & Levy, A. (2003). Capital Structure Choice: Macroeconomic Conditions and Financial Constraints. *Journal of Financial Economics, 68*(1), 75–109.

Kulkarni, G. K., & Balderas, J. U. (1998). An empirical study of the crowding out hypothesis: A case of Mexico. *Prajnan, 27*(3), 263–279.

Lagana, M., Martin, P., Köppen-Mertes, I., & Persaud, A. (2006). Implications for Liquidity from Innovations and Transparency in the European Corporate Bond Market. *European Central Bank Occasional Paper, Number 50,* August.

Laubach, T. (2009). New evidence on the interest rate effects of budget deficits and debt. *Journal of European Economic Association, 7*, 858–885.

Laurent, R. (1988). An interest rate-based indicator of monetary policy. *Federal Reserve Bank of Chicago Economic Perspectives, 12*, 3–14.

Laurent, R. (1989). Testing the spread. *Federal Reserve Bank of Chicago Economic Perspectives, 13*, 22–34.

Lee, M-J, & Kim, S-H. (2002). *Developing the corporate bond market: The Korean experience.* BIS Papers No. 26.

Leigland, J. (1997). Accelerating Municipal Bond Market Development in Emerging Economies: An Assessment of Strategies and Progress. *Public Budgeting and Finance, 17*(2), 57–80.

Litterman, R., & Scheinkman, J. (1991). Common Factors Affecting Bond Returns. *The Journal of Fixed Income, 1*(1), 54–61.

Longstaff, F. A., Pan, J., Pedersen, H., & Singleton, K. J. (2011). How sovereign is sovereign credit risk? *American Economic Journal: Macroeconomics, 3*, 75–103.

Luengnaruemitchai, P., & Ong, L. L. (2005). An anatomy of corporate bond markets: Growing pains and knowledge gains. IMF Working Paper.

Mall, O. P. (1999). Composite index of leading indicators for business cycles in India. *RBI Occasional Papers, 20*(3).

Mathieson, D. J., & Roldos, J. E. (2004). *Local securities and derivatives markets in emerging markets: Selected policy issues.* International Monetary Fund.

Maurya, A. K. & Mishra, O. N. (2016). The macro-economic determinants of corporate bond market in India. *Pacific Business Review International, 1*(1).

McCauley, R., & Remolona, E. (2000). *Size and liquidity of government bond markets.* BIS Quarterly Review.

Mehl, A., & Reynaud, J. (2005). *The determinants of 'domestic' original sin in emerging market economies* (Working Paper, No. 560). European Central Bank.

Mehl, A. (2006). *The yield curve as a predictor in emerging economies* (Working Paper Series, No. 691). European Central Bank.

Mensah, J. A., & Tkacz, G. (1998). *Predicting Canadian recessions using financial variables: a probit approach* (Working Paper, No. 5). Bank of Canada.

Mintz, I. (1969). *Dating postwar business cycles: Methods and their application to Western Germany, 1950–67* (Occasional Paper No. 107). NBER.

Mintz, I. (1972). Dating American growth cycles. In V. Zarnowitz (ed.), *The Business Cycle Today*. NBER, New York.

Mintz, I. (1974). Dating United States growth cycles. *Explorations in Economic Research*, *1*, 1–113.

Mishkin, F. S. (1990). What does the term structure tell us about future inflation? *Journal of Monetary Economics*, *25*, 77–95.

Mishkin, F. (1990). The information in the long-maturity term structure about future inflation. *Quarterly Journal of Economics*, *55*, 815–828.

Mitchell, W. C. (1913). *Business cycles*. Berkeley: University of California Press.

Mitchell, W. (1927). *Business cycles: The problem and its setting*. National Bureau of Economic Research Studies.

Mitra, A. (2009). Why corporate bond market in India is in Nelson's low-level equilibrium trap for so long? *(NSE) News*, March 8-16.

Mody, A. (2009). *From Bear Stearns to Anglo Irish: How Eurozone sovereign spreads related to financial sector vulnerability* (Working Paper No. 120). International Monetary Fund.

Mohan, R., & Ray, P. (2009). Development of the Indian debt market (Working Paper No. 410). Stanford Centre for International Development.

Mohanty, J., Singh. B., & Jain, R. (2003). Business cycles and leading indicators of industrial activity in India. *Reserve Bank of India Occasional Papers*, *21*(3), 235–269.

Muhammad, Z. B., Aminu, B. N., & Mubarak, A. S. (2012). Crowding In Or Crowding Out? Government Spending and Private Investment: The Case of Nigeria. *European Scientific Journal (ESJ)*, *8*(28). http://dx.doi.org/10.19044/esj.2012.v8n28p%25p

Muthu, S. (2010). Does public investment crowd out private investment in India? *Journal of Financial Economic Policy*, *9*(1), 50–69. https://doi.org/10.1108/JFEP-02-2016-0016

Nag, A. K., & Ghose, S. K. (2000). Yield curve analysis for government securities in India. *Economic and Political Weekly*, *35*(5), 339–348.

Nag, B., & Mukherjee, S. (2006). *Simultaneous equation models*. Indira Gandhi National Open University, School of Social Sciences.

Nath, G., Singh, S.P., & Dalvi, M. (2012). *Predicting power of yield curve: A study of Indian sovereign yield spread.* SSRN. https://ssrn.com/abstract=2078920.

Naoussi, C.F., & Tripier, F. (2013). Trend shocks and economic development. *Journal of Development Economics, 103*, 29–42.

National Stock Exchange (NSE) Report. (2012). *Indian Securities Market: A Review.*

Nomura. (2018). *Lead indicator index: Nomura Composite Leading Index (CLI).* Nomura Research Institute

OECD. (1987). *Leading indicators and business cycles in member countries 1960–1985.*

OECD. (1997). *Cyclical indicators and business tendency surveys.*

OECD. (2005). *Composite leading indicators for major OECD non-member countries—Selection of leading indicators and construction of composite indicators: Brazil, China, India, Indonesia, Russian Federation and South Africa.*

OECD. (2008). *Handbook on constructing composite indicators.*

Ouliaris, S., Pagan, A.R., & Restrepo, J. (2018). *Quantitative macroeconomic modelling with structural vector autoregressions: An EViews implementation.* EViews.

Pagano, M., & von Thadden, E. L. (2004). The European bond markets under EMU. *Oxford Review of Economic Policy, 20*(4), 531–554.

Pandey, R., Patnaik, I., & Shah, A. (2016). Dating business cycles in India. NIPFP Working Paper Series.

Paramanik, R.N., & Kamaiah, B. (2017). An empirical analysis of Indian business cycle dynamics. *Economic Annals, 62*(213), 7–25.

Park, J., & Shenoy, C. (2002). An examination of the dynamic behaviour of aggregate bond and stock issues. *International Review of Economics and Finance, 11*, 175–189.

Park, J-H. (2008). *Bond market development: The experience of the Republic of Korea.* Korea Institute of Finance.

Plummer, M.G., & Click, R.W. (2005). Bond Market Development and Integration in ASEAN. *International Journal of Finance & Economics, 10*(2), 133–42.

Poghosyan, T. (2012). *Long-run and short-run determinants of sovereign bond yields in advanced economies.* IMF Working Paper.

Rafael, R., & Ivan, Z. (2011). The use of SVAR analysis in determining the effects of fiscal shocks in Croatia. *Financial Theory and Practice, 35*(1), 25–58.

Raghavan, S., & Sarwono, D. (2012). *Development of the corporate bond market in India: An empirical and policy analysis.* Paper presented at the International Conference on Economics and Finance Research, IPEDR.

Raghavan, S., Sahoo, A., Hait, A., & Ghosh, S. (2012). *A study of corporate bond market in India: Theoretical and policy implications.* Development Research Group (DRG), Department of Economic and Policy Research, Reserve Bank of India.

Rajan, R. G., & Zingales, L. (2001). Financial systems, industrial structure, and growth. *Oxford Review of Economic Policy, 17*(4), 467–482.

Reddy, Y. V. (2002, March 11). *Developing bond markets in emerging economies: Issues and Indian experience.* Keynote address at the Asian Conference, jointly hosted by FIMMDA, PDAI, and Thai BDC, Bangkok, Thailand.

Reserve Bank of India. (n.d.). *Database on the Indian economy.* https://data.rbi.org.in/#/dbie/home

Reserve Bank of India. (2002, 2006). *Report on currency and finance 2000–01.*

Reserve Bank of India. (2007). *Equity and corporate debt market.* https://www.rbi.org.in/scripts/publicationsview.aspx?id=9243.

Reserve Bank of India. (2007). *Government securities market.* https://rbi.org.in/scripts/PublicationsView.aspx?id=9241.

Reserve Bank of India. (2025). *Handbook of statistics on the Indian economy 2024–25.* https://www.rbi.org.in/Scripts/AnnualPublications.aspx?head=Handbook%20of%20Statistics%20on%20Indian%20Economy

Reserve Bank of India. (2012). *Corporate debt market: Developments, issues, and challenges.* https://www.rbi.org.in/scripts/bs_viewcontent.aspx?Id=2783.

Reserve Bank of India. (2019). *India's corporate bond market: Issues in market microstructure.* https://rbidocs.rbi.org.in/rdocs/Bulletin/PDFs/2ICBMIMM141CFFF458BB4B3A9F4C006F4AE4897

Reserve Bank of India. (2019). *Financial sector: Regulation and developments.*

Reserve Bank of India. (n.d.). *Annual and monthly reports.* https://www.rbi.org.in/scripts/AnnualReportPublications.aspx.

Ringui, J. K. (2012). *A survey of factors determining development of corporate bond market in Kenya.* School of Business, University of Nairobi.

Roley, V. V. (1982). The effect of federal debt-management policy on corporate bond and equity yields. *Quarterly Journal of Economics, 97*(4), 645–668.

Rudebusch, G.D., & Wu, T. (2008). A macro-finance model of the term structure, monetary policy, and the economy. *Economic Journal, 118*(530), 906–926.

Rudebusch, G. D. (2010). *Macro-finance models of interest rates and the economy* (Working Paper 2010-01). Federal Reserve Bank of San Francisco.

Sahoo, S., & Bhattacharyya, I. (2012). Yield curve dynamics of the Indian G-Sec market: A macro-finance approach. *Indian Economic Review, New Series, 47*(2), 157–182.

Sarma, C. (2014). *The Indian bond market* (Working Paper, No. 196). Institute of South Asian Studies, National University of Singapore.

Schinasi, G. J., & Smith, R. T. (1998). *Fixed-income markets in the United States, Europe, and Japan: Some lessons for emerging markets* (Working Paper No. WP/98/173). Washington: International Monetary Fund.

Securities and Exchange Board of India. (n.d.). *Annual and Monthly Reports.*

Sethi, N., & Patnaik, U. S. K. (2007). International Capital Flows on India's Economic Growth: In View of Changing Financial Market. *The Indian Journal of Economics, 45*(348).

Sgherri, S., & Zoli, E. (2009). *Euro area sovereign risk during the crisis.* International Monetary Fund.

Shareef, K., & Shijin, S. (2017). The term structure of interest rates and macroeconomic factors: Evidence from Indian financial market. *Borsa Istanbul Review, 17*(4), 249–256.

Sharma, K. (2001). The Underlying constraints on corporate bond market development in Southeast Asia. *World Development, 29*(8),1405–1419.

Sharma, A. (2016). Exchange rate and business cycles in India: An analysis of lead and lag behaviour. *ZENITH International Journal of Multidisciplinary Research,* 6(9), 70–88.

Shivam, M., & Jayadev, M. (2004). *The interest rate term structure in the Indian money market.* Proceedings of The Sixth Annual Conference on Money and Finance in the Indian Economy, Indira Gandhi Institute of Development Research (IGIDR), Mumbai, India.

Sims, C., Stock, J. H., & Watson, M. W. (1990). Inference in linear time series models with some unit roots. *Econometrica, 58*(1), 113–144.

Singh, B. (2007). Corporate choice for overseas borrowings: The Indian evidence. *RBI Occasional Paper, 28*(3).

Singh, T. (2012). Does public capital crowd out or crowd in private capital in India? *Journal of Economic Policy Reform, 15*(2),109–133. https://doi.org/10.1080/17487870.2012.668767

Stock, J., & Watson, M. (2003). Forecasting Output and Inflation: The Role of Asset Prices. *Journal of Economic Literature, 41*, 788–829.

Subramanian, A., & Felman, J. (2019). India's Great Slowdown: What Happened? What's the Way Out? *Faculty Working Paper No. 370.* Center for International Development, Harvard University.

Sundararajan, V., & Takur, S. (1980). Public investment, crowding out, and growth: A dynamic model applied to India and Korea. *IMF Staff Papers 27*(4), 814–855.

Tahir, M. (2002). *Development of bond market in India.* JSEPA Workshop on the Development of Bond Markets in Asia, Singapore.

Tendulkar, R., & Hancock, G. (2014). *Corporate bond markets: A global perspective.* IOSCO.

The Working Group Report. (2016). *Development of corporate bond market in India.* The Financial Stability and Development Council

Sub-committee Report. https://www.sebi.gov.in/sebi_data/attachdocs/1471519221779.pdf

Thorpe, W. L., & Mitchell, W. C. (1926). *Business Annals: United States, England, France, Germany, Austria, Russia, Sweden, Netherlands, Italy, Argentina, Brazil, Canada, South Africa, Australia, India, Japan, China.* New York: National Bureau of Economic Research.

Valle, C. (2002). *Developing bond markets: A comprehensive view.* World Bank Report.

Vanhatalo, E., Kulahci, M., & Bergquist, B. (2017). On the structure of dynamic principal component analysis used in statistical process monitoring. *Chemometrics and Intelligent Laboratory Systems, 167,* 1–11.

Wells, S., & Schou-Zibell, L. (2008). *India's bond market: Developments and challenges ahead.* Asian Development Bank Working Paper Series on Regional Economic Integration No. 22.

World Bank. (2004). *Study on Korea's corporate bond market and its implications on China's bond market development.* World Bank Country Study Paper.

Xu, X., & Yan, Y. (2014). Does government investment crowd out private investment in China? *Journal of Economic Policy Reform, 17*(1), 1–12. https://doi.org/10.1080/17487870.2013.866897.

Yoshitomi, M., & Shirai, S. (2001). *Designing a financial market structure in post-crisis Asia.* ADB Institute, Tokyo.

Zamowitz, V., & Boschan, C. (1975). Cyclical Indicators: An evaluation and new leading indexes. In *Handbook of Cyclical Indicators.* Government Printing Office, Washington, D.C.

Zarnowitz, V., & Ozyildirim, A. (2002). *Time series decomposition and measurement of business cycles, trends, and growth cycles.* NBER Working Paper 8736.

Zoli, M. E. (2013). *Italian sovereign spreads: Their determinants and pass-through to bank funding costs and lending conditions* (Working Paper No. 13-84). International Monetary Fund, Washington, D.C.

Index

C

D

E

F

J

L

M

N

O

T

U

V

W

www.ingramcontent.com/pod-product-compliance
Lightning Source LLC
Chambersburg PA
CBHW041303210926
51850CB00001B/1
* 9 7 8 8 1 2 6 9 4 5 0 2 3 *